P9-DVD-372

ANCIENT TEXTILES FROM NUBIA

On the front cover:
Portion from a Carpet
entry 66.

Frontispiece:
Fragments of a Large Cover
entry 85.

ANCIENT TEXTILES FROM NUBIA

Meroitic, X-Group, and Christian Fabrics from Ballana and Qustul

Christa C. Mayer Thurman   Bruce Williams

An Exhibition Organized by The Art Institute of Chicago

The University of Chicago Oriental Institute Nubian Expedition
Excavations between Abu Simbel and the Sudan Frontier
Keith C. Seele, Director

The Art Institute of Chicago

May 26–August 5, 1979

THE ART INSTITUTE OF CHICAGO

Trustees:
James W. Alsdorf, Mrs. Julian Armstrong, Jr.,
Mrs. James P. Baxter, Edward H. Bennett, Jr.,
Edwin A. Bergman, Bowen Blair, E. Laurence Chalmers, Jr.,
Edward M. Cummings, Wesley M. Dixon, Jr., Marshall Field,
Stanley M. Freehling, R. Robert Funderburg,
Michael Goodkin, Charles C. Haffner, III,
William E. Hartmann, David C. Hilliard, Edwin E. Hokin,
John H. Johnson, Brooks McCormick, Charles A. Meyer,
John W. Moutoussamy, Bryan S. Reid, Jr., Arthur W. Schultz,
Edward Byron Smith, Mrs. Theodore D. Tieken,
Warner Arms Wick, Arthur MacDougall Wood,
William Wood Prince, George B. Young

Life Trustees:
John Gregg Allerton, Cushman B. Bissell,
William McCormick Blair, Mrs. Leigh B. Block, Leigh B. Block,
Mrs. Eugene A. Davidson, Frank B. Hubachek, Earle Ludgin,
Andrew McNally III, William A. McSwain,
Mrs. C. Phillip Miller, Mrs. Joseph Regenstein, Payson S. Wild,
Frank H. Woods

President Emeritus: William McCormick Blair

Ex Officio:
Jane Byrne, *Mayor of the City of Chicago*
Clark Burrus, *Comptroller of the City of Chicago*
Patrick L. O'Malley, *President, Chicago Park District*
William Swezenski, *Treasurer, Chicago Park District*

Officers:
Arthur M. Wood, *Chairman of the Board*
Bowen Blair, *Vice Chairman*
Brooks McCormick, *Vice Chairman*
Bryan S. Reid, Jr., *Vice Chairman*
George B. Young, *Vice Chairman*
Edward Byron Smith, *Treasurer*
E. Laurence Chalmers, Jr., *President*
Robert E. Mars, *Vice President for Administrative Affairs*
Donald J. Irving, *Vice President for Academic Affairs*
Larry Ter Molen, *Vice President for Development and Public
    Relations*
Linda Starks, *Secretary*

Copyright © 1979 The Art Institute of Chicago and
            The University of Chicago

Library of Congress Catalog Card Number: 79–52710
ISBN: 0–918986–25–7

Designed by Everett McNear

Photography by Deborah Hede with the exception of
entries 32, 36 and 146 which were photographed by
Howard Kraywinkel

Composition by Typoservice Corporation
Printed in the United States of America by
Congress Printing Company

TABLE OF CONTENTS

FOREWORD I

FOREWORD II

The textiles in this exhibit came to light as a result of archaeological salvage operations conducted by the Oriental Institute between 1962 and 1964. When Egypt (United Arab Republic) and UNESCO appealed for scholarly assistance in excavating areas about to be flooded by water rising behind the Aswan High Dam, the Oriental Institute responded by sending out several expeditions which worked in Egypt and the Sudan. One of these expeditions, directed by Professor Keith C. Seele, was granted a concession to work most of the region along the Egyptian Nile from Abu Simbel south to the Sudanese frontier. This expedition, which excavated many cemeteries ranging from prehistoric to medieval Christian times, uncovered the textiles here on exhibit. Most of the textiles come from Meroitic, X-Group, or Christian tombs, especially in the time range circa A.D. 100–600.

For those interested in learning something further about the archaeological background of the textiles, an introductory account of the excavations led by Professor Seele may be found in his posthumously published article "University of Chicago Oriental Institute Nubian Expedition: Excavations between Abu Simbel and the Sudan Border, Preliminary Report," which appeared in the *Journal of Near Eastern Studies* 33 (1974): 1–43. This gives a survey of the methods and results of the 1962–1964 expeditions. A detailed archaeological report of this work is now being prepared for publication.

The Institute wishes to acknowledge the work of the Egyptologists who made this exhibition possible: Keith C. Seele, the primary excavator; John A. Wilson, who coordinated so much of the UNESCO efforts; Carl DeVries, who worked on the reorganization of Professor Seele's records; and Bruce B. Williams, who is now readying the material for publication. We are also grateful to our benefactor William R. Boyd, who underwrote the costs of the initial archaeological survey of the area, and to an anonymous donor, who generously supported Professor Seele's research in Chicago and provided a subsidy for publication. A debt of gratitude is likewise owed to those who aided in the treatment and conservation of the textiles themselves: Christa Mayer Thurman at the Art Institute and Gustavus F. Swift, Barbara Hall, Robert Hanson, Elizabeth Tieken, and Raymond Tindel at the Oriental Institute. Finally, we wish to express our thanks to the National Endowment for the Arts for partial underwriting of expenses connected with conservation of the textiles (NEA Grant No. A72–0–956).

John A. Brinkman
Director
Oriental Institute

The Art Institute of Chicago became interested in these textiles from Egypt and the Sudan almost a decade ago. At that time, Mrs. Theodore D. Tieken, a member of the Textile Committee, approached the late John Maxon and Christa Thurman, our Curator of Textiles, about the materials excavated by the Oriental Institute in the early 1960s. Professor Keith C. Seele had asked Mrs. Tieken for advice about the excavated materials, still packed in plastic sacks and encrusted with sand, dirt, and decay. Professor Seele's problem had been compounded by the death of Louisa Bellinger, distinguished Textile Curator-Analyst of the Textile Museum in Washington, D.C., who had agreed to work on the material found during the excavations conducted by The University of Chicago Oriental Institute Nubian Expedition.

The problem was resolved when the Oriental Institute received a grant from the National Endowment for the Arts—a grant that made it possible for Christa Thurman to spend numerous weekends over an equal amount of numerous years carefully cleaning and arranging the materials. It was a slow and tedious process, but as the work progressed it became apparent to Mrs. Thurman that these textiles were too important to simply clean, sort, arrange and return to storage.

In 1975 the Exhibition Committee of the Art Institute approved an exhibition of these textiles, and the materials were transferred, on indefinite loan, from the Oriental Institute in 1976. During the last year the final cataloguing has been completed, a comprehensive photographic record has been assembled, and this exhibition has now been mounted. We are indebted to many people at the Oriental Institute and at The Art Institute of Chicago, most especially to Mrs. Thurman who for years has worked with these textiles and has developed this impressive exhibition. It has been a labor of love and the result accurately reflects her conservation talents and her exceptional scholarship. We are especially pleased to be a part of the efforts of the two Institutes: the one to retrieve these exceptional textiles, and the other to prepare and present them to our public.

E. Laurence Chalmers Jr.
President
The Art Institute of Chicago

Detail from a Carpet, entry 115.

ACKNOWLEDGMENTS

I acknowledge gratefully the help of many people, who, in one way or another contributed to the completion of this work. I am indebted to the late Professor Keith C. Seele, the late Gustavus F. Swift, Mrs. Theodore D. Tieken, John A. Brinkman, Carl DeVries and Barbara Hall for their trust in turning the textiles over to me. Their patience was continuously tested in that the project span a period of nearly eight years due to the fact in that I could only work on the material on weekends. Had it not been for Bruce Williams, co-author, who compiled the geographical, historical, and archaeological data as well as all grave information, this catalogue would probably have been even further delayed. His collaboration was of immense importance. It was an enjoyable experience to work with a true scholar.

Professor Dr. Walter Jenny and Norbert Bigler of CIBA-GEIGY AG., Basel, Switzerland, were most helpful in initial fiber analyses of five textiles (see pages 34, 48, 54, 125, 161) and the microscopic photographs of cross sections (page 48). With the purchase of a polarizing microscope for the Painting Conservation Department at The Art Institute of Chicago, Alfred Jakstas' consent to share that equipment with other departments and Inge Fiedler's technical knowledge and fascination in the difficult pursuit of sheep, camel and goat hair identification, a total of approximately a hundred fibers were processed. Her conclusions are to be found on page 49. We thank Mike Bayard, Honorary Consultant to The Painting Conservation Department, for his valuable assistance when it came to advice concerning fiber identification and for providing us with the scanning electron micrographs (SEM) illustrated on pages 50 and 51. Furthermore, we wish to thank Marion Weiman, Jr., Microscopist, for his arrangements so that the equipment at the SEM Laboratory, The University of Chicago, (funded by a grant from the National Institute of Health, Biotechnology Resources Section), could be used. And finally, it was Anne Benolken who printed the SEM micrographs. For the dye analysis, carried out on nearly one hundred samples, I am exceedingly grateful to Dr. Liliane Maschelein-Kleiner and her associate Luc R. J. Maes of the Institut Royal du Patrimoine Aristique, Brussels. Their findings are summarized on page 52.

My own staff, as always, performed admirably: Deborah Hede struggled for nine months with black and white as well as color photography, the development of negatives and subsequently the printing; Cynthia J. Cannon organized and prepared the typewritten manuscript for publication; Ilene W. Shaw assisted with final research questions; Lorna Filippini helped with the installation and together with Deborah Hede prepared over fifty frames required for the installation. The challenge of the over all installation was that of John Blatnick, Special Projects Consultant. George Schneider painstakingly drew the maps, chronology table and illustrations (pages 12, 19, 21, 42). Additional drawings were carried out by Joanna Steinkeller (pages 34–35). Special mention is in order when it comes to the most tedious, difficult and time consuming task of editing. This job was shared by Jean Luther and Pamela Bruton of The Oriental Institute; and Anselmo Carini and Mrs. Homer Rosenberg at the Art Institute, with further assistance from Pat Williams and Heather Taylor. I am also indebted to John Carswell, Barbara Hall and Bruce Williams in the selection and preparation of other objects found in those graves which contained textiles to augment the installation.

However, these acknowledgments would not be complete without a listing of the many individuals, who, over these many years periodically received either a frantic letter or a telephone call pertaining to "the Chicago Nubian nightmare." Foremost among those to be acknowledged is Max Saltzman, Los Angeles, who assisted with countless scientific and technical queries. Yet, there were others. Listed in alphabetical order they are: Ingrid Bergman, Sweden; Michael Bogle, North Andover, Massachusetts; Mark Burnham, Canada; Bernard V. Bothmer, New York; Elizabeth Crowfoot, England; Dows Dunham, Boston; Gudrun Ekstrand, Sweden; Charles Grant Ellis, Washington; the late Anne-Marie Franzen, Sweden; and Mrs. Keith C. Seele, Batavia, Illinois.

My final recognition goes to the memory of John Maxon who whole-heartedly encouraged me at the onset of this project and thereafter until his untimely death, to presevere and to complete this task.

Christa C. Mayer Thurman

The Oriental Institute
Nubian Expedition at Ballana
and Qustul 1962-1964

Diederika Seele
(Mrs. Keith C. Seele)

The UNESCO International Campaign to Save the Monuments of Nubia was launched in March of 1960. Egypt has always depended on the Nile. It brings not only its gift of water to a thirsty land but also its precious cargo of silt gathered as it travels from its source. Due to the yearly floods of the past, Egypt is a green valley wherever the Nile has reached. As flooding subsided, cotton, sugarcane, rice, and other crops necessary for feeding Egypt's population, as well as for its trade and commerce, were quickly planted. As early as 1902 a dam was constructed at the First Cataract at Aswan to irrigate more land for cultivation. This dam was 100 feet high, and it stored 980 million cubic meters of water. By 1912 it was necessary to raise the dam another sixteen feet in order to store 2,400 million cubic meters. The demands of a growing population were still not met, so during the period from 1929 to 1934 thirty more feet were added to the dam, making it possible to store 5,000 million cubic meters of water.

By the end of the 1950s Egypt faced a crisis. It was imperative to create more food-producing land. Increasing industrialization required new sources of electric power, and an entirely new dam had to be erected. As planned, it was to be 364 feet high and two miles wide, and would store 130,000 million cubic meters of water. At such a size it would create a great lake that would completely submerge Lower Nubia.

Nubia was an ancient land that extended along the banks of the Nile for some four hundred miles. In modern times, Nubia has extended from a point slightly north of the First Cataract at Aswan to one almost at the Fourth Cataract. It was divided by the Second Cataract into two unequal parts; Lower Nubia, the smaller part, belonged to Egypt while the larger part, Upper Nubia, belonged to the Sudan. Lower Nubia consisted of discontinuous strips of arable land on each side of the Nile; the adjacent country was desert. On the west bank of the Nile, blowing sand constantly threatened to bury the black soil under a golden blanket.

In spite of the fact that, compared to other parts of the Nile Valley, Nubia has little arable land, it has been an important part of the African continent for thousands of years. The historical events which have taken place there have had a significant influence on civilization. Civilizations were created, flourished, and fell there. Nubians created their own products and the country furnished routes over which products from the north and the south could be carried. From time to time Egypt, the giant to the north, conquered, ruled, and even settled various parts of it. Each of the Egyptian civilizations left important remains, some monumental, some humble.

This land, filled with the monuments of the past, was at one time a part of the great sweep of history. Much of it was doomed to disappear beneath the waters of the great lake created by the High Dam. To preserve as much of its past as possible, international cooperation was mandatory. The Director General of UNESCO, Vittorino Veronese, at the opening of the UNESCO international campaign, said, "Wondrous structures, ranking among the most magnificent upon earth are in danger of disappearing. . . . It is not easy to choose between a heritage of the past and the well-being of a people, living in need in the shadow of one of history's most splendid legacies: it is not easy to choose between temples and crops. . . . These monuments, the loss of which may be tragically near, do not belong solely to the countries who hold them in trust. The whole world has a right to see them endure. They are part of a common heritage which comprises Socrates' message and the Ajanta frescoes, the Walls of Uxmal, and Beethoven's symphonies. Treasures of universal value are entitled to universal protection."

The world responded. Many of the Nubian temples were moved to safe areas in Egypt or to distant places. Within the past year Americans have been able to see one of these temples displayed in its new home at the Metropolitan Museum of Art in New York.

Not only were there visible monuments in Nubia, there were also priceless records of history lying underground in the burial sites of those who dwelt in this land thousands of years ago. Scholars from many fields—Egyptologists, archaeologists, anthropologists, and historians—were very much aware of the short period of time remaining before the dam would cause the Nile to rise, and they responded to UNESCO's appeal.

At the urging of Professor Keith C. Seele the Oriental Institute of the University of Chicago was one of the first organizations to respond to the appeal. In March 1960 Professor Seele went to Egypt and the Sudan to observe the places available for excavation and to apply for concessions there. Ultimately, the Oriental Institute explored, recorded, and excavated sites in several areas, including an area near Kalabsha—thirty-one miles south of the First Cataract—and at Serra East, Dorganarti, and Semna South in the Sudan and at Qustul, Ballana, and Adindan at the southern end of Egyptian Nubia about 225 miles from Aswan.

Professor Seele became the director of the Oriental Institute's Nubian expeditions. The first of these was a joint effort with the Schweizerisches Institut für ägyptische Bauforschung und Altertumskunde in Kairo and was under the direction of professors Seele and Herbert Ricke. They spent the season of 1960 to 1961 copying the reliefs of the small temple at Beit el-Wâli and excavating sites in the area between Khor Dehmit and Kalabsha.[1] In the second season, the Oriental Institute Nubian Expedition worked alone at Serra East in the Sudan. Because Professor Seele was ill that season Professor George R. Hughes led the expedition. The seasons from 1962 to 1963 and from 1963 to 1964 were spent near the Sudanese border at Qustul, Ballana, and Adindan under the leadership of Professor Seele.[2] It was during these seasons that the textiles presented in this exhibition were found. Thereafter, two seasons of excavation at Semna South (1966 to 1967 and 1967 to 1968) were directed by Professor Louis V. Zabkar.

Excavating in Nubia was arduous and difficult. Work was done in a very remote area, accessible only by water. Supplies

Opposite page, top:
Detail from a Tunic Fragment, entry 100.

Center:
Detail from a Complete Carpet or Cover, entry 155.

Bottom:
Detail from a Sheet or Tunic (?) Fragment
entry 63.

had to be shipped some two hundred miles south of Aswan, for the Nubian villages, perched as they were on the barren hills overlooking the river, could not raise sufficient food. Sustenance was furnished by an occasional cluster of date palms and carefully tended small plots of vegetables near the river edge. Scrubby growth of brush furnished food for a few goats. Most of the able-bodied men had left their homes—either to seek employment in Cairo (they are highly regarded there as workers) or to engage in boat traffic (they are also highly regarded as rivermen). Because resources were so meager and so many able-bodied persons were gone, the excavators could not hope to hire much local help or to purchase many provisions.

The climate in Nubia poses many problems. There can be searing heat at times, and the choking storms of fine dust penetrate everywhere, causing havoc with camera equipment, machinery, and food. When the sun disappears below the desert's horizon in the winter season the weather rapidly becomes uncomfortably cold. During the winter season the expedition's work began at sunrise, but in springtime the sun became hot early in the day to the point that exposed metal could not be touched and work had to be started before sunrise. Dangers lurked from the bite of the cobra and the horned viper and from the sting of the scorpion. Since no treated water supplies were available at the site, water had to be taken from the Nile and boiled before being used.

An old Cook steamer, the *Fostat,* was purchased for housing the members of the expedition. Its hull was remodeled and its engines were removed to provide space for a photographic studio, workrooms for recording and storing artifacts, storage for a season's food supplies, and sleeping, dining, and living quarters for the staff of six to eight scholars. The *Fostat* was towed up the Nile by two tugboats, one of which was part of the expedition's equipment and able by itself to move the *Fostat* when she was in Nubian waters.

Aside from the staff of scholars, nineteen experienced Egyptian workers from the towns of Quft and el-Lahun were employed. Their ancestors had been trained in the 1890s by the famous British archaeologist Sir Flinders Petrie. The men from these towns have retained this training from generation to generation and are still often preferred for archaeological work.

A household staff completed the complement of expedition members, and a labor force of sixty or seventy Nubians from Qustul and Ballana was engaged when the expedition reached its work site.

The work area of Ballana and Qustul in Nubia was selected by Professor Seele as one that might produce results. In the years from 1929 to 1934 Professor Walter Emery had worked there and had made very exciting finds. Under tumuli, once considered to be natural mounds caused by drifting sand, there were royal burials. A king's entire retinue and his horses, camels, furniture, and silver treasures accompanied him in death. The discovery of this fact led to investigations of other tumuli, and these investigations revealed equally important royal materials, which remained in spite of the tomb robberies that had taken

place throughout the centuries. These tumuli belonged to the period designated by archaeologists as the X-Group, dated from A.D. 350 to 540 (late Roman and Byzantine periods). Professor Seele thought that in such an area there might also be tombs of persons belonging to the court and of other people who lived under the rule of these kings, so the Oriental Institute Nubian Expedition started work in this area. Its members were indeed successful, finding many graves of the X-Group and, in addition, materials of the immediately preceding Meroitic period. It was from the tombs of these periods that the textiles described in the catalogue were obtained.

The expedition members found the areas of Ballana, Qustul, and Adindan most rewarding. The cemeteries there ranged from the middle period of the A-Group, ca. 3500 B.C., to the Christian period.

Only one or two sites on tall outcrops of rocks can still be excavated. The High Dam has been erected, and the land slumbers beneath the waters of Lake Nasser. In museum laboratories, in university studies, and in libraries, scholars are sifting the results of the fieldwork. Publications are appearing that throw light on some of the questions from the past. The time spent in excavating the area was short, and there was always the haunting thought that probably many precious remains were being lost to posterity. At the Chicago exhibition we are able to see almost all of the textiles from the treasures that the generous Egyptian government permitted the Oriental Institute to retain from the total recovered. These textiles represent only part of the Meroitic to early Christian material in a much larger collection of all periods in ancient Nubia that includes a unique object now known to depict the earliest representation of a king (3400 to 3300 B.C.) yet known.

Professor Seele was an Egyptologist who spent his life in the study of the ancient hieroglyphic texts of Egypt, both in the field and at his desk at the university where he spent his entire academic career. He gave the last part of his life to the work in Nubia. After his return from the final days he spent there he devoted himself to the preparation and study of the thousands of objects he had brought back to the Oriental Institute. He was aware of his obligation to the Egyptian government to publish the results of the expedition's work.

Shortly before his death, Professor Seele asked Mrs. Christa C. Mayer Thurman of The Art Institute of Chicago to undertake the conservation and ultimately the publication of this highly specialized material, secure in the knowledge that she would bring to the task her extraordinary ability and competence and thus contribute to the knowledge of the history of a land now buried forever.

1. Herbert Ricke, George R. Hughes, and Edward F. Wente, *The Beit el-Wali Temple of Ramesses II,* OINE 1 (Chicago: University of Chicago Press, 1967). Herbert Ricke, *Ausgrabungen von Khor-Dehmit bis Beit el-Wali,* OINE 2 (Chicago: University of Chicago Press, 1967).
2. Keith C. Seele, "University of Chicago Oriental Institute Nubian Expedition: Excavations between Abu Simbel and the Sudan Border, Preliminary Report," *JNES* 33 (1974): 1–43.

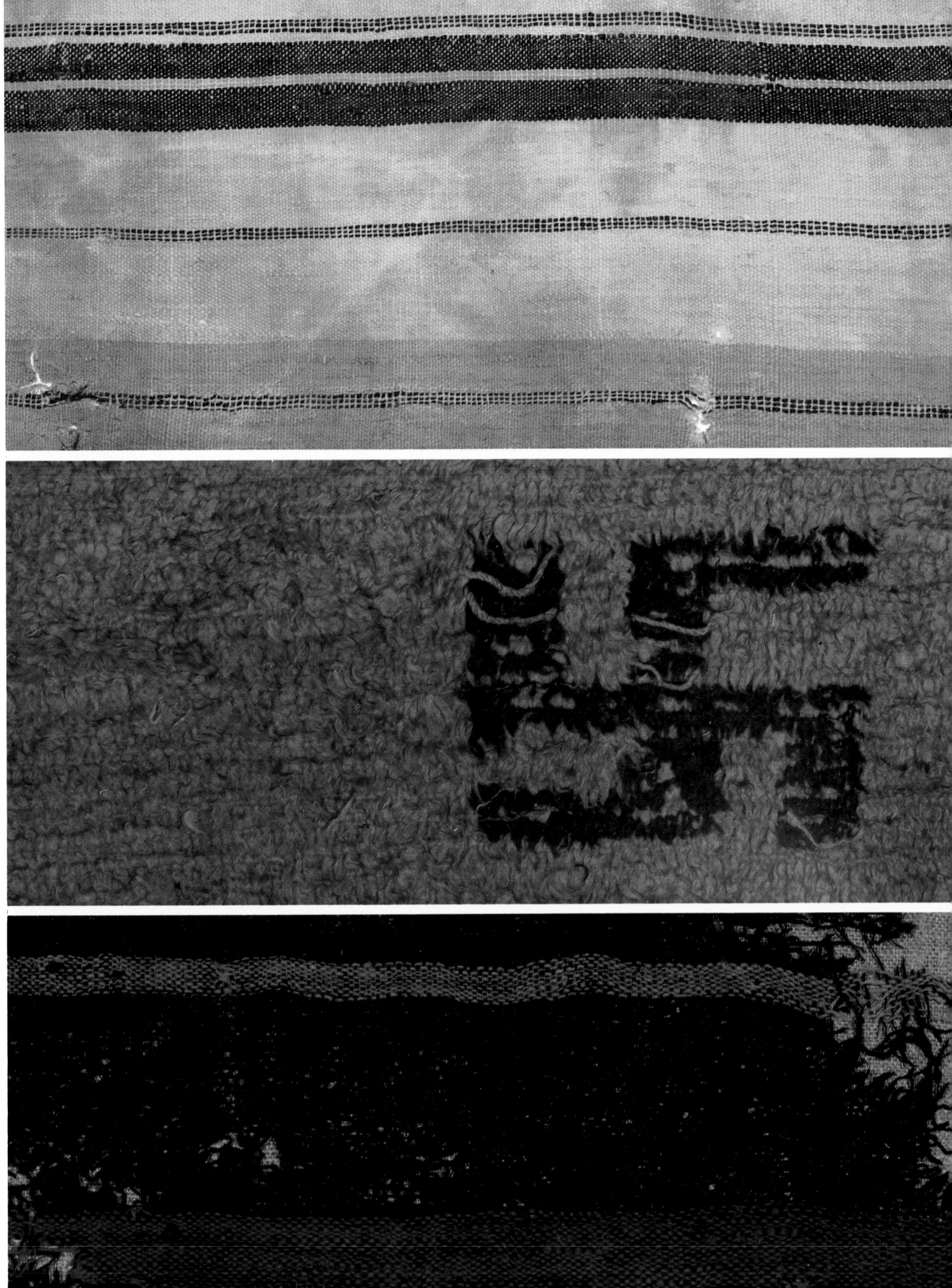

Chronology

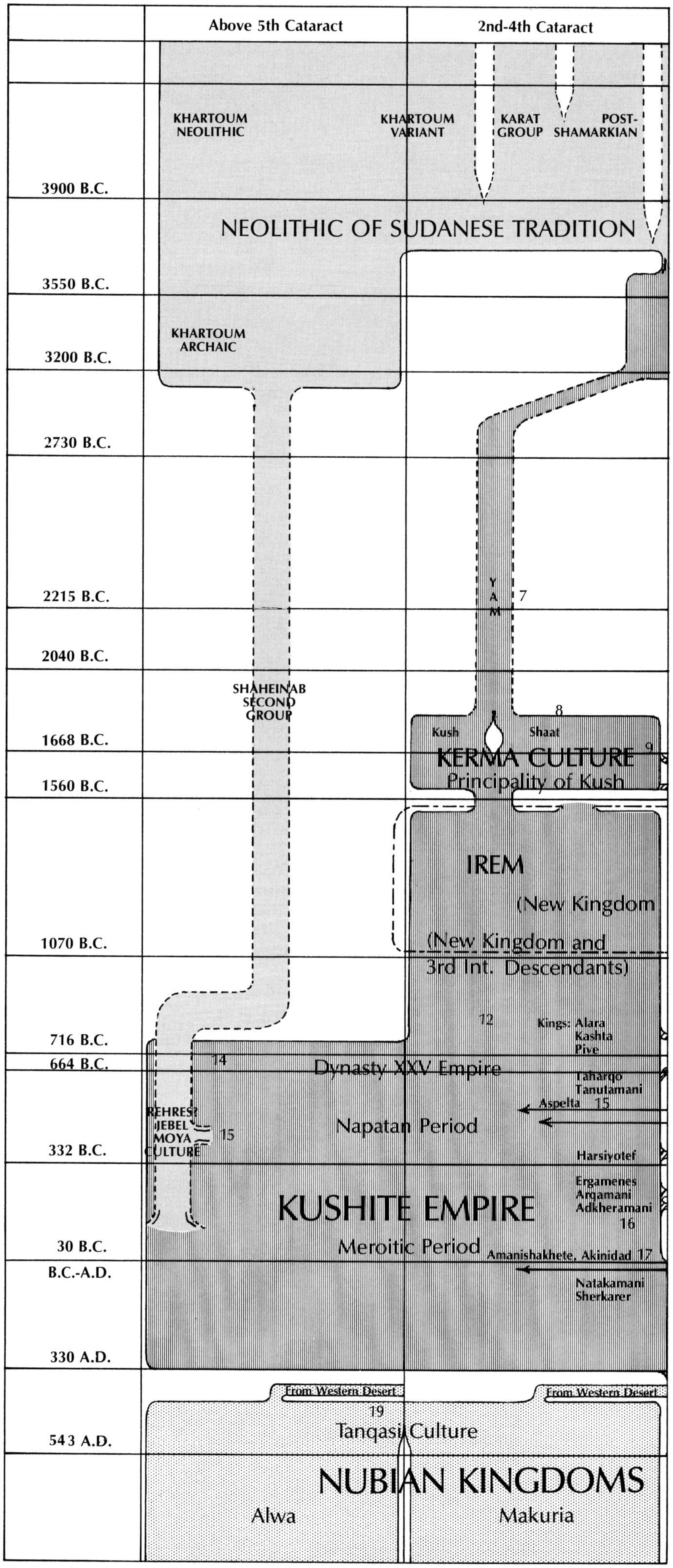

Legend	
————————	Encompasses connected or closely grouped material
- - - - - - - - -	Connection or grouping inferred
— - — - — - —	Military occupation and/or contact with some settlement
▨▨▨▨▨	Military occupation and/or control only
| |	Occupation present, but not known to be intense
{	Occupation expanded to adjacent area of neighboring region
⌐——¬	Movement of people
←————	Raid without intention of conquest
)) \	Major contribution to old cultural tradition; change from old to a new tradition
◊	Division, gap in tradition
▨▨▨▨▨	Mixed cultures

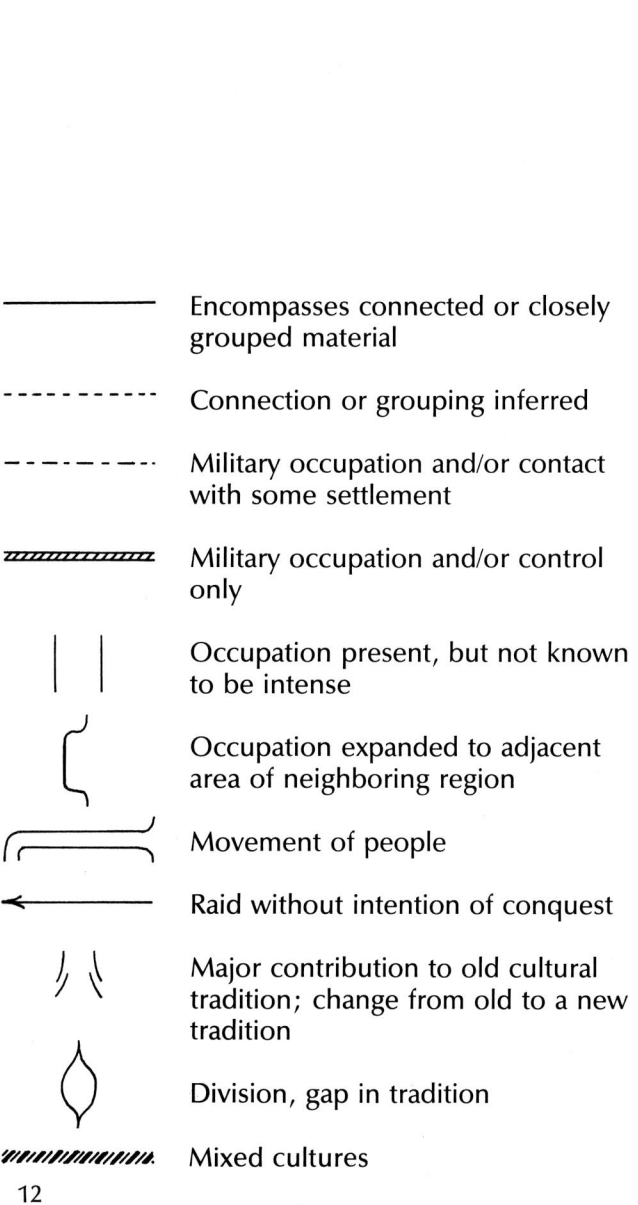

	Above 5th Cataract	2nd-4th Cataract		
	KHARTOUM NEOLITHIC	KHARTOUM VARIANT	KARAT GROUP	POST-SHAMARKIAN
3900 B.C.				
	NEOLITHIC OF SUDANESE TRADITION			
3550 B.C.				
3200 B.C.	KHARTOUM ARCHAIC			
2730 B.C.				
2215 B.C.		Y A M 7		
2040 B.C.				
	SHAHEINAB SECOND GROUP	8		
1668 B.C.		Kush · Shaat · KERMA CULTURE 9		
1560 B.C.		Principality of Kush		
		IREM		
		(New Kingdom		
1070 B.C.		(New Kingdom and 3rd Int. Descendants)		
716 B.C.		12 · Kings: Alara Kashta Piye		
664 B.C.	14	Dynasty XXV Empire · Taharqo Tanutamani		
	REHRES? JEBEL MOYA CULTURE 15	Napatan Period · Aspelta 15		
332 B.C.		Harsiyotef		
		KUSHITE EMPIRE · Ergamenes Arqamani Adkheramani 16		
30 B.C.		Meroitic Period · Amanishakhete, Akinidad 17		
B.C.-A.D.		Natakamani Sherkarer		
330 A.D.				
	From Western Desert	From Western Desert		
	19			
543 A.D.	Tanqasi Culture			
	NUBIAN KINGDOMS			
	Alwa	Makuria		

1st-2nd Cataract	Egypt	Eastern Desert	Libyan Desert and/or Darfur		
ABKAN	LOWER EGYPTIAN TRADITIONS			1	**NAQADA I**
2				3	**NAQADA II**
.3					**NAQADA III**
A-GROUP (KINGDOM AT QUSTUL)	UPPER EGYPTIAN KINGDOM(S) / LOWER EGYPTIAN KINGDOM(S)			4	
4 — from Eastern Desert / 5	**EGYPTIAN TRADITION**			5	**PROTODYNASTIC** Dynasties 0-II
6 (Old Kingdom domination or Occupation)				6	**OLD KINGDOM** Dynasties III-VIII
7 From Western Desert		Medjay	to Lower Nubia	7	
Setjau ◊ Irtjet ◊ Wawat **C-GROUP**	Theban Kingdom / Heracleopolitan Kingdom				**1st INTER** Dynasties IX-XI
Middle Kingdom conquest and military occupation) 8				8	**MIDDLE KINGDOM** Dynasties XI-XIII
9 Medjay-Eastern Desert	Medjay, Nubia / **Hyksos** / Medjay, Nubia	Medjay		9	**2nd INTER** Dynasties XIII-XVII
(New Kingdom Inhabitants of Lower Nubia) 10 conquest and occupation)				10	**NEW KINGDOM** Dynasties XVIII-XX
	(division, then finally multiple fragments)			11	**3rd INTER** Dynasties XXI-XXIII
				12	
(Kushite conquest of Egypt and rule) 13				13 14	**Dynasty XXV**
Psamettichos Cambyses		Meded		15	**LATER PERIOD** Dynasties XXVI-XXX
					PTOLEMAIC
TRIAKONTA-SCHOINOS **DODEKA-SCHOINOS**			Megabaroi?	16	
		Blemmyes		17	**ROMAN**
Petronius					
Akin 18		Bedja		18	
From Western Desert 20		**BLEMMYE CONFEDERACY**	**NOBATAE, NOBA** to Nubia and Sudan	19 20	**BYZANTINE**
X-Group Blemmye Tribes				21	
Nobatia		Bedja			**ARAB**

13

THE CHRONOLOGY TABLE

The illustrated chronology table is intended to chart the courses of some major peoples and events in Nubia and the northern Sudan, from the neolithic period to the advent of the Christian period in the sixth century A.D. The complexity of the table requires some apology; most people who make tables of this sort are content to use a few bars, making them wider or narrower or eliminating them altogether to represent changes. Unfortunately, the histories of peoples who occupied the area of Nubia and the northern Sudan are too complex to be represented in this way. The contrast between their histories and the history of Egypt illustrates the problem. The story of pharaonic Egypt is the story of a single civilization that existed in essentially one area. Foreigners entered Egypt from time to time, sometimes even ruling the country. In the end, they either became Egyptian or were expelled or, like the Greeks, formed small cultural enclaves within the overwhelmingly Egyptian population.

In the countries to the south things were different. These immense regions contained peoples whom we have provisionally assigned to five traditions. One of these traditions included a few Egyptians who from time to time settled in the south. Although we have usually characterized these traditions by region of origin (whether probable or known for certain), the areas in which they existed sometimes changed. In some instances two or more groups settled in the same region; sometimes one group ruled the others, but at other times they were both or all simply present in the same area at the same time. Sometimes a people moved from one place to another, leaving long stretches of the Nile Valley without evidence of population for extended periods.

The groups we are discussing often traded objects, materials, and ideas with each other, which makes it difficult to tell them apart. At least once, during the early New Kingdom, the cultures became so completely mixed that we have to use the teutonic term *Mischkultur* to describe the result.

Therefore, we have tried to show in the chart certain major events in political history, demography, and trade relations. We have attempted to follow the people of the five traditions through time, showing which regions they occupied at any point in time and—if they shared a region with others—which tradition was dominant. We have tried to make some distinctions in the nature of these territorial occupations by showing whether a given people occupied a certain region either intensively or sparsely and, if sparsely, whether their presence could be detected or had to be inferred. The table also records military occupation or military control.

1. In the early Naqada I phase (ca. 4000 B.C.), several groups of the Sudanese tradition, best known from occurrences in and near Khartoum, occupied the Nile Valley as far north as the Second Cataract. Groups of the Upper Egyptian tradition (Naqada I) were still concentrated there, and a number of groups of the Lower Egyptian cultures were to be found in and near the Egyptian Delta.

2. In later Naqada I, a major change in the distribution of the Naqada culture occurred when it colonized an empty area in northern Lower Nubia at Khor Bahan.

3. Although the objects and practices of this colony soon became distinct from Egyptian ones, the A-Group, as these later materials are called, remained similar in many ways to the Egyptian Predynastic. Close contact with Egypt continued. As the Naqada culture spread north to Lower Egypt in about 3500 B.C. and founded new kingdoms there, the A-Group spread south to the area near the Second Cataract, displacing the Neolithic of Sudanese tradition while adopting certain of its traits. At this time, the A-Group was organized into a kingdom of the Upper Egyptian type and probably had its capital near Qustul, where its kings were buried.

4. By the end of the Predynastic (Naqada III), Egypt was united by pharoahs of Upper Egypt. Under King Aha of the early First Dynasty the Egyptians displaced or destroyed the A-Group shortly after 3100 B.C.

5. Lower Nubia was left virtually empty, having perhaps only a few settlers from the Eastern Desert tradition during the periods of the later Protodynastic and the Old Kingdom (ca. 2900–2400 B.C.).

6. From the discovery of a colony at Buhen near the Second Cataract it appears that Egyptians controlled Lower Nubia during the Old Kingdom, although they did not occupy it intensively.

7. During the Sixth Dynasty (ca. 2400 B.C.) a new group, which was probably from the Western Desert, entered Lower Nubia; their archaeological remains are known as the C-Group. We know of three principalities they founded—Wawat, Irtjet, and Setjau, all north of the Second Cataract. At the same time, we know of a more powerful principality, Yam, near Kerma(?), in Upper Nubia. The culture of the country of Yam may have been descended from the culture of the A-Group and is probably the antecedent of the culture that appears at Kerma.

8. During the First Intermediate Period (ca. 2215–2040 B.C.) Egypt split apart and the C-Group expanded, even into Upper Egypt on the west side of the Nile. At the end of the First Intermediate Period, pharoahs of the Middle Kingdom attacked Lower Nubia in about 1950 B.C. and conquered it, ruling from a large complex of fortresses completed about a century later. The earliest texts record an opponent from above the Second Cataract, the principality

named Kush, probably at Kerma. Somewhat later documents record several principalities that include Kush and Shaat (Sai Island). Still later documents record several places in addition, but all apparently dominated or ruled by Kush and Shaat.

The C-Group continued to exist during this period in Lower Nubia, largely uninfluenced by Egypt though subject to it.

9. In the late Thirteenth Dynasty (ca. 1785–1668 B.C.) Egypt weakened again, and Egyptian troops that had been stationed at the fortresses began to stay on as permanent settlers, though they remained a distinct population.

During the same period of time Kush extended its rule over all of Upper Nubia and, as Egypt was being torn apart by the Hyksos (Asiatic) invaders, over Lower Nubia as well (about 1668 B.C.). The princes of Kush became valued allies of the Hyksos (1668–1560 B.C.) and possibly participated in campaigns in Egypt. The Egyptian garrisons remaining in Nubia now served the prince of Kush, and a people—the Medjay—entered Lower Nubia. Some of these people had served the Egyptians as scouts and police during the Middle Kingdom and they continued to do so during the New Kingdom.

10. As the Egyptians drove the Hyksos from Lower Egypt (ca. 1560 B.C.), they began the reconquest of Lower Nubia, apparently at the same time destroying the old renegade garrisons. This time they did not stop at the Second Cataract, but extended their conquests to the Fourth Cataract and possibly beyond that. The old forts were rebuilt and new ones added, complemented by new elements, the temple communities. The whole Egyptian Empire south of Aswan was ruled by an official called the "King's Son of Kush."

In Lower Nubia the four traditions that had coexisted during the Second Intermediate Period rapidly combined. By 1450 B.C. the heavily Egyptianized population had almost entirely disappeared from the countryside. Above the Second Cataract the native population continued, however, along with their local rulers, who were responsible to the Egyptians. Important elements of Egyptian culture were adopted by much of the population. During the New Kingdom, part of this area was known as Irem.

11. At the end of the Twentieth Dynasty (ca. 1080 B.C.) authority in Egypt was divided and her southern empire fell. Although Egypt was reunited for a

Top left, detail from Tunic (?) Fragments, entry 33.

Top right, detail from a Garment Fragment, entry 107.

Lower left, detail from a Portion of a Sash, entry 16.

Lower right, detail from a Carpet Fragment, entry 59.

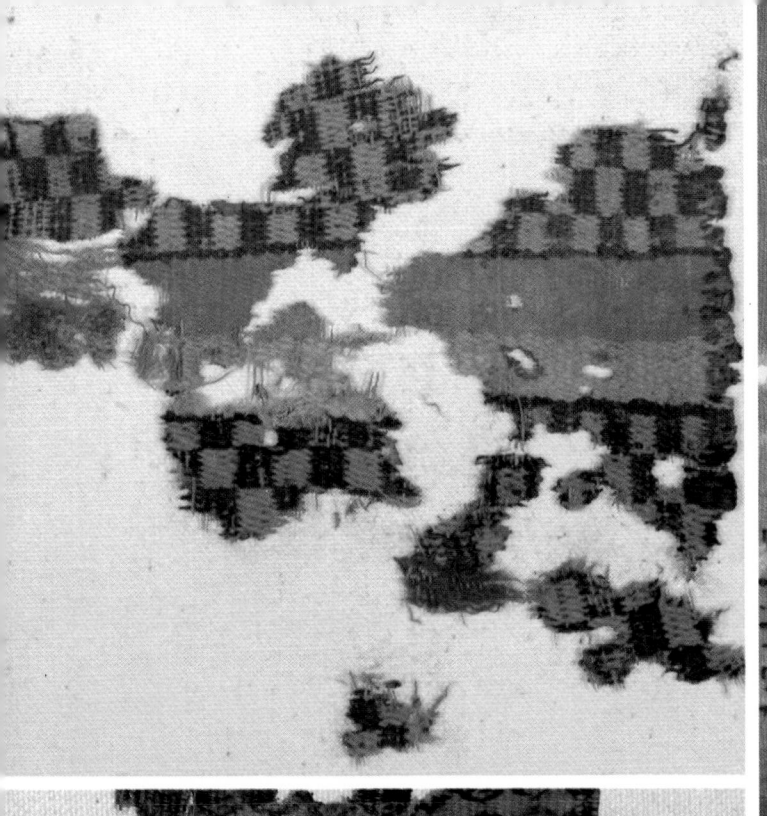

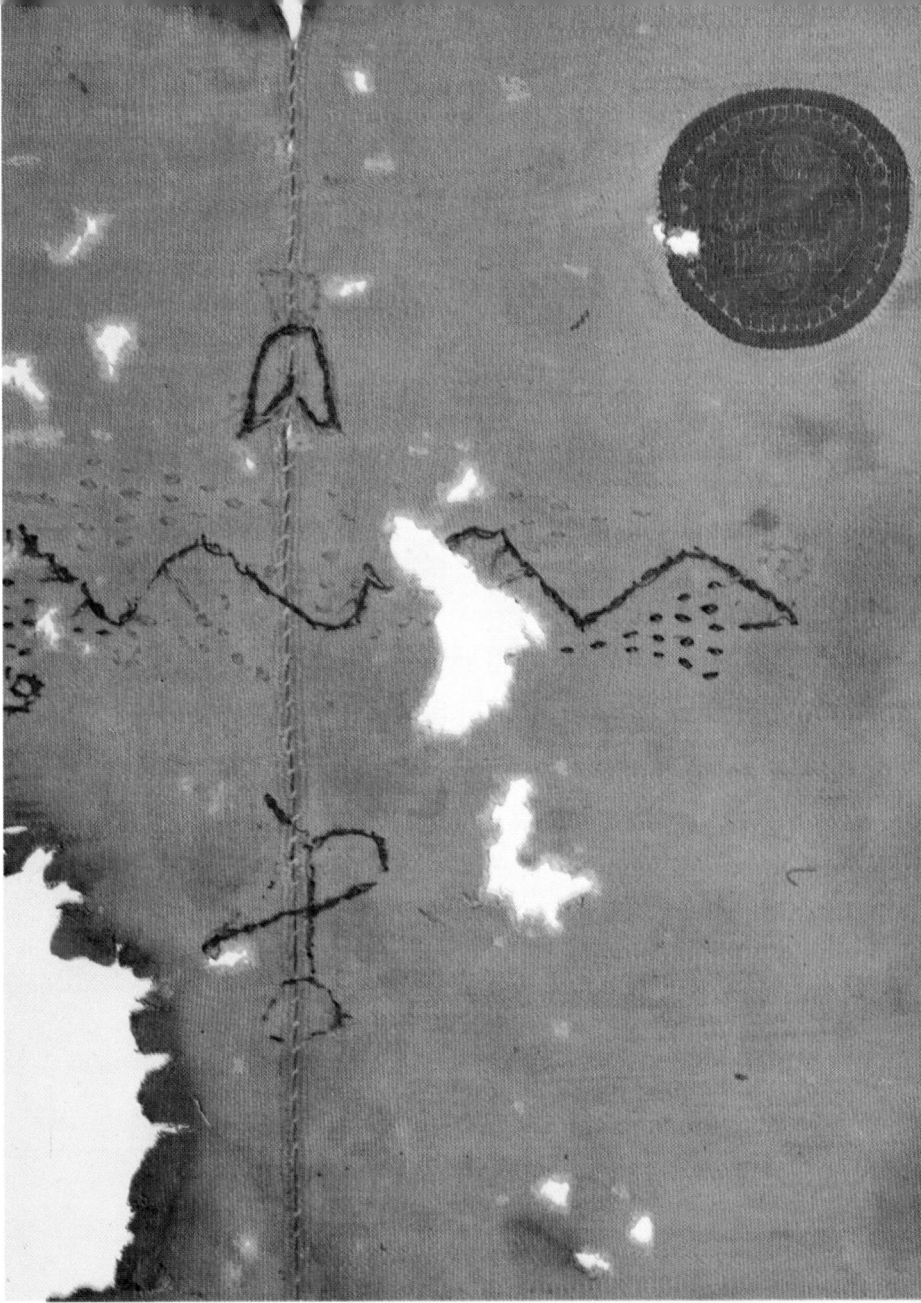

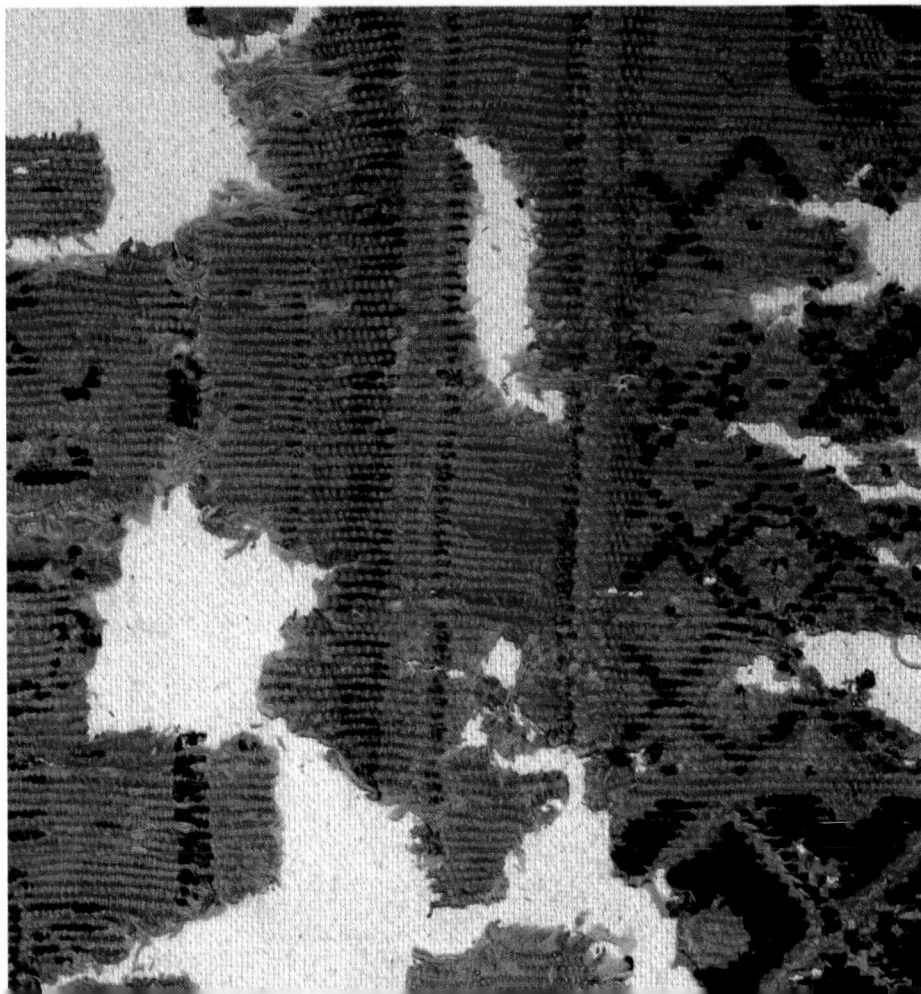

time during the Twenty-second Dynasty, the kingdom soon broke up into fragments.

12. The new rise of Kush is shrouded in obscurity. We know only that it began some five or six generations before its King Piye conquered Egypt in 716 B.C., as shown by the existence of tumulus burials in the old Kushite style at el Kurru, near Napata, later a great royal cemetery.

13. The rapid rise of Kush under Alara and Kashta culminated in the conquest of Egypt by King Piye (728 B.C.), who eliminated the petty kings of Egypt and united the country once again into an empire that stretched beyond the Fourth Cataract. Although the Kushite rulers were soon expelled from Egypt by the Assyrians (664 B.C.), their elimination of the petty kings and their patronage of the arts helped set the stage for one of the last great periods of Egyptian achievement, the Twenty-sixth Dynasty (to 525 B.C.). The conquest also renewed the close ties between Kush and Egypt, and important Egyptian cultural features, such as pyramids and hieroglyphs, reappeared in Kush.

14. As the Kushites were conquering Egypt, they were also expanding southward across the Bayuda region (see Map I) to Meroe. Soon after they were expelled from Egypt, Meroe became the empire's major center and later its capital.

15. The Kushite kings of the Napatan period (ca. 664–280 B.C.), called so because the kings of that time were still being buried near the old capital, Napata, increased their interest in the area near Meroe. Occasionally, they campaigned or attempted in some other way to expand in the direction of Egypt, taking advantage of periods when central authority in Upper Egypt was weak. However, they often had to fend off attacks in the vicinity of Meroe from the Rehres and, in the northern region, from the Meded of the Red Sea hills and from the Belhe, who apparently came from the west. At least two attacks were launched from Egypt.

16. By 280 B.C., the Kushite kings' control of the Isle of Meroe was consolidated, and the move of the capital to Meroe were completed when royalty was buried at Meroe instead of at Napata. The kings of the early Meroitic period took an interest in Lower Nubia and seem to have taken part in the revolts of Upper Egypt against the Ptolemies. As a result of the revolts, the Ptolemies established a buffer zone called the Dodekaschoinos, whose southern boundary was near the Wadi Alaqi; for a short time, they occupied the area from the Wadi Alaqi to the Second Cataract, which they called the Triakontaschoinos.

17. Taking advantage of Egypt's disaffection with Greek and Roman rule and a temporary evacuation of Roman troops from Upper Egypt, the Meroites attacked Aswan, probably hoping to raise a revolt (23 B.C.). This action provoked a major retaliation against Napata by the Roman prefect, Petronius. In a subsequent peace, Rome and Meroe accepted a boundary at the south end of the Dodekaschoinos.

18. Acceptance of each others' possession of part of Lower Nubia made possible a large-scale resettlement of this area, or at least the part under Meroitic control, which after 100 A.D. became known as the province of Akin. During the later third and early fourth centuries A.D. Akin was the most prosperous part of the crumbling Meroitic Empire, and it may have outlasted the fall of Meroe by some decades.

19. By 350 A.D. Meroe and the cities nearby were taken by people called the Noba, who settled in the old buildings. The presence of these people is attested by the appearance of the so-called Tanqasi culture. The area above the Third Cataract was later organized into two kingdoms, Alwa and Makuria, which persisted into Christian times.

20. By the early fourth century A.D., the Blemmyes, a confederacy of desert peoples near Upper Egypt who probably included some of the Bedja, attacked Upper Egypt and settled in the Dodekaschoinos, which had been abandoned by the Romans. To a lesser extent they settled in other parts of Lower Nubia. Their mobile forces ranged from Kharga Oasis in the west far into the Eastern Desert. The Romans invited the Nobatae to counter the presence of the Blemmyes, and the Nobatae, after destroying Meroitic higher culture, established a series of kingdoms between the First and Third cataracts. In the sixth century these kingdoms were consolidated by Silko into the kingdom of Nobatia. Known archaeologically as the X-Group, these Nobatian kingdoms included distinct and substantial elements from the previous Meroitic inhabitants, and their people seem to have merged at least in part with local Blemmyes.

21. By ca. 543 A.D. the Nubian kingdoms were ready for Christianity, which came to them in the form of Monophysitism, associating the Nubians with the Coptic and other Eastern churches as opposed to Orthodox Byzantium.

B.W.

LIST OF ABBREVIATIONS

JARCE   *Journal of the American Research Center in Egypt.* Boston and Princeton, N.J., 1962–.

JEA   *Journal of Egyptian Archaeology.* London, 1914–.

JNES   *Journal of Near Eastern Studies.* Chicago, 1942–.

LAAA   *Annals of Archaeology and Anthropology of the University of Liverpool.* Liverpool, 1908–48.

MIO   *Mitteilungen des Instituts für Orientforschung.* Berlin, 1953–.

OINE   Oriental Institute Nubian Expedition. Chicago, 1967–.

Urk. 3   Heinrich Schäfer. *Urkunden der älteren Äthiopenkönige.* Vol. 1. Urkunden des ägyptischen Altertums, Abt. 3. Leipzig, 1905.

ZÄS   *Zeitschrift für ägyptische Sprache und Altertumskunde.* Leipzig and Berlin, 1863–.

The Geographical, Historical, and Archaeological Background of Ancient Nubia and Northern Sudan

Bruce Williams
Research Associate
Oriental Institute

The textiles listed in this catalogue were discovered by the members of the Oriental Institute Nubian Expedition in the years 1962 to 1964.[1] They were found at Ballana and at Qustul, just north of the Sudan frontier in what is today called Nubia, in tombs dated to the Meroitic, X-Group, and early Christian periods, that is, to the years from 100 to 600 A.D.

Nubia as a modern geographical entity has been considered to be whatever part of the Nile Valley was occupied by people who speak Nubian. Before the construction of the High Dam these people occupied the area that extended from Aswan almost to the Fourth Cataract; today there are large colonies of Nubians north of Aswan and in the eastern Sudan.[2] We cannot speak of constant boundaries for any time in the past, because the areas occupied by different groups (not all of them well identified)[3] varied considerably.[4]

A major reason for the variability of political and ethnic boundaries in Nubia is illustrated by the distinct topographical difference between Nubia and Egypt.

In Egypt the Nile flows through a comparatively wide valley in the desert. Although the river is occasionally constricted by prominent outcrops and cliffs of sandstone and limestone or sometimes flows close to the desert cliffs on one or the other side of the valley, in almost every region it has a broad fertile floodplain. Before the construction of modern dams it used to inundate this plain once a year, making a comfortable existence possible for a very large population at a time well before the First Dynasty. The Egyptian valley is in almost complete contrast to the adjacent areas east and west. Although the Red Sea hills receive some moisture, the area of these hills can support only a few people, who are largely engaged in tending flocks or trading with the inhabitants of the valley. To the west, the completely dry Libyan Desert is broken by oases; some fairly large, but these are a long walk from the Nile and none are capable of sustaining a population equal to that of even the most miserable province of ancient Egypt.[5] With its overwhelming resources and well-defined territory, Egypt was certainly· equipped to maintain and extend a single culture and massive population, which could hardly be much altered or diluted by contact with the tiny alien groups contiguous to it.

South of Aswan the resources of the Nile Valley are much less conspicuously superior to those of surrounding regions. The valley is not as well defined by cliffs and hills, though they certainly exist. On either side of the river very narrow crescents of usable alluvial plains lie opposite stretches of barren desert. The area between the Second and Third cataracts is even more barren. Although areas in what is called the Dongola Reach are more promising, some stretches above it, near Abu Hamed, are almost devoid of sustenance. Above the junction with the Atbara, rainfall makes a poor vegetation possible today; the area may have been somewhat more productive in ancient times. For transport above Aswan the river, broken by six cataracts over outcrops of hard igneous rock, offers only limited opportunities; most long-distance trade goes at least partly overland. Thus, in resources for both communication and production the Nile and its valley south of Aswan are less superior to the desert than they are in Egypt.

At its most prosperous time (later Meroitic period, about 100–300 A.D.) the population in the area between Dal at the Second Cataract and Aswan may have numbered about 60,000, which is less than the mean for any of the nomes in Egypt throughout history.[6] During most of the other periods the population was much smaller; frequently, long stretches of valley were virtually uninhabited.

With such slim resources along the Nile in Nubia and the Sudan even a small number of newcomers could make a large impact on the relatively sparse population supported by the valley in antiquity. Moreover, the deserts on either side of the Nile south of Aswan have a somewhat greater potential for affecting life in the valley. The Red Sea hills are substantially more extensive here than they are east of the valley in Egypt, making a larger area available for the necessarily limited population. Although oases in the Libyan Desert are fewer and smaller than those of Egypt, Seleima and Dunqul are close to the valley and are connected by roads with wells to the greater oases to the north and to the more productive steppe and hill country in the far south.

Our knowledge of the ancient peoples of this region is almost completely confined to the people of the valley. What little knowledge we have of ancient peoples from beyond the valley's boundaries comes mainly from evidence left by those who from time to time spilled into the valley itself. This evidence is often poor or ambiguous; often it is difficult to discover and interpret. In many cases our ideas about the origins of some things that appear alien will have to be revised, but it would be extremely unwise to deal with the history of this region without keeping in mind that many things we see in the valley had their origins elsewhere and without trying, however tentatively, to indicate some directions for those origins.

Because local documentary sources are so rare and not generally tied to specific archaeological groups, the history of the area of the Nile Valley south of Aswan is often obscure or confused. Our knowledge of materials is inadequate. For some periods, materials are difficult to find or to date. Even when specific materials and documents have been associated, investigators have raised issues which throw doubt on that association.[7] Although the Nile Valley between the First Cataract and the southern end of the Second Cataract has been intensively, if unevenly, explored by archaeologists, epigraphers, anthropologists, and geophysical scientists, the inhospitable regions to the east and west, as well as the occasional oases, have hardly been touched and the evidence procured has sometimes been ambiguous. The valley south of the Dal cataract is poorly known. Major monuments, royal tombs, pyramids and temples, even the great city of Meroe itself have been explored and some of them splendidly published, but the study of major monuments is far from complete and the archaeology of humbler materials has hardly begun.

Despite all these lacks, two general histories of this area

have been written in the last generation.[8] In numerous books, tracts, and articles, scholars have dealt with specific periods or tried to relate some group of archaeological materials to some fragment of documentary evidence. However, a great difficulty presented by the material has not yet been resolved—the fact that the history of the Nile Valley above Aswan and the adjacent regions is not a unified one, that is, it is not the story of a single people living in the same place through time.

At present, five major threads of tradition can be followed for this region, beginning at or before the fourth millennium B.C. and in some cases possibly continuing to the present. Because the peoples who maintained these traditions occupied first one part and then another of the general area, few parts of which have been thoroughly explored, the traditions are often difficult to trace. Because peoples of these cultures traded features of their cultures with one another, distinguishing one group from another is also sometimes difficult.[9]

The best known of these traditions is northern and found in the Nile Valley in Egypt. Toward the middle of the fourth millennium B.C. the Naqada culture of Predynastic Egypt spread along the entire valley between Gebel Silsila and the Mediterranean Sea. As it spread, its control over the astonishing resources of the broad valley in Egypt also grew. It became and remained the ultimate market for goods from the south and north; at the same time it was the major source of manufactured goods and often of agricultural products for people to the south. Because of Egypt's overwhelming cultural, political, and economic resources, much—and often most—of the histories of peoples south of Aswan were generated by their contacts with Egypt and their confrontation with Egyptian culture.

Two more threads of tradition can be found in the vast group of cultures that spread in neolithic times from the Sudan in the east across the Sahara almost to the Atlantic.[10] One is known to us best from neolithic sites in and near Khartoum; it is traced mainly by distinctive pottery found as far north as the Second Cataract, where some of its characteristic objects and practices were taken up and carried forward in the A-Group, which replaced it in this area and belongs largely to another tradition.[11] The homeland of the other Sudanese-Saharan tradition has not yet been found. Among other characteristics this western/Libyan tradition strongly emphasized cattle. The people of this tradition buried their dead under fairly high stone circles, and they made a characteristic heavy-walled, dark-faced incised pottery.[12] The tradition is first revealed only occasionally—as alien objects and practices in Predynastic and Archaic Egypt and in the A-Group to the south. The most distinctive flowering of this tradition in Nubia is found in the C-Group, a culture that lasted from about 2300/2200 B.C. to about 1550/1500 B.C., but it occurred again, even as late as the fourth century A.D.[13]

The archaeological remains of the fourth thread of tradition are very simple. The tradition is almost certainly centered in the Eastern Desert and is first seen in a few simple burials of Late Archaic or Old Kingdom date in Lower Nubia (which is between the First and Second cataracts).[14] It is revealed in Egyptian documents that mention the people called Medjay, who often served Egypt as scouts and policemen. Archaeologically, the best-known appearance is as the so-called Pan Graves, which are found in Nubia and Egypt and date to the Second Intermediate Period;[15] perhaps a number of poorer burials south of the Second Cataract can be included as well.[16] During the New Kingdom the people of this tradition continued to be known as Medjay and appeared as Meded in Kushite documents from the second half of the first millennium.[17] They appear to have been involved with the Blemmyes[18] and may even be the Bedja of our own day.[19]

The fifth and last tradition is the Kushite. The Kushite tradition was the central one in ancient Nubia; in a sense, the history of Nubia before Christianity should be written as the history of this tradition and its relations with the others. Like Egypt, Kush was closely associated with the river. Although the archaeological evidence is discontinuous, especially in the Late Archaic and Old Kingdom periods, it seems clear that many objects and practices which later reappeared repeatedly in the Kushite tradition were already in use in the A-Group.[20] The A-Group had its origin in the Naqada culture of Predynastic Egypt as a colonization of northern Lower Nubia.[21] Developing many distinctive characteristics, it spread southward as the Naqada culture spread northward, adopting some of the materials and possibly some of the practices of the Sudanese cultures it encountered and replaced in the region of the Second Cataract; at about the same time A-Group Nubia was united under a kingship of Upper Egyptian type with its capital near Qustul.[22] The A-Group came to a sudden end during the First Dynasty, possibly because of Egyptian military action,[23] and no pre-Kushite remains are known that can be dated within the next several hundred years.[24] However, Sixth Dynasty inscriptions refer to a powerful principality, Yam, associated with the area at or above the Third Cataract;[25] this principality may be an ancestor of the Kushite tradition. Shortly after 2000 B.C. the name Kush first appeared—as that of an opponent of Egypt in Nubia and as the object of some Egyptian campaigning.[26] During the Second Intermediate Period in Egypt, about 1650 B.C., the principality of Kush built a remarkable empire. The area extended from the Fourth Cataract, or somewhere above it, to the First Cataract, and had as subjects people of at least four of the five major traditions discussed, among them the Egyptian garrisons in the forts of Lower Nubia, the C-Group, and the Pan Grave people.[27] Despite the astonishing complexity of her empire, Kush, as represented by the tombs of its princes at Kerma, still used some distinctive objects and customs handed down from Predynastic Egypt and the A-Group. These include a distinctive royal tomb substructure, human sacrifice, certain pottery shapes, and even some forms of art.[28]

After the end of the Second Intermediate Period a revived Egypt conquered not only Lower Nubia but the entire Kushite

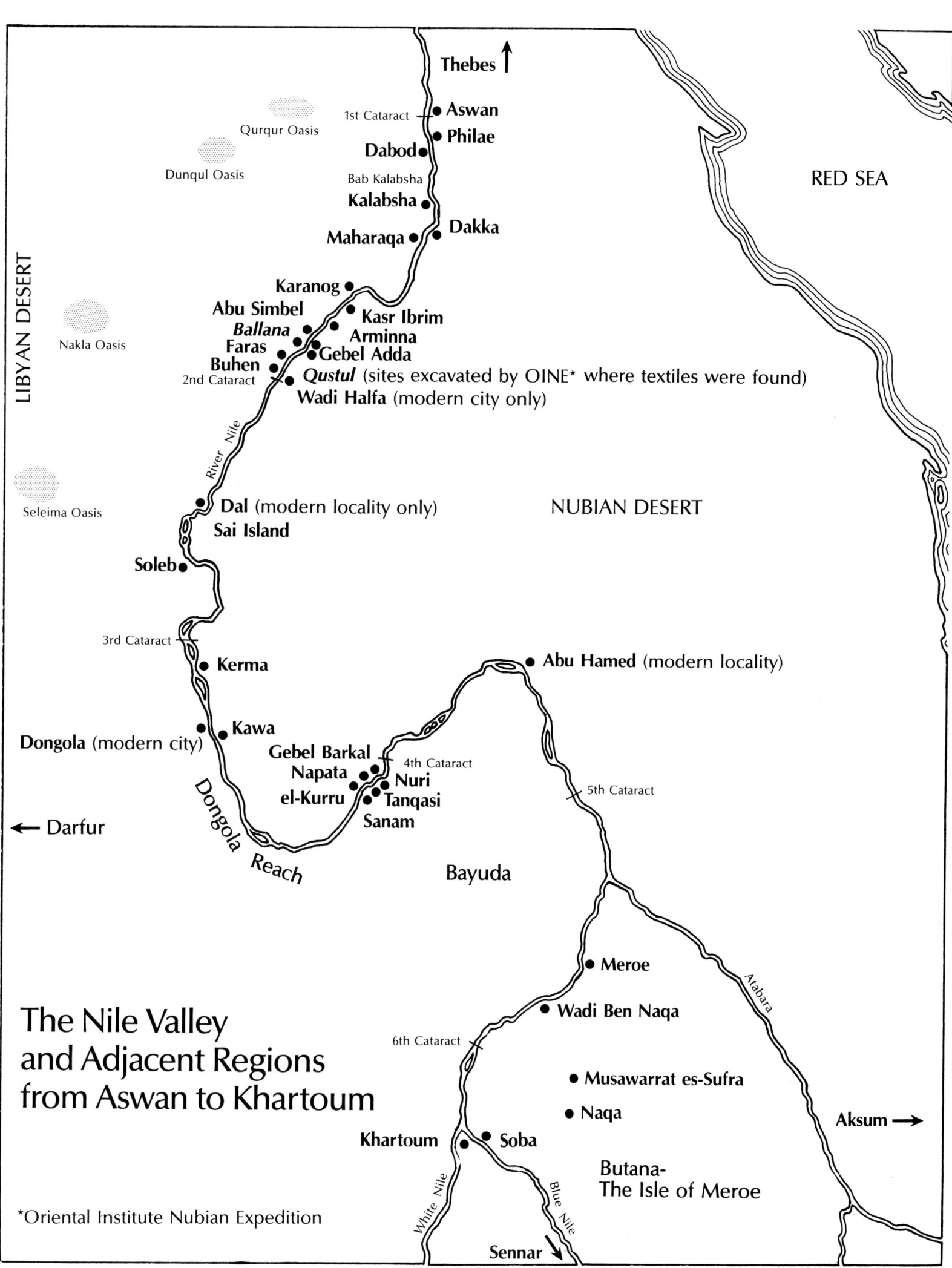

Thebes ↑

1st Cataract — ● **Aswan**
● **Philae**
Dabod ●

Qurqur Oasis

Dunqul Oasis

RED SEA

Bab Kalabsha
Kalabsha ●
● **Dakka**
Maharaqa ●

LIBYAN DESERT

Nakla Oasis

Karanog ●
Abu Simbel
● **Kasr Ibrim**
Ballana ●
● **Arminna**
Faras ●
● **Gebel Adda**
Buhen ●
2nd Cataract ✕ *Qustul* (sites excavated by OINE* where textiles were found)
Wadi Halfa (modern city only)

River Nile

Seleima Oasis

● **Dal** (modern locality only)
Sai Island

NUBIAN DESERT

Soleb ●

3rd Cataract —
● **Kerma**
● **Abu Hamed** (modern locality)

● **Kawa**
Dongola (modern city) ●
Gebel Barkal
4th Cataract
Napata ● ● **Nuri**
el-Kurru ● ● **Tanqasi**
5th Cataract
Sanam

← **Darfur**

Dongola Reach

Bayuda

The Nile Valley
and Adjacent Regions
from Aswan to Khartoum

● **Meroe**

● **Wadi Ben Naqa**

Atbara

6th Cataract ✕

● **Musawarrat es-Sufra**

● **Naqa**

Aksum →

Khartoum
● **Soba**

**Butana-
The Isle of Meroe**

White Nile

Blue Nile

Sennar ↓

*Oriental Institute Nubian Expedition

19

Empire. Egypt absorbed the area from the First to the Fourth cataracts, but local princes—perhaps even the Kushite dynasty itself—continued to exist under Egyptian control.[29]

Although this first Kushite Empire of the Second Intermediate Period had remained truer in some ways to its Egyptian Predynastic heritage than did Egypt herself, the Egyptian Empire's control of Kush meant the introduction of new and contemporary Egyptian ideas, practices, and techniques.[30] For the first time an Egyptian population was added to the local one above the Third Cataract.[31] Temples with fully developed priesthoods were established at such centers as Soleb, Kawa, and Napata.[32] Napata became not just a fortress and a town but the major center in Nubia for the worship of the god Amun.

In Lower Nubia the old C-Group population had adopted many Kushite and Pan Grave practices for burials, and Egyptian ways and objects finally became dominant about 1500 B.C.[33] By about 1450 B.C. the population there had nearly disappeared, leaving only a few people in and near the Egyptian fortresses.[34] Above the Third Cataract the native population, with their princes, remained; all of the Southern Empire of Egypt was ruled by an official called the King's Son of Kush.

With the exception of a few minor revolts, little disturbed the Egyptian presence in Kush until almost the end of the New Kingdom.[35] At that time a King's Son of Kush, Panehsy ("The Nubian"), intervened militarily in a dispute involving the High Priesthood of Amun at Thebes. He was not successful and retreated from Egypt; it is assumed that he then separated the rule of Kush from that of Upper Egypt, which ultimately fell to the High Priest of Amun.[36] In any case, there is no evidence that Egypt's rule in the area south of Aswan continued during the Twenty-first Dynasty and later, though a Libyan king of the Twenty-second Dynasty made a limited intervention there of some sort.[37]

In fact, there is no direct evidence that there was any population at all in Lower Nubia during this period. Virtually nothing is known of events in Kush then, for the art of writing had either been lost or was being ignored. However, if the fact that Egyptians continued to reside in Lower Nubia during the Second Intermediate Period is any guide to their conduct when Egyptian control in Nubia ceased,[38] they may have also continued to reside in Kush, probably serving as priests at Kawa and Napata and as officials of whatever government existed in the area.[39] Some time after the country to the south seceded from Egypt (about 1080 B.C.) and at least five generations before the Kushite king Piye conquered Egypt (728 B.C.), the viceroyalty of Egyptian origin gave way to a principality or kingship ($\beta\alpha\sigma\iota\lambda\iota\sigma\kappa\sigma\varsigma$[?]) of the Kushite tradition.[40] That the priests of Amun at Napata had some role in this change can be inferred from the fact that they, along with palace officials and the army, had the right to confirm the succession and, until the third century B.C., the right to order the king's death.[41]

The structure of the earliest tombs of these Kushite sovereigns was based on Kushite burial traditions of Kerma.[42] After Kush conquered Egypt, however, important Egyptian elements were reintroduced to Kush and adapted to local usage. These elements included hieroglyphic writing and canons of art, and the pyramid form came to be used for the Kushite royal tombs. This pyramid form and the chapel that accompanied the tomb was not like the vast pile built for the pharoahs of the Old Kingdom; it was a considerably larger version of the tall and slender pyramid placed over many Egyptian private tombs of the New Kingdom, especially the later New Kingdom. Such pyramids were erected over New Kingdom tombs at Soleb in Nubia.[43]

When Piye conquered Egypt, founding the Twenty-fifth Dynasty there, he eliminated a number of local Libyan rulers who had rival claims to her headship. Kushite interest in the earlier achievements of Egyptian literature and art helped to bring about one of the last great flowerings of Egyptian culture. Although the adoption of Egyptian arts, especially the art of writing, benefitted Kush, the intervention did not end happily for her. She had followed the Egyptian policy of opposing Assyria in Asia, and the result was that in three campaigns, which culminated in Assurbanipal's sack of Thebes in 664 B.C., the Kushite Twenty-fifth Dynasty was entirely swept from Egypt.

Confined to the area above Aswan and ruling effectively probably only above the Second Cataract, Kush sought new fields of activity, especially to the southeast, where involvement had already begun.[44]

The Dongola Reach, which had been the center of Kush, was separated from productive land to the south by the grim territory between the Fourth and Fifth cataracts at the great bend of the Nile.[45] However, above the Fifth Cataract, beyond the place—a little south and somewhat east of Napata—where the Nile is joined by a seasonal freshet, the Atbara, the river runs through open steppe and scrub land.[46] Although the land is dry now, in the past a slightly greater rainfall and some arrangements for collecting and storing the rainwater would have made it productive enough to sustain a substantial agricultural and pastoral population.[47] Communication with Napata was maintained across the Bayuda steppe (the area inside the great bend) by way of the oasis of Abu Klea.[48]

Thus, the center of Kushite civilization was moved southward and a new center was established at Meroe, which was in the region between the Atbara and the Blue Nile along the east side of the Nile. The region came to be known to classical writers as the Isle of Meroe and is known now as the gezira ("isle") or Butana. Although the Meroitic civilization, as the later phases of the Kushite kingdom are known, spread some distance into this gezira and up the Blue Nile as far as Sennar,[49] the major centers remained near the Nile.[50] This strangely formed bi-regional state may have remained united throughout its history. If it split apart politically, it was at most only twice, and then the divisions were of very limited significance and duration.[51]

Within a few hundred years, that is, just after 300 B.C., the kings of Kush were being buried at Meroe under the same kind of slender stone pyramids, with chapels, that had been used at

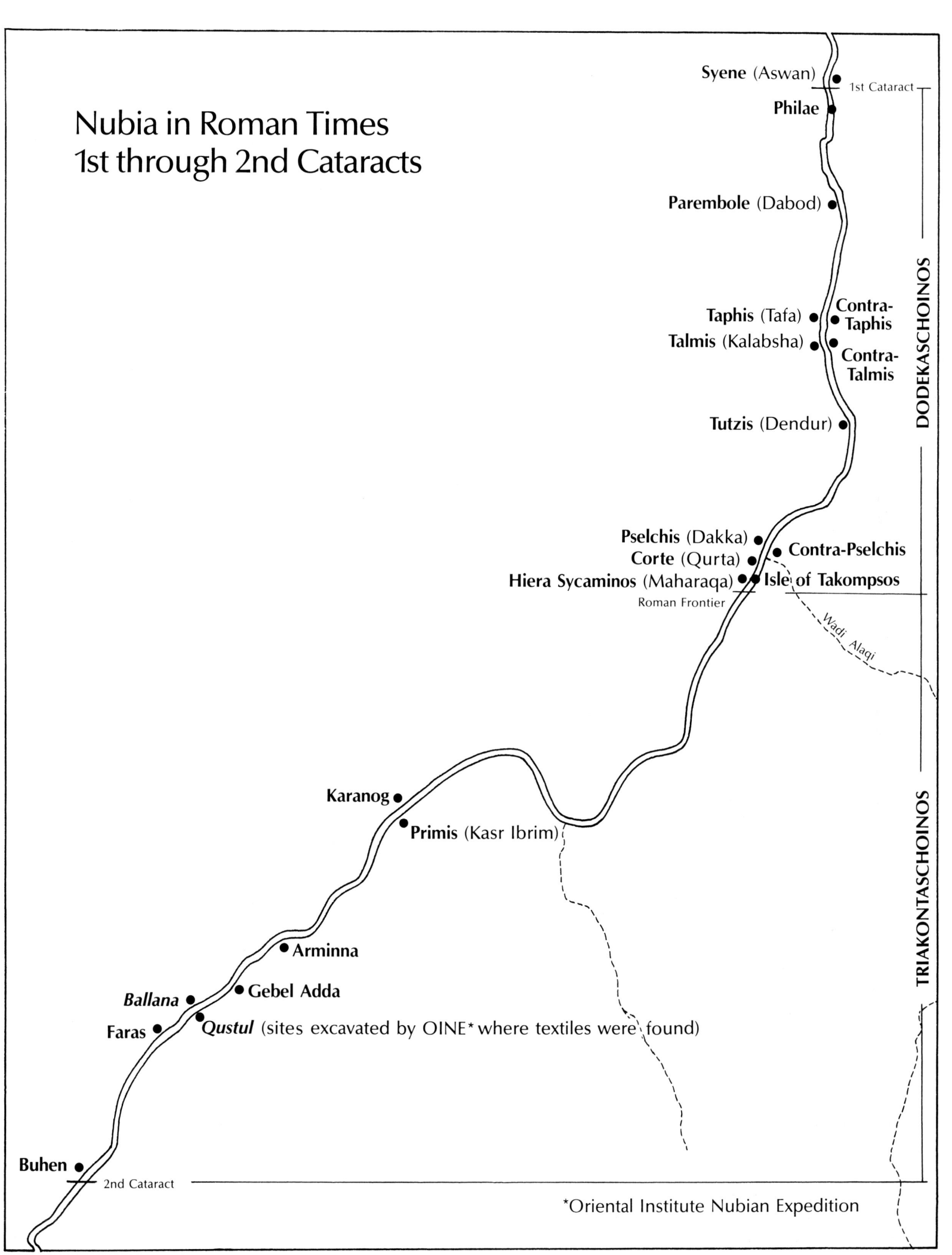

Nubia in Roman Times
1st through 2nd Cataracts

Syene (Aswan) ● 1st Cataract

Philae ●

Parembole (Dabod) ●

DODEKASCHOINOS

Taphis (Tafa) ● ● **Contra-Taphis**

Talmis (Kalabsha) ● ● **Contra-Talmis**

Tutzis (Dendur) ●

Pselchis (Dakka) ● ● **Contra-Pselchis**
Corte (Qurta) ●
Hiera Sycaminos (Maharaqa) ●● Isle of Takompsos

Roman Frontier

Wadi Alaqi

TRIAKONTASCHOINOS

Karanog ●

● Primis (Kasr Ibrim)

● Arminna

Ballana ● ● Gebel Adda

Faras ● ● *Qustul* (sites excavated by OINE* where textiles were found)

Buhen ●
2nd Cataract

*Oriental Institute Nubian Expedition

el Kurru and Nuri near Napata. The area of the Dongola Reach was reduced in importance. While Egypt preserved her independence until she was conquered by the Persians in 525 B.C., the Kushite civilization, with its center at Meroe, continued, although fairly isolated, to develop its remarkable bicultural heritage. Kushite objects and practices (along with some from farther south, perhaps) existed alongside a heavily Egyptianizing "higher culture." Kushite, or Meroitic, elements gradually entered this official culture. Local gods, such as the lion-headed Apedemak, became prominent along with Egyptian deities; Amun, or Amani, remained the official royal deity. Modifications of the old pharaonic headdresses came to be preferred;[52] Meroitic kings and queens were increasingly shown with local dress, jewelry, and weapons,[53] and according to local standards of beauty (some of the queens are simply enormous!).[54] The most interesting change was in the language of the inscriptions. Although the Egyptian language continued to be used for some time on monuments, the local language, Meroitic, came to be written in two scripts. One, of hieroglyphs derived from Egyptian, was used for monumental purposes. The other was an alphabet of 23 letters derived from Egyptian hieroglyphics and Demotic.[55] These scripts appear to have been developed in the late third or second centuries B.C.[56] The language is largely undeciphered. Although the scripts can be read, the inscriptions remain substantially unintelligible; moreover, the language has not yet been successfully related to any other.[57] In any event, the inscriptions would not inform us much about specific events, for they are largely funerary formulae that recite names, titles, and family relationships.

Because of the lack of source material, Napatan and Meroitic history is often little more than a list of names, especially after 1 A.D. We know the names because they were inscribed in the pyramid chapels, which were excavated early in the twentieth century. The excavator constructed a sequence of pyramids by relating each pyramid to all the others by type of shape, chamber, and decoration, making a series that is believed to be almost complete. This sequence is connected to the history of Egypt, the Near East, and the classical world by only four or five events that are scattered over a period of 600 years. Each king was assigned a date according to the place that his pyramid occupied in the sequence, and an estimate of the length of his reign was based on the relative size, complexity, and wealth of his funeral arrangements.[58]

The record of specific events in Kush is made up of the few events mentioned above that link Napata and Meroe to Egyptian and classical civilization and the few recorded in classical or Kushite sources only. From the time of Taharko in the seventh century B.C. to the campaign of Ezana in the fourth century A.D., these events can be counted on the fingers.

Soon after Kush lost Egypt, she was beset with external difficulties. Anlamani (623–593 B.C.?) reported an attack of the Belhe (later known as Blemmyes) on Kawa and other Kushite settlements, which he claimed to have repulsed.[59] Internal dif-

ficulties occurred also. Aspelta, his successor, may have had to publicly record on a stela the punishment of a priest of Amani. Later, Aspelta's name was erased from the stela.

Aspelta was, however, able to move his army forward toward Egypt as far as the "Pure Mountain."[60] Although Egypt was distracted by the threat of Babylon, Psammetichos II of the Twenty-sixth Dynasty forestalled Aspelta by sending southward an army that appears to have campaigned well into the Dongola Reach, perhaps even beyond Napata. The campaign was recorded by the pharoah himself and by Greek and Carian soldiers who scrawled graffiti at Buhen and especially at Abu Simbel. Some of these soldiers may have been left in Lower Nubia as a garrison.[61]

Cambyses, king of Persia, conquered Egypt in 525 B.C. and attempted to conquer Ethiopia as well, but he was forced to give up the venture because the country was so inhospitable. Thereafter, Aswan was garrisoned by Jewish troops from Judah, and we read little of disturbed relations during the period of Persian rule in Egypt (fifth century B.C.), although this may be due to the scarcity of historical texts.[62]

About a century after the Persian conquest of Egypt, Irike-Amanote of Kush (431–405 B.C.) recorded the events surrounding his accession to the throne. Before his coronation at Napata he had to deal with an invasion of the Rehres,[63] directed against the vicinity of Meroe itself, and after his coronation he again had to deal with intruders, the Meded (i.e., the people known earlier as the Medjay), before visiting the temples at Kawa.[64]

After Irike-Amanote, his second successor, Harsiyotef (ca. 404–380 B.C.) continued the policy of confrontation with the Rehres and the Meded.[65] In the second year of his reign he slaughtered the Rehres. In Year 5, he went against the Meded and after three campaigns finally obtained the formal submission of their chief.[66]

His next campaign was against Aqnat (Akin? Lower Nubia?), where he went to deal with two enemies, Berga and Sa-amaniso, whom he defeated as far as Aswan.[67] If the reign of Harsiyotef is correctly dated even approximately, this campaign took place during the period when the Twenty-eighth and Twenty-ninth dynasties (404–380 B.C.) were freeing Egypt from the Persian yoke. The sequence of Harsiyotef's campaigns indicates a thrust of policy; probably he was seeking opportunities in Upper Egypt. If so, he was thwarted, not by resurgent Egypt, but by an old enemy, the Rehres, who were close at hand. The brief expansion of the late Napatan Kingdom was halted and perhaps reversed.

In Year 16, Harsiyotef faced the rebellion of a city. Although a slaughter is claimed in the text, the usual refrain is omitted and we can assume that all was not as he would have liked.[68]

The situation worsened in Year 17, when the Rehres, apparently revived, attacked the vicinity of Meroe; after a battle they were repulsed but not destroyed. In Year 23, they returned and were finally slaughtered. We hear nothing more of ambitious campaigns on the part of Harsiyotef, but a minor action was subsequently undertaken—significantly, after a conference with Amani.[69]

The next event we know of occurred a century later, when Meroe battled an invader named *hmbdswn*, possibly Khabbash, known to have been in revolt against Persia in Upper Egypt from 338 to 336 B.C.[70] Two generations later a king known from classical sources as Ergamenes (probably Arkamani-qo) was ruling. Arkamani-qo was the first ruler buried at Meroe and was said to have had a Greek education. It was also said that he had disregarded a priestly summons to suicide and, indeed, that because of the summons he had attacked and slain the priests of Amani.[71]

A split may have occurred in the kingdom at this point, indicated by a group of pyramids at Napata that are contemporary with the early ones at Meroe, but this division and a later one are matters of controversy though they may be related to the events discussed below.[72]

All through the reigns of the first three Ptolemies in Egypt, Lower Nubia appears to have continued to be virtually unoccupied. However, toward the end of the reign of Ptolemy III Euergetes I there were disturbances in Egypt that portended the revolts which later shook the kingdom.[73] It would appear that Arkamani, then king of Meroe, extended his northern frontier to Aswan and built a small temple at Philae, already a religious center.[74] After Ptolemy IV Philopator came into control of all Egypt, he occupied the region just south of Aswan called the Dodekaschoinos, making additions to the temple of Arkamani at Philae and building a temple of his own at Dakka, opposite the opening of the Wadi Alaqi.[75]

After the mighty but dangerous victory over Antiochus of Syria at Raphia, Philopator was beset toward the close of his reign by a major revolt in Upper Egypt. A local pharoah, Harmachis (205/4–200/199 B.C.), was established in power.[76] Once again Arqamani took the Dodekaschoinos; he then made additions to the temple of Philopator at Dakka.[77] It is difficult to believe that Arqamani was not involved in the events in Upper Egypt, for there was little point to involving himself in barren Lower Nubia.

Our knowledge of subsequent events is more definite. Ptolemy V Epiphanes is attested at Elephantine in 199 as well as in 198 and 196; the last recorded date of Harmachis is July/August in 199.[78] By 194, however, Upper Egypt was again in revolt, this time under Ankhmachis, a new king, who counted his years from those of Harmachis and thus considered himself a successor.[79] It was probably at this time that the Meroite, Adkheramani, built the temple at Dabod.[80] The revolt was finally quashed in 186 with the aid of Greek troops, probably after some battles and sieges had taken place in Middle Egypt.[81] Ankhmachis was captured and his son as well as his *Nubian* troops were slain.[82] Since these troops were not called Blemmyes or Megabaroi, peoples well known at the time, they must have been Meroitic soldiers.[83] Meroitic policy threads through these revolts; it would appear that under Arkamani and Adkher-

amani the Meroites were attempting to revive the days of the Twenty-fifth Dynasty, using Egyptian dynasts in revolt from the Ptolemies as stalking horses.[84] How nearly they succeeded is shown by the extremely dangerous situation of Epiphanes between 197 and 190, when at times his writ was not respected outside Alexandria and barely respected within it.

Epiphanes reoccupied Upper Egypt in 186; the event is recorded in the inscription at Philae. Although his successor, Ptolemy VI Philometor, established a special military command at Thebes, he did not consider possession of the Dodekaschoinos sufficient protection and moved his forces forward to the Second Cataract.[85] In the process, settlements were founded or renamed. Although we hear nothing of this area, known as Triakontaschoinos, between the time of Ptolemy VI Philometor and the time of Augustus, records are fragmentary, and subsequent revolts in Upper Egypt cannot be clearly connected with Meroe. Upper Egypt continued to be disturbed—by the revolt of Harganophor in the time of Ptolemy IX Alexander I[86] and by others—until a three-year guerilla war culminated in the sack of Thebes by Ptolemy X Soter II in 85.[87]

It was against this background of disorder that the Ptolemies and the Meroitic rulers and their Egyptian allies or cobelligerents struggled not just for Nubia but for Upper Egypt or more.[88] After the victory of Epiphanes, however, Egyptians began to settle in the Dodekaschoinos, especially near Dakka at Awam, as shown by burials,[89] and the Ptolemies became involved in Nubia. The involvement was essentially for purposes of defense, but it also had an economic purpose (gold could be mined there) and a political purpose (prisoners could be sent there to work the mines).[90]

In the first century B.C., as the Ptolemaic grip on Egypt slackened once again, the Meroitic Kingdom began to edge northward again, moving into the abandoned area of Triakontaschoinos and apparently establishing garrisons near the Second Cataract and at Ibrim. Garrisons probably were not intended to secure the area for settlement but as watch posts for possible opportunities over the frontier; in these circumstances the area would hardly have been suitable for civil settlement.

After the battle of Actium, Rome became the ruler of Egypt. As usual, the turbulent Thebans greeted novelty with revolt, but in an astonishing performance Roman legions quelled the revolt in fifteen days.[91] Thereafter, the second prefect Aelius Gallus felt secure enough to strip Upper Egypt of Roman troops so as to attempt the conquest of South Arabia.

In the absence of troops, the Meroites, probably under Akinidad,[92] who had the support of his mother, Amanirenas (the *kdke*; in Greek, Candace), attacked and sacked Philae and Aswan, pulling down the statues of Augustus and enslaving a number of the inhabitants.[93] Only the barest facts are given about this encounter, but the futility of the action is immediately apparent. It would appear that Akinidad was trying to raise a revolt against the Romans (as his predecessors had participated in revolts against the Ptolemies), perhaps hoping that the long trek to the Dongola Reach might keep the Romans from coming after him there if he failed in the attempt. If that was in his mind, he misjudged Roman power and determination.

Petronius, who replaced the discredited Gallus, began by demolishing both the Meroitic army and Meroitic positions in Lower Nubia. After taking Ibrim, he stabbed deep into the Dongola Reach to take and sack Napata, the second capital of the kingdom.[94] This lesson in Roman diplomacy having been delivered, the Meroites sued for peace. Petronius met the envoys at Aswan, where he added to the lesson in Roman energy a lesson in the depth of Roman power—he sent the envoys to Samos to see the emperor. Augustus, whose concern was simply to maintain a secure frontier, allowed the Meroites to cease paying tribute and ceded all Roman claims to the territory south of the Dodekaschoinos. As a result of established peace all of Lower Nubia was ultimately opened to civil settlement.[95]

It would be difficult to exaggerate the importance for subsequent events in Lower Nubia of the settlement that Augustus made with the Meroites. Even before the Libyans took over the government of Egypt more than nine hundred years earlier, the two great regions of that country had been ready to part politically. Because Kush had a close relationship with the worship of Amun (Amani), Upper Egypt was willing enough to be under southern control and thus became a tempting target for Kushite ambition. This potential for mischief in Upper Egypt became a major problem for the foreign rulers of Egypt. Every time they appeared to be growing weak, the Kushites pushed toward the frontier.

The first time they did so after the Twenty-fifth Dynasty had been expelled from Egypt, they were forestalled by Psammetichos, as they may have been by Cambyses three quarters of a century later. Their next attempt was carefully prepared during the time Egypt was gaining independence from Persia. They forced dangerous tribes into submission, got the support of Amani's priests, and reached Aswan. However, rebellion at home and the invasion of Meroe by the tribe of Rehres ended this attempt and the time was lost; the powerful Thirtieth Dynasty arose in Egypt before the death of Harsiyotef. The next attempt was possibly in the time of Khabbash, about whom we know little, but the Persians returned, soon replaced by Alexander and the mighty early Ptolemies. As the Ptolemaic grasp on Egypt weakened and Egyptian resentment of the Macedonian rule increased, the Meroites advanced toward Aswan again, this time participating in the dangerous revolts that shook the thrones of Philopator and Epiphanes. Once again Kushite ambition was thwarted, and the ever-present danger from Kush, recorded at Edfu by the Ptolemies, was finally removed when Petronius sent the Meroitic envoys to Samos.

The major reason for the repeated Meroitic failures in the north was not the dangerous flaw in Meroitic society that Ergamenes corrected—the conflict between the throne and the priests of Amani—in spite of the fact that rebellion helped to frustrate Harsiyotef. It was not the geographic flaw—the inability of the Nile Valley above Aswan to support a population large enough to fend off the tribes that finally overwhelmed it. The major reason was the fact that for the Meroites the world had grown larger. Piye was able to defeat the Libyan potentates partly because these potentates had only their own resources to rely on. The Assyrian opponents of Kush, however, had behind them the might of a military and bureaucratic empire. The Saites used the hardened strength of Greek mercenary soldiers. The Persians, the Ptolemies, and the Romans were able to draw on their resources of almost limitless levies and numerous professional soldiers (as at Aswan). Not until Petronius, however, were the Meroites made to understand how the world had changed and what that change meant for their ambitions.

Little is known of Meroitic history after the time of Augustus. After a spurt of new building, reconstruction, and repairs, building seems to have been reduced from even the modest scale of the first century B.C.[96] Trade with Rome continued, and perhaps increased over that of Ptolemaic times, as the resettlement of Lower Nubia played a greater role in Meroitic affairs.

Before the second century A.D. the Meroitic Kingdom had two centers—the Isle of Meroe and the area of Napata in the Dongola Reach, which were linked by a road across the Bayuda steppe. The earlier center waned in importance over time. In Lower Nubia the activities of the Meroites were limited to the building and restoration of a few temples and the maintenance of a few garrisons at points such as Ibrim and Faras;[97] but in the second century A.D., settlement spread away from the fortress areas, and Lower Nubia was soon a third center of the Meroitic Empire.[98] The development of this region was perhaps the chief event in the Meroitic Kingdom after 100 A.D.[99]

The most informative document of Meroitic history may be the one that is associated with the end of Meroe itself. Ezana, king of Aksum, the Abyssinian kingdom closely related to the cultures of South Arabia, recorded in about 350 A.D. that he, claiming the kingship of Kush, had defeated the Noba. These people were living in or near the Butana "in Kasu," some in cities of brick "which the Noba had taken" from the Kasu, which presumably were cities of the old Meroitic Empire.[100]

Ezana's conquests mark the end of the Kushite Empire and the Kushite Kingdom if not the tradition. The peoples whom Ezana had conquered, the Noba, or Nubians, had moved into and taken over the area of the old Meroitic Kingdom. There they created a culture usually referred to as Tanqasi.[101] In Lower Nubia to the north, the arrival of people who were probably related to the Tanqasi culture is marked by the reappearance of low tumuli that covered burials with bodies in contracted positions. This Lower Nubian culture, the X-Group, was at first ruled by local kinglets at major points along the Nile. Later, many of these kingdoms were consolidated by a certain Silko. The rulers of Lower Nubia maintained a number of customs derived from the Kushite tradition that were evident in the barbaric splendor of their tombs at Ballana and Qustul.

Lower Nubia in the Later Meroitic and X-Group Periods

When the Meroitic settlers first expanded their settlements beyond the immediate vicinity of the fortresses, Lower Nubia had not been intensively occupied beyond the Dodekaschoinos for over a thousand years. There are, however, certain difficulties in determining the amount of activity in Lower Nubia. Most of the cemeteries away from the fortresses were no longer in use about midway through the Eighteenth Dynasty.[102] The fortress cemeteries were in use beyond that time, as were some near Qustul.[103] During the Nineteenth and Twentieth dynasties, changes that affect our evidence occurred in Egyptian burial customs. Pottery and other objects in daily use were no longer deposited with the body, which was increasingly treated as though it were a statue; religious texts and shawabtis were relied on to provide those who could afford them with the necessities of life in the underworld.[104] As a result we no longer have the large number of well-defined groups of artifacts necessary to build an adequate picture of daily life during the Third Intermediate and Late periods, especially in Upper Egypt. Moreover, we cannot disregard the possibility that after burial was desecularized, Egyptians living outside Egypt might have wished to be buried in Egypt, as was done during the Middle Kingdom.[105] It is therefore quite possible to exaggerate the scarcity of the population in Lower Nubia during this millennium. A major reduction in rural population and a retreat to the major centers is documented for the New Kingdom, but we can perceive no evidence at all of settlements during the first two thirds of the first millennium. At most, there must have been only a few, poor, permanent inhabitants.

Although it has been proposed that this almost complete lack of population was due to a reduction in the water levels of the Nile,[106] this explanation flies in the face of what evidence we have. Taharko spoke of floods in a temple, and the Nile levels at Thebes are reported to be rather higher there than they were during the New Kingdom.[107]

Two reasons for the scarcity of population present themselves as plausible. First, Egypt and newly independent Kush had reason to distrust each other. Both the adventure of Panehsy in Upper Egypt and the intervention of Sheshonk in Nubia would have made a no-man's-land between the two powers desirable, especially since the kings of Lower Egypt often held only precarious power in Upper Egypt.[108] (Piye, in fact, conquered all of Egypt from Thebes.) The stories that Ethiopia accepted Egyptian deserters, the evidence that Psammetichos II in the Twenty-sixth Dynasty and the Kushite, Harsiyotef, campaigned over the border, and the affair of ḥmbdswn all seem to indicate that military activity along the frontier was a continuing affair. Border problems from the time of the Ptolemies to the time of Augustus have also been reviewed above. These details should indicate that additional skirmishes or even significant campaigns surely occurred about which nothing is known. Further, there was little reason for settlement there; the country itself had relatively little value except for the gold mines, whose operation required much effort and expense. Only when there was substantial trade was Lower Nubia valuable. Also, the interests of both Egypt and Kush were expanding in opposite directions. In this period Napata was shifting its interest southward, and Egypt, because of its increased exploitation of the Delta's prodigious agricultural resources, could trade agricultural products for metallic wealth and exotic products available from the growing Mediterranean trade of the Phoenicians and the Greeks.[109]

The first resettlement of any size that we can detect to the south of Aswan was Egyptian and was made in the Ptolemaic period, presumably after the victory of Ptolemy V Epiphanes. The primary purpose was to secure the dangerous southern frontier, although a fairly lively trade in Hellenistic artifacts indicates trade with Meroe.[110]

After peace was made by Augustus, we begin to see, probably in the first century A.D., signs of permanent Meroitic settlement in the area of Faras.[111] The settlements spread from there to all parts of Lower Nubia south of the Dodekaschoinos.[112] This large-scale resettlement has usually been attributed to the saqiya, because it has been supposed that this part of Nubia could not have supported a large population if the ability to raise water had not been increased by the use of this waterwheel. Qawadus, the pots usually used on a saqiya, have been found in Meroitic sites.[113] However, these pots are also found in graves, which indicates that there were alternative uses for them (e.g., the making of beer). Moreover, if the saqiya were the only or the main reason for the resettlement of Lower Nubia, the Dongola Reach had much greater promise. The saqiya probably played an important role in resettlement, but the real reason should be sought in the one feature that gave Lower Nubia an advantage over all the other stretches of the valley south of Aswan—its proximity to Egypt. Because the uprisings in Upper Egypt had been quelled and there was therefore no opportunity in Egypt for Meroitic meddling, Lower Nubia was not likely to raid to the north and therefore suffer counter-raids. Moreover, opportunities for trade were growing. Although Egypt was easily able to provide basic supplies for the miniscule Roman garrison there, the Roman Empire had a continuing and growing desire for southern products such as gum arabic. At the same time, the spread of the domestic camel put more than a weapon into the hands of more distant and nomadic peoples;[114] they now had a carrier of trade. Routes such as the Darb el Arbaᶜin could be opened. All in all, Lower Nubia offered a place for transshipment or smuggling into the Roman Empire.

In Egypt, on the other hand, conditions were on the decline for the average citizen. Some had taken to abandoning their livings and fleeing, some to bandit groups and, later, some to monasteries.[115] Some, perhaps, fled to Nubia. We should look to this anachoresis as the source of most of the new techniques to be seen in Meroitic Lower Nubia.

Almost predictably, the culture of Meroitic Lower Nubia

seems to have been a mixture of habits and customs from the Kushite homeland in the south and some new ideas and techniques from Egypt.

It is difficult to compare Lower Nubia with the homeland in the Dongola Reach and Butana. The people of the homeland continued to follow the traditions of the Napatan Kingdom. Little has been studied of their town and grave sites.[116] From the royal inscriptions we learn of three groups that had special importance in the state—the king and the king's relations, the priesthood, and the army.[117]

Although, for obvious reasons, royal institutions did not exist in the province in the north, many formal features of that society appear to be like those of the south but on a smaller scale. In the third century A.D. the rule of Lower Nubia descended in the Dodekaschoinos from that of the estate of Isis, under the agents of Isis, to a "General of the River."[118] Other officials, also hereditary, ruled major centers[119] under the "Prince of Akin,"[120] who resided outside the province. Officials in Lower Nubia kept in touch with the center at Meroe.

The Meroitic gods were in evidence in temples in the larger centers and in the fact that a large proportion of the surviving funerary texts use the term *priest* to refer to the person for whom they were dedicated and to the relatives of those persons. The language of inscriptions is Meroitic; the slightly altered dialect used indicates that it was in fairly common use.[121]

The other major social element we can detect in Meroitic Lower Nubia came from Egypt. Most of the names in Lower Nubia are Meroitic; a few are Egyptian. Major burial customs, including tomb shapes, appear to have been derived from those of Ptolemaic and Roman Egypt. The major tomb shape, the shaft with end chamber, is one of these importations.[122] However, most burials are Kushite. There is no attempt to turn the body into a "statue" as had been the custom in Egypt for more than a thousand years, and the Kushite tendency to bury elaborate but useful grave goods with the dead is dominant, though there are coffin burials that more closely reflect Egyptian practice.[123]

Elements other than names and tomb substructures point to a strong Egyptian influence. Pottery, in shapes congenial to Kushite usage, was made on the wheel and often decorated almost like the Hadra vases with Hellenistic designs. The other designs on pots are roughly Kushite.[124] The most obvious Egyptian contribution was the art of viticulture.[125] This delicate and complex technology required trained and experienced people, and Egypt is the only place from which they could have come to this area. Of course, imported goods from Egypt were common: beads, including millefiori, glass vessels, and the iron jewelry of Late Roman Egypt.[126]

Artistic traditions from the south may have continued. Antecedents of the charming polychrome designs on cups and jars, so typical of Meroitic Lower Nubia, are probably to be traced to the more elaborate incised metal cups found from earlier times in the Meroitic heartland.[127]

In this attractive, prosperous society the traditions of the deserts near and far do not appear. Handmade pottery is local. No non-Meroitic or non-Egyptian names occur in the texts.[128] The towns, with their well-built houses for "patricians" and "plebeians," do not offer any evidence of extensive slaveholding. The picture we derive of Meroitic Lower Nubia is that of a mixed Meroitic–Egyptian culture. Some desert people may have been present, such as Blemmyes, Megabaroi, and Nobatai, but it appears that, if present, such people were more probably scouts, mercenaries, and traders than settlers. In any case, they had very little effect on the culture as we know it.

The Meroitic Lower Nubian population was engaged in trade, manufacturing, and agriculture under the political sovereignty of Meroe, which was exercised semiautonomously by local officials, whose positions were at least partly hereditary. The society came into being toward the end of the first century A.D. or during the second; its heyday was in the second half of the third century and it continued into the fourth, at which time new and discordant elements were introduced.[129]

From an archaeological point of view the first and most easily detectable change was the establishment of a new group just south of Aswan near Kalabsha.[130] Archaeologists found evidence of the group in four places, three of which were dug by a joint expedition of The University of Chicago Oriental Institute Nubian Expedition in cooperation with the Schweizerisches Institut für ägyptische Bauforschung und Altertumskunde in Kairo. On Gebel Khor Abu Sina there is a necropolis made up of tall well-built dry-stone circles enclosing domed-corbelled burial chambers that have an entry on the east side and offering places in front of them.[131] The pottery associated with these remarkable structures is unlike anything found elsewhere in Nubia (except for Sayala); it is handmade and has white-filled impressed and incised designs[132] possibly descended from the old C-Group incised bowl. Along with these pots there were some Late Roman coins and other objects[133] and tapered cups of the type usually referred to as early X-Group.[134] Only one Meroitic painted sherd[135] was found at the sites dug by the Oriental Institute team, and there were some lamp fillers.[136] Coins from Cemetery E, which also contained the distinctive pottery already mentioned, were dated to the mid-fourth century.[137] It is almost inconceivable that these tombs on Gebel Khor Abu Sina belong to any but chieftains of the Blemmyes. This group existed in the age when the camel had greatly increased the mobility of the inhabitants of the deserts, so it is not surprising that its cultural relations were with western rather than eastern traditions.

The second change, represented by materials found at Qustul, is more important, but due to problems with archaeological chronology and a relative lack of attention to major changes in the habits and customs in the populations of this area it has not been clearly demonstrated.

The earliest tombs of the X-Group found at Qustul are the burials of a few warriors, who were sometimes rudely thrust into Meroitic tombs.[138] One striking example is a man buried in semi-contracted posture along with his military equipment, leather armor, bow, arrows with vicious barbs, archer's loose, and anklet made of feathers strung around the lower leg. He was laid in a Meroitic tomb the original occupant of which had been carelessly thrown from the chamber into the shaft. His burial and a few others like his seem so alien that they must be the first after a conquest or migration. The semicontracted posture instead of the more "civilized" extended position, the absence of pottery, and the prominence of weapons and military equipment and of portable goods such as rugs bespeak a people used to moving and fighting.[139] Subsequent burials of this type include a low tumulus raised over a simple shaft with side chamber, the body in semicontracted position, and the same kind of portable goods, which occasionally include a pottery vessel.[140] The final development of this type of grave culminated in the immense mounds of the royal tombs of Qustul. The grave goods are warlike but include much pottery and less portable wealth. People are now often buried lying on their backs.[141]

Other major changes can be detected in the towns and cemeteries of Lower Nubia. Where found, Meroitic temples have been violently destroyed and not rebuilt.[142] Many towns continued at the same sites, but many sites were abandoned,[143] and those that continued soon became impoverished.[144] The colorful pottery of local origin died out quickly and was rapidly replaced by drabber vessels inspired by shapes used in the Dodekaschoinos.[145] Shapes indicate that the vessels were put to the same uses as before, but the vessels have lost their attractiveness. Glass practically disappeared from private tombs; tombs of the wealthy more often contained metal vessels. The Meroitic language rapidly disappeared as a language of inscriptions; only a few inscriptions survive.[146] Greek became the written language, but was very seldom used.[147]

Although the political, social, and economic relations of Meroitic Nubia were swept away, the archaeology indicates that the population found by the X-Group newcomers did not disappear. Inferior though they were, old burial customs continued—sometimes alongside the tumuli of the great lords, sometimes in separate cemeteries. The end-chamber and brick-vault tomb with no tumulus, body in extended position, and pottery still frequently occurred.[148] Little wealth was deposited in these tombs, and the objects tended to be more portable than before. The tombs of Meroitic tradition continued, as did so many settlements, but on a reduced and much humbler scale and without the special identifying features of Meroitic higher culture—temples, pyramids, ba-statues, and offering tables with inscriptions.

Although the evidence for dating the earliest warrior burials and simpler tumuli is not as obvious as that for dating the Blemmye necropoleis, they are clearly of earlier date than the great tumuli of Ballana and Qustul of the late fourth to the sixth centuries. According to the stratigraphy the earliest burials are of later date than the Meroitic tombs of the third and possibly the early fourth centuries. It would therefore be difficult to avoid identifying the newcomers as the Nobatae referred to by classical authors.[149]

The social and economic picture of these times is often in depressing contrast with that of Meroitic Lower Nubia's great age.

In the north, Blemmyes first attacked Egypt, then settled in the old Dodekaschoinos, where they continue to be attested.[150] They appear to have merged later with the populations already there and to the south, or at least to have used the material cultures of these populations to some extent, forming the amalgam first noted by Reisner as the X-Group. A special form of tumulus continued to be used in the Dodekaschoinos.[151]

In the south, especially near the eventual capital in the Ballana–Qustul area, Nubia remained bicultural. The Nobatian overlords maintained strong and individual habits, detectable in their burial customs, some of which must have seemed fearsome and barbaric to the older Meroitic inhabitants. Tumulus burials, hecatombs of sacrificed animals, and numerous human sacrifices accompanied the burials of kings and great persons.[152] The older traditions continued among the people who supplied the Nobatian overlords with many goods and, presumably, services.[153] Their role as suppliers led to the misleading impression that there was cultural uniformity in Lower Nubia.[154]

The political history of this period is poorly known. The incursions and invasions of the Blemmyes into Lower Nubia and their subsequent activities there and in Upper Egypt have been noted in classical sources and some local documents.[155] Procopius recorded that the Nobatae were invited into Lower Nubia in the time of Diocletian as a counterbalance to the Blemmyes.[156] The date of the invitation may have been some time later, but Procopius may have correctly recorded the order of events. Under the Nobatae, who were almost certainly Nubians, the area between the Third and First cataracts was divided into a number of kingdoms with Nobatian and Blemmye rulers.[157] In the sixth century, one Nobadian kinglet named Silko united them under a single rule.[158] By defeating the Blemmyes, who were staunch supporters of Isis, and uniting Lower Nubia, Silko set the stage for the conversion of the three Nubian kingdoms, Nobadia, Makuria, and Alodia, to Christianity. The conversion was effected by Monophysite missionaries sent from Constantinople by Empress Theodora in or about 543 A.D.

NOTES:

1. The excavations were organized and directed by Prof. Keith C. Seele of the Oriental Institute of the University of Chicago, who was responsible for preparing the final publication until his death in 1971. Thereafter, the project was continued by Prof. Carl E. DeVries until 1975. Keith C. Seele, "University of Chicago Oriental Institute Nubian Expedition: Excavations between Abu Simbel and the Sudan Border, Preliminary Report," *JNES* 33 (1974): 3–12, 20–24. Special acknowledgement is made to Jean Luther and Pamela Bruton of the Oriental Institute for their editorial work on this text.
2. W. Y. Adams, *Nubia, Corridor to Africa* (London: Allen Lane, 1978), p. 14, fig. 1, and p. 45.
3. The most obvious example is the problem of the identification of the X-Group. The carriers of this material culture are considered to be primarily the descendants of the people who lived in Lower Nubia during Meroitic times (W. Y. Adams, "Meroitic North and South," *Meroitica* 2 [1976]: 23–24). For a

slightly different view see B. Trigger's commentary on this article (*Meroitica 2*, pp. 113–17). In addition, most scholars identify the X-Group as Nobatian. W. B. Emery and L. P. Kirwan identified the X-Group tumuli at Qustul as Blemmyan (*The Royal Tombs of Ballana and Qustul* [Cairo: Government Press, Bulaq, 1938], pp. 18–24). This identification was denied by Ugo Monneret de Villard ("Le necropoli di Ballana e di Qostul," *Orientalia* 9 [1940]: 61–75) and ultimately by Kirwan himself ("Tanqasi and the Noba," *Kush* 5 [1957]: 37–41).

4. The southern boundary of Egypt was north of Aswan in the First Dynasty as is shown by the Egyptian name of the southernmost nome of Upper Egypt, Ta-Seti, which is the earliest name given the country to the south, also Ta-Seti. The name *Kush* was first applied to a country near the Third Cataract (J. Vercoutter, "Pour une localisation du pays Kush au moyen empire," *Kush* 6 [1958]: 39–68), then for a time, to the entire Egyptian southern empire and finally applied mainly to the area of the Butana above the Atbara.

5. This assumes a population in ancient Egypt of about 2.5 to 3 million. Karl Baedeker (*Ägypter und der Südan*, 8th ed. [Leipzig: Karl Baedeker, 1928]) gives 29,000 for the population of *both* Kharga and Dakhla oases.

6. Bruce Trigger, *History and Settlement in Nubia*, Yale University Publications in Anthropology, no. 69 (New Haven: Department of Anthropology, Yale University, 1965), p. 160. This is compared to 1/42 x 3,000,000, which is over 71,000.

7. Adams, "Meroitic North and South," pp. 1–26; see ibid., pp. 27–117 for the varied reactions.

8. A. J. Arkell, *A History of the Sudan to 1821* (London: University of London, The Athlone Press, 1961), and Adams, *Nubia, Corridor to Africa*.

9. Specific criteria for distinguishing one tradition from another were developed by Manfred Bietak (*Studien zur Chronologie der nubischen C-Gruppe: ein Beitrag zur Frühgeschichte Unternubiens zwischen 2200 und 1550 vor Chr.*, Österreichische Akademie der Wissenschaften, philosophisch-historische Klasse, Denkschriften, vol. 97 [Vienna: Hermann Böhlaus Nachf., 1968]) for the cultures contemporary with C-Group, ca. 2300–1550 B.C. Much of the following discussion of traditions extends beyond the chronological limits set by his study. On ibid., pp. 117–27, specific characteristics of Pan Grave Kerma, and Egyptian New Kingdom objects are given. Those of C-Group are given on pp. 92–116. For the Sudanese archaeological tradition, though with emphasis on its western appearances, see Gabriel Camps, *Les civilisations préhistoriques de l'Afrique du Nord et du Sahara* (Paris: Doin éditeurs, 1974), pp. 221–57.

10. Camps, *Civilisations préhistoriques de l'Afrique du Nord*, pp. 223–24.

11. The relations between Abkan and the A-Group are discussed in Hans-Åke Nordström, *Neolithic and A-Group Sites*, Scandinavian Joint Expedition to Sudanese Nubia, vol. 3/1 (Uppsala: Scandinavian University Books, 1972), pp. 17 and 28–29. It will also be dealt with in OINE 3, forthcoming, ch. 2, "The Pottery (of Cemetery L)," and ch. 5, "Conclusion."

12. Bietak, *Chronologie*; OINE 3, ch. 2.

13. Herbert Ricke, *Ausgrabungen von Khor-Dehmit bis Beit el-Wali*, OINE 2 (Chicago: University of Chicago Press, 1967), pp. 37–42.

14. These materials were once referred to as B-Group in Lower Nubia. Criticism by H. S. Smith ("The Nubian B-Group," *Kush* 14 [1966]: 69–124) effectively demonstrated that the criteria for assigning tombs to this period were arbitrary or so generalized that they applied to other periods as well; tombs assigned to B-Group could instead be assigned to A- or C-Groups. This writer believes, however, that there are a few tombs which should be given a late Archaic and Old Kingdom date (see OINE 4, forthcoming). The argument to be made really has nothing to do with Smith's point, the intent of which was the destruction of the B-Group as it was established by G. A. Reisner and C. M. Firth.

15. Manfred Bietak, *Ausgrabungen in Sayala-Nubien 1961–1965: Denkmäler der C-Gruppe und der Pan-Gräber-Kultur*, Österreichische Akademie der Wissenschaften, philosophisch-historische Klasse, Denkschriften, vol. 92 (Vienna: Hermann Böhlaus Nachf., 1966), pp. 43–78.

16. Bruce Williams, "Archaeology and Historical Problems of the Second Intermediate Period" (Ph.D. diss., The University of Chicago, 1975), pp. 577–79.

17. M. F. Laming Macadam, *The Temples of Kawa, I: The Inscriptions*, Oxford University Excavations in Nubia (London: Oxford University Press, 1949), p. 58 (the Irike-Amanote inscription).

18. The identification of the two terms is not fully demonstrated. The Blemmyes are the people usually referred to in Greek and Coptic texts from Egypt and the Mediterranean (Jakob Krall, *Beitrag zur Geschichte der Blemmyer und Nubier*, Kaiserlichen Akademie der Wissenschaften in Wien, philosophisch-historische Klasse, vol. 4 [Vienna: Carl Gerold's Sohn, 1898], [Gebelein docu-

ments], p. 6 and n. 1). The people of the Axumite Greek texts are called Bedja ($\text{B}\epsilon\gamma\alpha$, $\text{Bov}\gamma\alpha\tilde{\iota}\tau\epsilon\varsigma$). In a biography of Shenute, the Coptic–Greek text refers to Blemmyes ($\text{N}\iota\beta\alpha\lambda\eta\mu\mu\text{ov}\iota$) translated into Arabic as Bedja (البجاة). An Arabic text of 758 A.D. recently discovered at Ibrim refers to the Bedja while Coptic texts from the same hoard refer to Blemmyes (J. Martin Plumley, "An Eighth-Century Arabic Letter to the King of Nubia," *JEA* 61 [1975]: 241–45, see line 45 and note, p. 245 especially). Although some relation between the two terms can be presumed, we cannot be sure that they have the same meaning. The Arabic and Coptic texts at Ibrim may refer to the same people, but we cannot be sure that the Coptic texts are not using *Blemmye* as an archaistic label for a people to whom it did not belong or, on the other hand, that the Arabic, in using the term *Bedja*, is not transferring a name familiar from the old Arabian–Axumite situation to a new, less appropriate one. It remains possible that one term encompassed a part of the other at one time or another.

19. The words *Blemmye* and *Bedja* have in common the fact that both were used to designate peoples who were at least partly located in the Eastern Desert and who from time to time either raided the valley, seized parts of it, or attacked traders who came from it. The Blemmyes, however, do not appear to have been associated solely with the Eastern Desert. Their field of activity seems to have included as well the Libyan Desert oasis as far as Kharga Oasis (Krall, *Beitrag zur Geschichte der Blemmyer und Nubier*, p. 12). The name may designate a confederacy of some sort (N. B. Millet, "Meroitic Nubia" [Ph.D. diss., Yale University, 1968], pp. 203–18, 269–304, esp. pp. 288, 304).

20. See OINE 3, ch. 5, "Conclusion."

21. Werner Kaiser, "Stand und Problem der ägyptischen Vorgeschichtsforschung," *ZÄS* 81 (1956): 108, fig. 5; Trigger, *History and Settlement*, p. 69.

22. See OINE 3, ch. 2, "The Pottery"; Trigger, *History and Settlement*, p. 74; OINE 3, ch. 5, "Conclusion."

23. Nordström, *Neolithic and A-Group Sites*, p. 32; OINE 3, ch. 5, "Conclusion."

24. Brigitte Gratien, *Les cultures Kerma: essai de classification*, Publications de l'Universitié de Lille, vol. 3 (Villeneuve d'Aseq: Centre nationale de la recherche scientifique, 1978). On pp. 133–260, Dr. Gratien distinguishes four phases of the Kerma culture. Without discussing the merits of these phases in detail, it is clear that fine pottery of the earliest phase (Kerma ancien, ibid., pp. 153–54, fig. 43, 12b; fig. 44, 12a–c) is C-Group, Sixth Dynasty or later in date.

25. Trigger, *History and Settlement*, p. 95. A number of candidates for the place name Yam can be found in the later Execration Texts (G. Posener, *Princes et pays d'Asie et de Nubie* [Brussels: Fondation égyptologique Reine Elisàbeth, 1940], pp. 59, 60 [B 17, 18]).

26. Kush appears as the principal place in Upper Nubia in the Execration Texts (Posener, *Princes et pays*, pp. 48 [A 1], 55 [B 2]).

27. Williams, "Archaeology and Historical Problems," pp. 599–626. The Egyptian population near the forts in Lower Nubia seems to have increased throughout the period. For other groups, see Bietak, *Chronologie*, pp. 92–116.

28. OINE 3, ch. 5, "Conclusion."

29. We have specific information only on local princes in Lower Nubia (William Kelly Simpson, *Heka-nefer and the Dynastic Material from Toshka and Arminna*, Publications of the Pennsylvania–Yale Expedition to Egypt, no. 1 [New Haven and Philadelphia: The Peabody Museum of Natural History at Yale University and the University Museum of the University of Pennsylvania, 1963], pp. 26–27). For the continuation of the Kerma K cemetery, see Williams, "Archaeology and Historical Problems," pp. 551–52, 636–37.

30. Perhaps the most fateful importation was the prominence of Amun in the Nubian temples, especially at Napata. In addition, the native inhabitants, especially those living below the Second Cataract, mostly adopted Egyptian burial practices (Simpson, *Heka-nefer*, pp. 26–27).

31. Michela Schiff Giorgini, *Soleb II: les nécropoles* (Florence: Sansoni, 1971). The New Kingdom cemeteries (pp. 79–340) contained many tombs of the Upper Egyptian type, with shaft and chamber substructures and pyramid superstructures.

32. Torgny Säve-Söderbergh, *Ägypten und Nubien* (Lund: Hakan Ohlssons Boktrykeri, 1941), pp. 193–94.

33. Bietak, *Chronologie*, p. 157.

34. C. M. Firth, *The Archaeological Survey of Nubia: Report for 1909–1910* (Cairo: Government Printing Office, 1915), pp. 21–23; F. Ll. Griffith, "Oxford Excavations in Nubia—Cont.," *LAAA* 11 (1924): 115–17; Giorgini, *Soleb II*, pp. 79–340; Georg Steindorff, *Aniba*, vol. 2 (Glückstadt, Hamburg, New York: J. J. Augustin, 1937), p. 101, nos. 29 and 30. Note, for example, that Ramesside names are found at Aniba. See also Adams, *Nubia, Corridor to Africa*, pp. 241–43. Concentration near the forts is documented.

35. K. A. Kitchen, "Historical Observations on Ramesside Nubia," in *Ägypten und Kusch (Festschrift Fritz Hintze)*, ed. Erika Endesfelder, Karl-Heinz Priese, Walter-Friedrich Reinecke, and Steffen Wenig, Schriften zur Geschichte und Kultur des Alten Orients, vol. 13 (Berlin: Akademie-Verlag, 1977), pp. 213–25.

36. K. A. Kitchen, *The Third Intermediate Period in Egypt* (Warminster: Aris and Phillips, 1973), §§ 208, 209, 211, 251.

37. Ibid., § 251 (the intervention of Sheshonq I).

38. Williams, "Archaeology and Historical Problems," pp. 626, 630–32; H. S. Smith, *The Fortress of Buhen: The Inscriptions*, Egypt Exploration Society, vol. 48 (London, 1976), pp. 67–69. Smith notes the great strength of the settlement at Buhen and Mirgissa after the fall of the Middle Kingdom.

39. Adams, *Nubia, Corridor to Africa*, pp. 258–59. No specific evidence can be cited on this point, but it must be assumed that the strong cult of Amun in Kush had been maintained by someone with a claim to represent a legitimate priesthood, which first appears in documents about the time of Piye.

40. Dows Dunham, *El Kurru*, Royal Cemeteries of Kush, vol. 1 (Cambridge, Mass.: Harvard University Press, 1950), pp. 2–3.

41. Inge Hofmann, *Studien zum meroitischen Königtum*, Monographies Reine Elisabeth, vol. 2 (Brussels: Fondation égyptologique Reine Elisabeth, 1971), p. 29.

42. For the later tumulus with trench and side chamber see Dunham, *El Kurru*, p. 12, fig. 1a, and p. 19, fig. 4a. For an early prepared-bed burial, see p. 30, fig. 11a.

43. Giorgini, *Soleb II*, pls. VI–VII (T 32). Ramesside scarabs from T 32 are on pl. XII, and discussed on pp. 288–92.

44. Dows Dunham, *The West and South Cemeteries at Meroë*, The Royal Cemeteries of Kush, vol. 5 (Cambridge, Mass.: Harvard University Press, 1957), pp. 304 (W648), 362 (S132), 431 (S130), 441 (S193). These include objects with the names of Kashta, Shebitku, and Tanutamani, but are only *termini post quem*. The first mention of Meroe is in the inscription of Irike-Amanote. Hofmann, *Studien zum meroitischen Königtum*, p. 12.

45. Adams, *Nubia, Corridor to Africa*, pp. 32–33.

46. G. H. Wainwright, "The Position of Ast-Raset," *JEA* 33 (1947): 59.

47. Adams, *Nubia, Corridor to Africa*, p. 32; J. W. Crowfoot and F. Ll. Griffith, *The Island of Meroë and Meroitic Inscriptions*, pt. 1, The Archaeological Survey of Egypt Memoir 19 (London, 1911), pp. 6–29.

48. Wainwright, "The Position of Ast-Raset," pp. 58–62. P. L. Shinnie, "A Note on Ast Raset," *JEA* 41 (1955): 128–29. For other wells on the Bayuda route, see O. G. S. Crawford, *Castles and Churches in the Middle Nile Region*, Sudan Antiquities Service Occasional Paper no. 2 (Khartoum, 1953), pp. 36–39. He wanted to identify the fortress at Fura as Meroitic, though the age of another site so identified at Jedkol has been questioned. See H. N. Chittick, "Notes on the Archaeology of the Middle Nile Region," *Kush* 2 (1954): 94–95.

49. D. M. Dixon, "A Meroitic Cemetery at Sennar (Makwar)," *Kush* 11 (1963): 227–34.

50. Fritz Hintze, "Preliminary Report on the Butana Expedition, 1958," *Kush* 7 (1959): 171–95.

51. Evidence for these "Intermediate Periods" is found only in the existence of two groups of Meroitic (royal?) pyramids at Barkal (Napata) dated to the third and first centuries B.C. respectively that parallel the long sequence of those at Meroe. G. A. Reisner, "The Meroitic Kingdom of Ethiopia, A Chronological Outline," *JEA* 9 (1923): 34–77, esp. 63–67, 75. The first Napata Group equals groups e–g in typology and thus dates, beginning approximately with Barkal XI, ending with VII, parallel to Begrawiya S VI, which is dated to Arkamani-qo (Ergamenes), and ends approximately with Begrawiya NL III, still in the third century. The second Napatan Group made the group Barkal VI to Barkal X equal the group Begrawiya N XX to Begrawiya N VI (Amanishakheto) at Meroe in the first century. Dunham (*Royal Tombs of Meroe and Barkal*, The Royal Cemeteries of Kush, vol. 4 [Boston: Museum of Fine Arts, 1957], pp. 4–5) rejected the second division of the kingdom because royal monuments of the period were found at both Meroe and Barkal. Macadam (*The Temples of Kawa, I*, pp. 74–75, and *The Temples of Kawa, II* [London: Oxford University Press, 1955], pp. 19–20), who also found reason to identify inscriptions at Kawa with the owners of pyramids at Meroe in the third century, attempted to deny the existence of the earlier division as well. Still later, Hintze (*Studien zur meroitischen Chronologie und zu den Opfertafeln aus den Pyramider von Meroe*, Abhandlungen der Deutschen Akademie der Wissenschaften zu Berlin, Klasse für Sprachen, Literatur und Kunst, Jahrgang 1959, no. 2 [Berlin: Akademie Verlag], pp. 21–33) came to accept both dynasties, but later appeared to reject the first ("Meroitic Chronology: Problems and Prospects," in *Meroitica* 1; *Sudan im Alterum*, ed. Fritz Hintze [Berlin:

Akademie Verlag, 1973], pp. 127–43), basing his rejection on evidence derived by Wenig ("Bemerkungen zur Chronologie des Reiches von Meroe," *MIO* 13 [1967]: 1–44) in which the first secondary dynasty was subsumed in the regular sequence and the second was actual but related to the Meroitic northern push which ended in the sack of Aswan. (See below pp. 23–24; Hintze, *Meroitica* 1, p. 136. This was only the last, not the only, push northward.) Any explanation of these groups of pyramids must take into account the occurrence of connections between Barkal and Meroe during the time of the first group (Dunham, *Royal Tombs of Meroe and Barkal*) and Kawa and Meroe during the time of the second (Macadam, *Temples of Kawa I* and *Temples of Kawa II*) and also take into account the facts that one tomb at Barkal is actually that of a queen and kings are represented in some chapels of the second group. Explanations advanced so far have assumed that each king built only one pyramid. We cannot ignore the fact that these so-called splits in the kingdom immediately preceded major campaigns or programs northward (below, pp. 23–24). It would appear safer to assume that the secondary groups of pyramids of the third and first centuries B.C. at Gebel Barkal were constructed as a result of some administrative and political (religious?) arrangements associated with an impending expansion of the kingdom. (Steffen Wenig, "Nachmals zur 1. und 2. meroitische Nebendynastie von Napata," *Meroitica* 1, pp. 147–59).

52. Hofmann, *Studien zum meroitischen Königtum*, pp. 18–19.

53. Examples can be seen in P. L. Shinnie, *Meroe: A Civilization of the Sudan* (London: Thames and Hudson, 1967), pls. 10–11.

54. Ibid.

55. Karl-Heinz Priese, "Zur Entstehung der meroitischen Schrift," *Meroitica* 1, pp. 273–306, especially table I, a–d (note equivalence of hieroglyphic, hieratic, Demotic, and Meroitic forms).

56. Ibid., p. 273.

57. Trigger, "Meroitic Language Studies; Strategies and Goals," *Meroitica* 1, pp. 243–72, esp. 259–72. Id., "The Classification of Meroitic: Geographical Considerations," in *Ägypten und Kusch*, pp. 421–35.

58. Reisner, "The Meroitic Kingdom of Ethiopia," pp. 34–77; Hintze, *Studien zur meroitischen Chronologie*; Wenig, "Bemerkungen zur Chronologie des Reiches von Meroe," pp. 1–46.

59. Macadam, *The Temples of Kawa I*, p. 47.

60. *Urk.* 3, p. 86, no. 2. Note that the deity is Dedwen, Foremost of Ta-Seti.

61. Hofmann, *Studien zum meroitischen Königtum*, pp. 66–73; Serge Sauneron and Jean Yoyotte, "La Campagne nubienne de Psammétique II et sa signification historique," *Bulletin de l'Institut français d'archéologie orientale* 50 (1952): 157–207. Both conclude that the soldiers of Psammetichos II reached Napata. In addition to this campaign, Diodorus (I. 60) records an attack on Egypt in the time of an Amasis, intended to be Ahmose I. If this campaign is assigned to the wrong Ahmose, and actually belongs to Amasis (and is partly garbled with accounts of the Twenty-fifth Dynasty), there may have been an attempt on Egypt from the south during late Dynasty XXVI, led by Actisanes; Amani-natake-lebte (ca. 538–519 B.C.?) might be a candidate for the leader.

62. Herodotus 3. 25. For a basic description and bibliography of the Elephantine colony, see Emil G. Kraeling, "New Light on the Elephantine Colony," *Biblical Archaeologist* 15 (1952): 50–67.

63. Karl-Heinz Priese ("The Kingdom of Kush, the Napatan Period," in *Africa in Antiquity: The Arts of Ancient Nubia and the Sudan*, vol. 1, *The Essays* [Brooklyn: The Brooklyn Museum, 1978], p. 81) reads the name of this people as Adadas; we will here continue with a literal hieroglyphic transliteration.

64. Hofmann, *Studien zum meroitischen Königtum*, p. 23. Macadam, *The Temples of Kawa I*, pls. 17–26 and pp. 50–67.

65. *Urk.* 3, pp. 113–33.

66. Ibid., pp. 126–28.

67. Ibid., pp. 128–29.

68. Ibid., p. 129.

69. Ibid., pp. 130–33.

70. Fr. Hintze, *Studien zur meroitischen Chronologie*, pp. 17–20. H. Schäfer, *Die aethiopische Königsinschrift des Berliner Museums* (Leipzig: J. C. Hinrichs'sche Buchhandlung, 1901). The name, as dealt with by Hintze, is hmbdswn. However, unlike the records from other reigns, the records of the campaigns here are so generalized and nonspecific that the possibility must be raised that Nastasen was copying an earlier inscription, or adapting one to suit his purposes.

71. Diodorus 3. 6. Dunham, *Royal Tombs at Meroe and Barkal*, p. 6. This assumes an identification of Arkamani-qo with Ergamenes (Hintze, "Meroitic Chronology, Problems and Prospects," pp. 131–32).

72. See n. 51.

73. W. F. Petrie et al., *History of Egypt,* vol. 4, *A History of Egypt under the Ptolemaic Dynasty,* J. P. Mahaffy (London: Methuen and Co., 1899). The domestic problems of Euergetes and the beginning of the great temple-building project are discussed on pp. 109–26. We actually know little about the events in this reign. The distraction of war in Syria that came early in the reign of Philopator (219 B.C.) could have offered an opportunity for Kush in the south.

74. A. E. P. Weigall, *Report on the Antiquities of Lower Nubia, 1906–1907* (London: Oxford University Press, 1907), pl. XVI. See p. 42 for erasure by Ptolemy V Epiphanes, but the date is conjectural.

75. Günther Roeder, *Der Tempel von Dakke,* Les Temples immergés de la Nubie (Cairo: Imprimerie de l'Institut français, 1930), pp. 98–171, gives the Ptolemaic portion.

76. P. W. Pestman, "Harmachis et Ankhmachis, deux rois indigènes du temps des Ptolémies," *Chronique d'Egypte* 40 (1965): 157–70. For the chronology see pp. 159–60. See N.B. at end of notes.

77. Roeder, *Der Tempel von Dakke,* pp. 171–306, which give the portion executed by Arqamani.

78. Pestman, "Harmachis et Ankhmachis," p. 165.

79. Ibid., p. 164, also p. 159, citing Berlin 3146.

80. Bertha Porter and Rosalind Moss, *Topographical Bibliography of Ancient Egyptian Hieroglyphic Texts, Reliefs and Paintings,* vol. 7, *Nubia, the Deserts and Outside Egypt* (Oxford: Oxford at the Clarendon Press, 1951), p. 4, gives references to Adkheramani at Dabod; p. 5 gives references to Ptolemy VII.

81. This is attested by a graffito at Abydos; Pestman, "Harmachis et Ankhmachis," p. 163, n. 2.

82. Kurt Sethe, "Die historische Bedeutung des 2. Philä-Dekrets aus der Zeit Ptolemaios Epiphanes," *ZÄS* 53 (1917): 35–49, esp. pp. 44–45.

83. For the early occurrence of Blemmyes and Megabaroi, see Millet, "Meroitic Nubia," p. 9. See also G. Möller, "Mhbr = Μεγαβαρος," *ZÄS* 55 (1919): 79–81. Sethe, "Die 2. Philä-Dekrets," p. 44. They are called nhᶜsw or nhsw.

84. Jakob Krall, "Studien zur Geschichte des alten Aegypten II: Aus demotischer Urkunden," *Sitz. Ber. Wien Akad. d. Wiss.,* vol. 105 (1884): 368–72. Krall makes many of these points on slimmer evidence, citing, however, a war between Egypt and Ethiopia, vaguely alluded to in Agatharchides (see ibid., p. 371).

85. W. Dittenberger, *Orientis Graeci Inscriptiones Selectae* (Leipzig: S. Hirzel, 1903–1905). No. 111 gives the basic evidence. See also Millet, "Meroitic Nubia," pp. 10–11.

86. Claire Préaux, "Esquisse d'une histoire des révolutions égyptienne sous les Lagides," *Chronique d'Egypt* 11 (1936): 533.

87. Ibid., pp. 538–52, esp. p. 548.

88. After Philopator, the high-water mark of rebellion was reached by the combined revolt of Lower Egypt, the Alexandrian populace, and Upper Egypt. See ibid., p. 532.

89. C. M. Firth, *The Archaeological Survey of Nubia, Report for 1908–1909,* vol. 1, pp. 32–34.

90. Diodorus 3. 12–14, quoted from Agatharchides.

91. Cornelius Gallus, Aelius Gallus's predecessor, made a first move in relation to Nubia, claiming the Triakonaschoinos and appointing a *tyrannos* for the area as well as placing Meroe *in tutelam,* moves probably related to the revolt he had just crushed. J. G. Milne, *Greek Inscriptions,* Catalogue général des antiquités égyptiennes du Musée du Caire (Oxford: Oxford University Press, 1905), no. 9295, pp. 38–39. The rather vague wording of the inscription may indicate a claim rather than a reality.

92. F. Ll. Griffith, "Meroitic Studies IV," *JEA* 4 (1917): 159–73. Three or four campaigns are described.

93. Strabo 17. 820–21; Pliny the Elder *Nat. Hist.* 6. 181–87. Pliny explicitly states that the name Candace was handed from queen to queen. See also Inge Hofmann, "Der Feldzug des C. Petronius nach Nubien und seine Bedeutung für die meroitische Chronologie," in *Ägypten und Kusch,* pp. 189–205. On p. 99, she expresses doubt about the sack of Napata. Hofmann doubts the actuality of any campaign against the Meroitic homeland, considering it a propagandistic invention intended to help Augustus through a period of political difficulty. While Napata might not have been reached, the campaign is too explicitly described to be pure fiction, as is the part of the Candace and the statement by Strabo that Napata was her capital. If we interpret earlier Meroitic building in Lower Nubia as evidence for a Meroitic push northward that involved a political claim to the Dodekaschoinos, then a *royal* inscription in Dakka could hardly be treated other than as a reflection of a claim to the area (see ibid., pp. 204–5). There the inscription would have been recorded only after control of the area had been taken from Rome, which happened during the attack of 23.

94. Strabo 17. 820–21. Napata is the "queen's royal residence." Throughout, the enemies of Petronius are the queen and her son.

95. Ibid.; Millet, "Meroitic Nubia," pp. 23–28. Some places had already been settled. The description of the Petronius campaign mentions Pselchis (Dakka), the fortress Premnis (Primis, Ibrim); and Pliny (*Nat. Hist.* 6. 181) added Bocchis, Forum Cambusia, Attenia, Stadissas on a cataract, and Napata (with Strabo). Bocchis could be Faras (Millet, "Meroitic Nubia," p. 18). If these campaigns were more ambitious than is usually supposed, in keeping with greater Meroitic ambitions in Egypt, then a longer list might be appropriate.

96. This happened after the reign of Natakamani and Queen Amanitere. See Hofmann, "Der Feldzug des C. Petronius nach Nubien," p. 199.

97. Activity at Faras is documented in F. Ll. Griffith, "Oxford Excavations in Nubia, Continued," *LAAA* 13 (1926): 22. Id., "Meroitic Studies V," *JEA* 11 (1925): 23, pl. XXVIII–6. Objects from the "Western Palace" at Faras included an ostracon with a Greek inscription of the second or first century B.C. For Meroitic activity in the area during the second century, see Brian Haycock, "Landmarks in Kushite History," *JEA* 58 (1972): 239–40.

98. See pp. 25–26.

99. See p. 26. This is perhaps due to the poverty of written records after 1 A.D.

100. Erich Dinkler, "König Ezana von Aksum und das Christentum: ein Randproblem der Geschichte Nubiens," in *Ägypten und Kusch,* pp. 121–32, esp. pp. 125–26.

101. P. L. Shinnie, "Excavations at Tanqasi, 1953," *Kush* 2 (1954): 66–85; H. N. Chittick, "A New Type of Mound Grave," *Kush* 5 (1957): 73–77; L. P. Kirwan, "Tanqasi and the Noba." So far, very few of these mounds have been excavated, so we know little of the extent of the materials, though the shaft and side-chamber substructure does indicate a date close to that of the X-Group, as does the posture of the bodies, which are in a semicontracted position on their sides.

102. This dramatic change in the material has been noted from the beginning of Nubian archaeology. C. M. Firth, *The Archaeological Survey of Nubia, Report for 1910–1911* (Cairo: Government Printing Office, 1927), p. 28.

103. Publication of these materials is projected for OINE 6. See Keith C. Seele, "Excavations between Abu Simbel and the Sudan Border," p. 15, for Ramesside burials.

104. H. E. Winlock, *Excavations at Deir el Bahri* (New York: The Macmillan Co., 1942), pp. 94–95 (Henttawy), 96–97 (group of burials), 98 (Ankhshepenwepet), 178–79 and 194–99 (Nauny, called Entiuny [sic]). These illustrate the typical burial at Thebes in the early first millennium B.C.

105. H. S. Smith, *The Fortress of Buhen, Inscriptions,* pp. 67–69.

106. Adams, "Meroitic North and South," p. 14; Trigger, Commentary on "Meroitic North and South," pp. 105–7.

107. The quay at Karnak records that the Nile was high rather than low during the first millennium, including Year 7 of Ramses IX, Years 3, 12, and 19 of Osorkon II, Year 2 of Shabako, Year 3 of Shebitku, Years 6, 7, and 9 of Taharko, Years 10, 17, and 19 of Psammetichos I, and Year 29 of Amasis. Karl Butzer, "Studien zum vor- und frühgeschichtlichen Landschaftwandel der Sahara," *Akademie der Wissenschaften und der Literatur, Abhandlungen der mathematische-naturwissenschaftlichen Klasse,* Jahrgang 1959, no. 2 (Wiesbaden: Akademie der Wissenschaften und der Literatur in Mainz), pp. 46–122; see p. 113, where, however, he attributes the inundation of Year 38 of Osorkon III to Psammetichos. Ventre Pasha, "Crues modernes et crues anciennes du Nil," *ZÄS* 34 (1896): 95–107. Jürgen von Beckerath, "The Nile Level Records at Karnak and their Importance for the History of the Libyan Period," *JARCE* 5 (1966): 43–55.

108. K. A. Kitchen, *The Third Intermediate Period in Egypt (1100–650 B.C.),* § 206–323, esp. 210, 290–94, 298–300.

109. Pierre Montet, *Les constructions et le tombeau de Psousennès à Tanis,* La nécropole royale de Tanis, vol. 2 (Paris: Direction générale des relations culturelles, 1951). For lapis see pl. CX. An Akkadian cylinder seal is on pl. XXX (p. 46). A bead inscribed in cuneiform is on pl. CXII (pp. 139–43). Gold was still probably mostly Egyptian or from the desert, though gold from the north is noted for the period of the New Kingdom (A. Lucas, *Ancient Egyptian Materials and Industries,* 4th ed., rev. and enl. by J. R. Harris [London: Edward Arnold, 1962], pp. 227–28). Silver, on the other hand, was probably Asiatic, with some, perhaps, from Libya (ibid., pp. 247–48). Silver objects at Tanis included the coffin of Sheshonq, remains of another silver coffin (Montet, *Les constructions et le tombeau de Psousennès à Tanis,* p. 72, no. 684), a coffin of Psussenes (pp. 130–32), and vessels (pp. 82, no. 773, 83, no. 775; stands, p. 96, nos. 391–92; ḥs-vase, p. 99, no. 394; spouted vessel, no. 395; serving vessel, p. 102, no. 400; others, pp. 102–4, nos. 401–2, 404–8, and p. 163, no. 634). Gold remains prominent for jewelry and vessels, but more

vessels are being made of silver, and it is used for large objects such as coffins.

110. Shinnie, *Meroe*, pp. 104, 120, 122, 124, 127, 130; Brian Haycock, "Landmarks in Cushite History," *JEA* 58 (1972): 230.

111. For Buhen see Haycock, p. 235. For Faras, see Griffith, "Oxford Excavations in Nubia," *LAAA* 11, pls. XV–LXXI. Note Barbotine pottery on pl. XLIX.

112. For a list of sites as of 1964, see Trigger, *History and Settlement*, pp. 186–97, appendix 3.

113. Adams, "Meroitic North and South," p. 15.

114. Adams, *Nubia, Corridor to Africa*, p. 304. However, the specific date for the introduction of the camel is uncertain. Strabo (815. 17. 1. 45) mentions camel merchants operating in the Eastern Desert from Coptos as having existed for some time and as having changed their method of operation by constructing cisterns along their route. Diodorus, a generation or so earlier, does not mention the camel in Egypt, despite his lively interest in the fauna, wild and domestic.

115. H. Idris Bell, *Egypt from Alexander the Great to the Arab Conquest* (Oxford: Oxford at the Clarendon Press, 1948), pp. 77, 93, 119, and p. 148, n. 9 to ch. 4.

116. Trigger, Comment on "Meroitic, North and South," p. 104.

117. Hofmann, *Studien zum meroitischen Königtum*, esp. pp. 11–15.

118. Millet, "Meroitic Nubia." For "General of the River," see pp. 33–34, 42–43, 55–56, and 77–107. For "General of the Desert," see also pp. 107–11.

119. Ibid., p. 35, for examples of officials in major centers.

120. Ibid., pp. 37–40 and 112–28.

121. Ibid., grammatical notes, pp. 226–48.

122. C. M. Firth, *The Archaeological Survey of Nubia, Report for 1908–1909*, vol. 1, pp. 30–31 and 31–32.

123. See catalogue entries Q 306 (3) and Q 317 (not in catalogue).

124. C. Leonard Woolley and D. Randall-MacIver, *Karanog: The Romano-Nubian Cemetery*, Eckley B. Coxe Junior Expedition to Nubia, vol. 4 (Philadelphia: University Museum, 1910), pl. 43 G 738, 528; pl. 45 G 712 (shoulder decoration). Compare static "Kushite design" based on Egyptian motifs, mostly "Neferzeichen" (pls. 41, G 271; 42, G 156; 43, G 685; 44, G 626, 702, 442; 45, G 535; 46, G 100, 583; 48, G 717, 712), and drawings that appear to show motion (pls. 41, G 566, 129; 42, G 162; 43, G 189, 8293; 45, G 112, 712, the last with a bronze bowl, pls. 26–28). Both groups of decoration should be compared with objects from Meroe (Dunham, *The West and South Cemeteries of Meroe*, p. 25, fig. 18e–W 832 23–3–602 [bronze bowl], p. 31, fig. 22c [latter style], p. 96, fig. 73e–f), which combined the Hellenistic and Kushite elements, details, and designs as often as did Lower Nubian Meroitic pottery (see also p. 97, fig. 74, fig. 90i, which combined moving with static design, p. 448, fig. 242; see especially p. 148, fig. 108b–e, the lid of a bronze box inlaid with colored stone; on p. 360, fig. 191 is the finest example).

On the basis of the above-cited examples, painted Meroitic pottery should be considered derived from the earlier and more elaborate traditions of decorating vessels of bronze and faience in Meroe.

125. W. Y. Adams, "The Vintage of Nubia," *Kush* 14 (1966): 262–83.

126. Woolley and MacIver, *Karanog, The Romano-Nubian Cemetery*, pls. 37–39, 40.

127. See n. 124.

128. Trigger, Comment on "Meroitic North and South," p. 115.

129. Millet, "Meroitic Nubia," pp. 29–33.

130. Three sites excavated by the Oriental Institute Nubian Expedition in the Kalabsha area actually had the distinctive pottery. They were Cemetery B at Gebel Khor Abu Sina, Cemetery C at Khor Kalabsha, and Cemetery E north of Bab Kalabsha (Ricke, *Ausgrabungen*, pp. 37–42, finds, pp. 43–70). The pottery also occurred at Sayala in the "taverns" (Karl Kromer, *Römische Weinstuben in Sayala (Unternubien)*, Österreichische Akademie der Wissenschaften, philologisch-historische Klasse, Denkschriften, vol. 95 [Vienna: Hermann Bohlaus Nachf., 1967], figs. 30–31, pls. 32, 34. Another site with this pottery was excavated by a Czech expedition; a coin of Constantius I (337–361 A.D.) was found here. Steffen Wenig, *Africa in Antiquity: The Arts of Nubia and the Sudan*, vol. 2, *The Catalogue* (Brooklyn: The Brooklyn Museum, 1978), pp. 106–7.

131. Ricke, *Ausgrabungen*, pp. 37–41.

132. Ibid., pls. 24–28, passim.

133. Ibid., p. 39, fig. 57, pp. 43–46, figs. 64–65 (glass).

134. Ibid., pls. 25, B 6/1; 27, B 8/3, 8/4, 8/10; 28, B 11/7.

135. Ibid., pl. 26 B 12/2, also impressed, pl. 28 B 1/1.

136. Ibid., pl. 24, C 5/1.

137. Ibid., p. 39 and fig. 57.

138. See catalogue descriptions, tomb Q 378; see also tomb Q 394.

139. Ibid.

140. See catalogue descriptions, tombs, Q 2, 7, 10, 11, 13, and 149, for example. See below fig. 2.

141. Bodies in semicontracted position seem to have continued in private tombs. See catalogue descriptions, tombs Q 27, 68. Bodies in extended position, discussed below, include Q 134 and 141.

142. Adams, *Nubia, Corridor to Africa*, pp. 398, 415.

143. Ibid., pp. 393–95. Of the fifty-five cemeteries (which were either partly or entirely X-Group) that Adams considered, only thirteen began in Meroitic times..

144. Ibid., pp. 414–15, also 398–400.

145. William Y. Adams, "Progress Report on Nubian Pottery; I. The Native Wares," *Kush* 15 (1967–68): 26.

146. Millet, "Meroitic Nubia," pp. 203–11 and 272–304, for possible post-Meroitic inscriptions.

147. Woolley and MacIver, *Karanog, The Romano-Nubian Cemetery*, pp. 103–5.

148. See catalogue description. A number of tombs cited with Cemetery R belong to this tradition. See below fig. 1.

149. Procopius *De Bello Persico* 1. 19. 59A; Priscus (ed. Niebuhr) 153. These authors deal with the Nobatae most vividly. See also Woolley and MacIver, *Karanog, The Romano-Nubian Cemetery*, pp. 104–5.

150. Millet, "Meroitic Nubia," pp. 191, 196–212. Silko (Inscr. 1.3) refers explicitly to the Blemmyes in the Dodekaschoinos. As Millet points out, Blemmye activity was not limited to the Dodekaschoinos and Upper Egypt. Krall (*Beitrag zur Geschichte der Blemmyer und Nubier*, p. 12) notes an alleged raid on Kharga. See also Adams, *Nubia, Corridor to Africa*, p. 423.

151. C. M. Firth, *The Archaeological Survey of Nubia, Report for 1910–1911*, p. 117, fig. (cem 112, Wadi Allaqi), plan VIII.

152. Emery and Kirwan, *The Royal Tombs at Ballana and Qustul*; Shafiq Farid, *Excavations at Ballana* (Cairo: General Organization for Government Printing Office, 1963).

153. For continuing Meroitic burial customs see catalogue description, many of the tombs cited under Cemetery R.

154. Trigger, *History and Settlement*, pp. 134–40; Adams, *Nubia, Corridor to Africa*, p. 420.

The argument is that archaeology here discloses not one but three distinct groups in Lower Nubia by the end of the fourth century A.D., the "X-Group of Blemmye tradition" near Kalabsha, the "X-Group of Meroitic tradition" in various cemeteries south of the Dodekaschoinos, especially Arminna, and the "X-Group of Nobatian tradition," also in various cemeteries south of the Dodekaschoinos and perhaps within it. These groups are linked by common use of mass-manufactured goods into an archaeological phase, but distinguished by burial customs, certain hand-made goods, and certain associations, such as the emphasis on portable goods in the humbler graves of the Nobatian group. The so-called problem of continuity in the town sites is solved by the remarkably clear statement of Ezana that he took the cities of the Noba, both those of reeds and those of brick, which the Noba had taken—from the Kasu (see n. 100).

155. Woolley and MacIver, *Karanog, The Romano-Nubian Cemetery*, pp. 99–105; Millet, "Meroitic Nubia," pp. 191–219.

156. Procopius *De Bello Persico* 1. 19. 59A. There is a certain tendency to doubt Procopius because he wrote two centuries after the events mentioned (Adams, *Nubia, Corridor to Africa*, pp. 419–23). It must be remembered, however, that Procopius was a high Byzantine official, privy to official records and correspondence. Although he might have misinterpreted and misdated some items of evidence or misunderstood their significance, such as the summoning of the Nobatae from Oasis (which might have been, in fact, a place where Roman and Nobatian envoys met to avoid possible Blemmyan interference or detection of any meeting, which was possible if they met on the Nile), actual events discussed probably took place.

157. Adams, *Nubia, Corridor to Africa*, p. 423. Here he refers to a letter between two kinglets found at Ibrim in 1976.

158. Woolley and MacIver, *Karanog, The Romano-Nubian Cemetery*, pp. 104–5 (the Silko inscr.).

N.B. After this essay was in final proof, this writer received a copy of *Göttinger Miszellen* 29 (1978) in which Karl-Th. Zauzich proposed new readings for Harmachis and Ankhmachis ("Neue Namen für die Könige Harmachis und Anchmachis, pp. 157–58) Hr-wn-nfr and ꜥnh-wn-nfr. The change would mean that the revolt of ὑργονοφορ (Hargonoephor) is to be identified with the earlier king. See p. 23.

Figure 1 a–c: Q 61—A tomb of X-Group of Meroitic Tradition

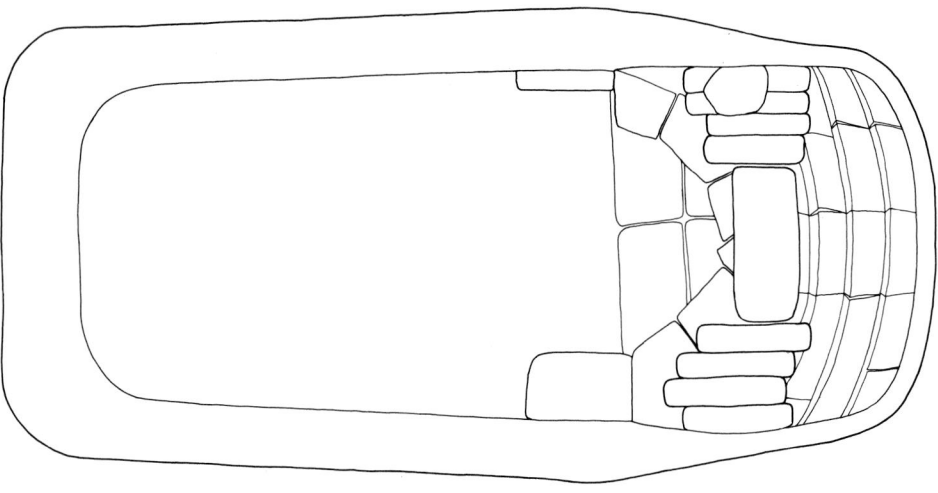

a) plan of shaft and vault (exterior)

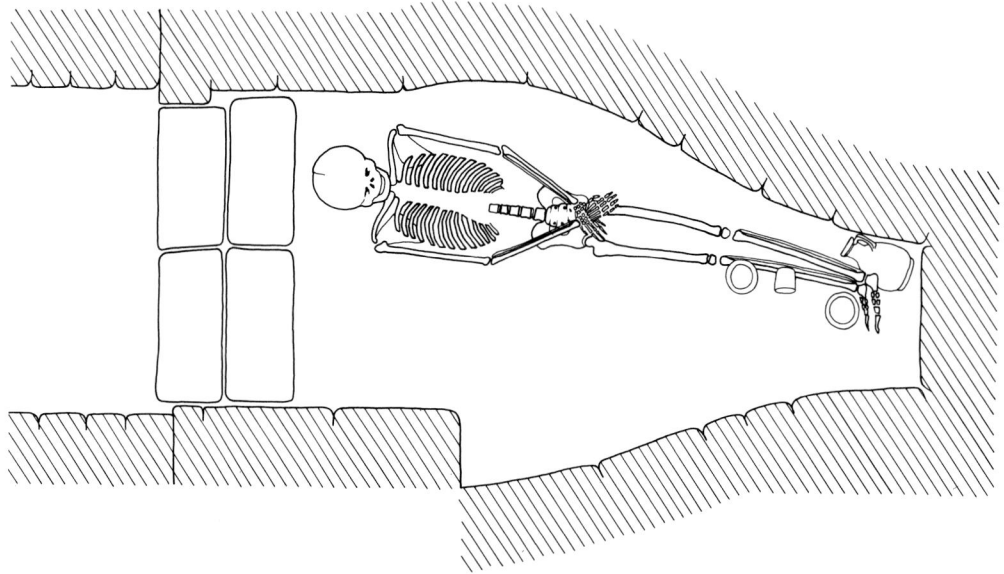

b) plan of burial chamber

c) cross section

THE CIRCUMSTANCES OF DISCOVERY

The textiles published here were found at Ballana and Qustul in tombs dated to the Meroitic, X-Group, and Christian periods, the largest group of tombs excavated by the Oriental Institute Nubian Expedition. Most of the textiles were used as wrappings for the body, though clearly some were originally intended for other purposes. Some of these purposes were indicated by the location of the textile. Occasionally a cloth was found on the head or around the waist.

The typical Meroitic tomb[1] in which a textile was found contained a burial of Kushite type. At its most elaborate, it was a tall, slender brick (or sometimes stone) pyramid with a niche high in its front side for a crude sandstone ba-statute (a figure of a falcon's body with a human head or, sometimes, a figure depicting a complete human body to which was attached the rear half of a falcon). In front of and below this niche there was an offering table, also of sandstone and often incised with crude reliefs of funerary deities pouring libations. These tables often carried an inscription in the Meroitic language around their edges, giving the name and titles of the deceased and names and titles of their relations. The substructures of these pyramids were of a variety of types. Most elaborate was a rectangular pit with a mud-brick arched chamber built in it. Less elaborate, but—like the rectangular pit—often with a superstructure was a shaft with a chamber at the end. Normally, the body was placed with one end in the chamber, the other end in the shaft. Although all types could lack superstructure the simple ones rarely had any. Less elaborate among the tomb types was a shaft with narrow side chamber, normally with some sort of stone or brick blocking along the side of the chamber. There was also a simple shaft with a shelf on both of its sides and roofed by two rows of bricks leaning together in a simple inverted V. The body was laid on its back in the side chamber with its hands crossed above the pelvis. Occasionally it was placed on a bed, a standard Kushite burial practice from the time of the A-Group. At Qustul the deceased was sometimes placed in a coffin made of hollowed palm log. The body was wrapped in a textile, and objects were placed with the body. They included pottery—especially, fine vessels with elaborately painted decorations. Jewelry often included elaborate beads, particularly those made of glass in the fused-mosaic style called millefiori. Glass vessels were common, as were metal ones. Weapons were found, but not commonly.

In the succeeding period, that of the X-Group, the lines of two traditions can be traced at Qustul. The Meroitic burials continued, but there were distinct changes: all surface installations of the Meroitic type—the pyramid, the ba-statue, and even, somewhat later, the offering table (devoid of reliefs and inscription long before, however)—disappeared. The more elaborate burial substructures became relatively rare, and the simple ones more common. Important changes in the grave goods took place, partly because old crafts, such as elaborate painting on pottery, died out in Nubia and were replaced by new ones from Egypt.

Figure 2: Q 378—An early burial of X-Group of Nobatian Tradition placed in a Meroitic Grave
Not shown: The rectangular brick superstructure, debris and remains of Meroitic burial thrown out of the shaft

The other tradition, the X-Group of Nobatian tradition, became dominant in Lower Nubia. Fully developed, the burial customs of this group differed substantially from those of the Meroitic group. The superstructure of the tomb was a low tumulus, occasionally surrounded by a stone circle. (At Qustul the ceremonies of the cults of the dead were carried out in square brick chapels arranged in long lines that had little to do with the arrangement of the cemetery.) The substructure was usually one of the simple Meroitic types, the shaft with narrow side chamber, although royal tombs at Ballana and Qustul had complexes of brick chambers. The body was usually semicontracted, that is, it was placed on its side with the thighs at right angles to the body, the feet folded under the hips, and the hands placed in front of the face or chest. This arrangement, in which the body often protruded somewhat into the shaft, was awkward and shows that this new tradition was making use of a design less than perfectly suited to the semicontracted burial.

At first, the objects placed in these tombs were simple; they consisted primarily of military equipment and textiles, even including an occasional rug or bag. Later, pottery and other less portable household items were added; they sometimes indicated considerable opulence (the royal tombs were filled with every available kind·of finery). Curiously enough, glass vessels were rarely found in these tombs. As before, textiles occurred mostly as body wrappings, but also as clothing and rugs and other objects of daily use. Many of the wrappings were decorated or dyed (no longer the simple sheets of Meroitic times), and almost all were of animal fiber rather than of the cotton or linen fiber of earlier times.

After the Christianization of Nubia in the mid-sixth century A.D., there was another and more drastic change in the burials, in keeping with the new beliefs about the afterlife. At first, the old shaft and side chamber were used, often with a blocking of flagstones. Later, a simple shaft with ledges around it near the bottom was dug, and the body was placed at the bottom of the shaft and covered with flagstones laid on the ledges. If there was a superstructure it was a simple rectangular platform only a few centimeters high and made of stone or brick. A lamp might be placed on the platform or in a niche cut at the head end of the grave, usually in the shape of an inverted J. Apart from textiles used for wrapping or a lamp, which was deposited as a symbol of the Resurrection, objects of daily use were rare. The body was no longer contracted, but placed in an extended position on its back, with its hands above the pelvis. It was usually wrapped in a fabric, which may have been made especially for the purpose. The textile was usually secured by tapes, which were often tied in an elaborate crisscross pattern from the head of the corpse to its toes (a technique used in Christian Egypt).

B. W.

1. Woolley and Randal-MacIver, *Karanog: The Romano-Nubian Cemetary,* Eckley B. Coxe Junior Expedition to Nubia, vol. 4, (Philadelphia: University Museum, 1910), plates 112–114. This shows a substructure of Meroitic date. The common substructures were similar to Figure 1a–c.

Figure 3 a–c: Q 164—A later burial of Meroitic Traditi◦

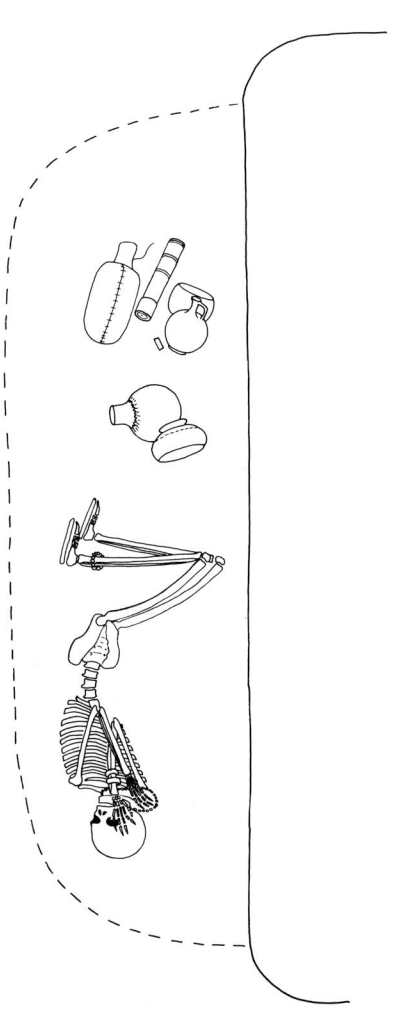

a) plan of burial chamber

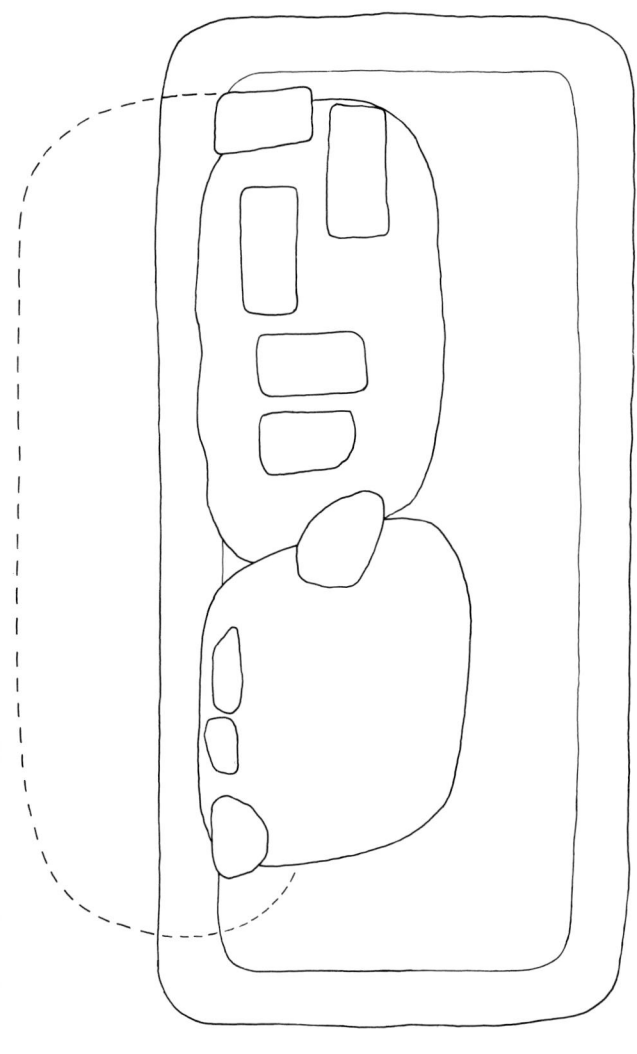

b) plan of shaft and blocking

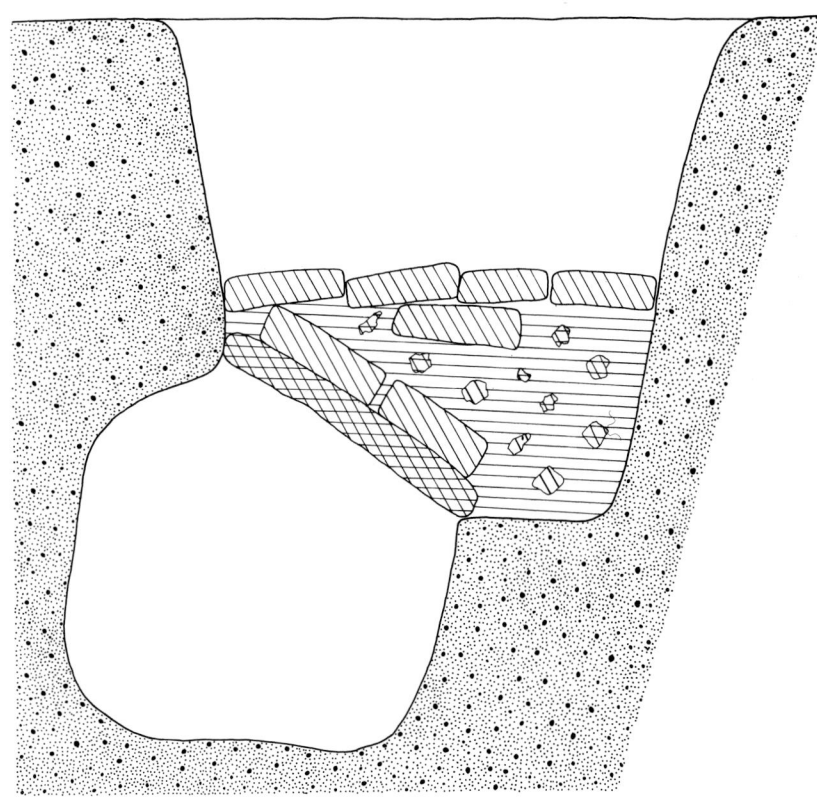

c) cross section
Not shown: Circular tumulus and shaft plan

The Textiles

Christa C. Mayer Thurman
Curator
Department of Textiles
The Art Institute of Chicago

All of the Late Nubian textiles published in this catalogue were those excavated and retained by the Oriental Institute Nubian Expedition in seasons 1962–63 and 1963–64.[1] This collection of ancient textiles was assigned 109 field numbers, but when studied was found to consist of 188 actual fabrics and dated to the Meroitic, X-Group, and Christian periods, as seen in Table 1. They were not treated in the field.[2]

It is one of the most significant collections in North America of textiles from Nubia, comparing favorably with a collection of 160 small fragments at Brandeis University, also excavated by the Oriental Institute expedition to Sudanese Nubia, of similar date.[3] Because the part of the Nile Valley from which Nubian fabrics came is now flooded, such archaeological collections are of special significance. A much larger but later collection of Islamic date (641–ca. 1800) was excavated at Gebel Adda just north of Qustul. It is on loan from the National Geographic Society to the Royal Ontario Museum in Toronto.[4]

The largest collection of Meroitic, X-Group, and early Christian textiles was made by the Scandinavian Joint Expedition and published in 1975. This group included 6,000 fragments from 168 tombs, including approximately 142 that are contemporary with the textiles presented here. The number of textile objects actually recovered by this expedition is not certain, but it is probably somewhat larger than the number in this collection.[5]

Textiles from the Nile Valley have not commonly been published despite the fact that there exists in museums a fairly extensive corpus of fabrics in general.

As will be discussed in greater detail, most of these textiles had been used as burial wrappings. Few, however, were originally intended as funerary cloths, and a variety of types was in fact discovered. These were primarily sheets and garments, with a few rugs and other objects, made of several different kinds of fibers and dyed with various substances.

MATERIALS
The Fibers

Most of the fibers used to make the textiles in this collection are of animal origin, from sheep, goats, or camels, though the animals could not be distinguished with certainty in most cases.[6] Other fibers used were linen and cotton, one silk, and a few of horsehair, coarse grass or reed.

The identification of fibers was based on an examination of nearly one hundred of them through a polarizing microscope (100–250×) and a scanning electron microscope. The remaining textiles were identified with the aid of a Bausch and Lomb stereo microscope (30×), the more completely identified fibers serving as a standard of reference.

The majority of the twenty-seven Meroitic textiles were of cotton. Only a few were of linen, animal, or mixed animal and vegetable (Table 2). X-Group fabrics, which were far more numerous, were almost all of animal fiber. Only two of each type were of cotton or linen only, and three were mixed, vegetable-fiber decoration added to animal-fiber fabrics. One was of silk. In the late X-Group and Christian periods the numerical proportions of the various types changed, and the totals are one linen, seven cotton, and seventeen animal fibers. Although the second change is relatively minor, the first—from Meroitic to X-Group—is major and must certainly represent a substantial change in preference for certain fabrics, the availability of vegetable fibers, or the customary uses of material.

Animal Fibers

Because of their poor condition, it could not be determined in most cases whether the textiles were made of fibers from sheep, goats, or camels. A small fragment of sheepskin shows that sheep were present in the area. Camels and goats are well-known animals in X-Group contexts.[7]

Although few animal-fiber fabrics were used in the Meroitic textiles, various animals whose fibers could be utilized had been available in the Nile Valley for millennia. Sheep are among the most ancient of domestic animals and were available in some numbers in the Nile Valley. The most likely source of wool would have been domestic breeds available in Egypt of the period. These included hairy thin-tailed sheep (including those with *ammon*-shaped horns), wooled thin-tailed sheep, and (wooled) fat-tailed sheep.[8] The Ptolemaic government had taken a special interest in this industry, introducing a species of sheep that yielded better wool. Production of wool was sponsored by the state. During Ptolemaic and Roman times there was an extensive trade in this product, and its use began to increase.[9] Goats were imported early into Egypt, apparently those of the screw-horned type; camels had been known for some time in the ancient Near East and had recently become common in

Table 1 Field Numbers and Textile Objects by Date

Date	Field No.	No. of Textiles
Meroitic	17	27
Meroitic/X-Group	5	6
X-Group	69	126
X-Group/Christian	8	14
Christian	12	12
Doubtful	1	1

Table 2

Date	Linen	Cotton	Animal*	Horsehair	Animal and Cotton	Animal and Linen	Silk	Grass and Reed	Total
Meroitic	5	15	6						26
Meroitic/X-Group	1		4					2	7
X-Group	2	2	114	1	1	2	1	1	124
X-Group/Christian		5	8						13
Christian	1	2	9						12

* It is uncertain whether the fiber came from goats, camels, or sheep

Egypt.[10] The extent to which these animals were used for their fiber is uncertain.

Vegetable Fibers

Linen. Eight fabrics were made entirely of linen and two had traces of it, though the latter were largely of animal fiber (70 and 92). Linen is the product of the flax plant *Linum usitatissimum,* which is found in Egypt. It had possibly been introduced there early, at least by the Badarian period.[11] Flax continued to be a popular fiber, and a vigorous trade in it and linen was maintained in the Ptolemaic Period.[12] Specific mentions of flax in Nubia are few, but in the New Kingdom there is reference to "flax fields of the king" at Aniba in Lower Nubia.[13]

The processes used to prepare harvested flax for spinning and weaving are complex and include rippling, retting, skutching, roughing, or hackling.

Cotton. Nineteen textiles in this collection were identified as cotton; an additional fabric contained some cotton threads, though it was made mostly of animal fiber (145).

It is presently believed that cotton is the vegetable fiber most recently introduced for the making of cloth in this area, though it is well known from Indus Valley contexts of the late third millennium B.C.[14] It is assumed to have been introduced to Egypt via the Red Sea routes.[15] However, it remains possible that a kind of cotton plant was available nearby; Pliny reported the existence of "wool-bearing" trees in Upper Egypt and Ethiopia, which may be Sudanese cotton.[16] The oldest known fragments of cotton textile from the Nile Valley appear to be contemporary with the cotton from Ballana and Qustul. They were found at Karanog in Lower Nubia and at Meroe and were apparently of Roman date.[17] Analyses by the research laboratories of the British Cotton Industry Research Association showed them to be cotton of Sudanese, or some other equally coarse, type.[18] In any case, the cotton industry became important in the Sudan. Ezana of Aksum, in the description of his campaign to the Nile about 350 A.D., said, "I destroyed their provision of corn and cotton and cast them into the Seda river [Nile?]."[19]

Knowledge of the cotton plant in this area may have been available much earlier, however. An Indian expedition to Afya found sheep dung containing cotton seeds and fibers near A-Group houses. Tests revealed little difference in either the width or the length of the convolutions of the fibers of these samples and those of modern cotton. If the context is reliable, cotton could have been known as a plant in Nubia as far back as 3100 B.C. although there is no evidence of its use in textiles at that time.[20]

Silk. Silk originated in China, spun from the fibers made by the *Bombyx mori* of the family *Bombycidae* of the *Lepidoptera.* This true silk is not to be confused with the wild silk of Tussah type, which is produced by more than six different species of worm in India.[21] Silk textiles appeared in the early Roman Empire, but sericulture is not thought to have appeared in Khotan until 419 A.D.[22] It was taken to Byzantium by two famous monks

Procopius and Theophanes, who used hollow walking sticks to smuggle silkworms from Khotan. With the spread of Islam the industry reached Arabia, Syria, Persia, Egypt, and North Africa.

One small fragment of silk was found in an X-Group tomb (40). Two contemporary pieces of silk were also found in the excavations of X-Group royal tombs at Qustul. The two fragments found were described by A. Lucas as follows:

> Two specimens were examined, both in two colours, one being red and yellowish-brown and the other black and the same yellowish-brown. Both the specimens have a very modern appearance and look like silk.
>
> The fibre in both specimens (the warp as well as the weft threads) is all alike and is silk, though it is not a mulberry silk, that is to say it is not composed of fibres produced by the catipillars (sic) *Bombyx mori,* but is a "wild silk" of the nature of Tussah silk from caterpillars that are not cultivated like the *B. mori.*[23]

The design illustrated on plate 110, figure C, is similar to the example published here, but Lucas' description does not include thread counts or other technical features, and his reasons for identifying the silk as a wild silk are not clear.[24]

One further example of silk in Nubia, which was no doubt imported, has been reported from Gebel Adda. It is from a medieval Christian tomb.[25]

The Colors

Due to oxidation and contamination, the color of most fabrics was altered and resulted in irregular appearance. For this reason, neither of the Munsell color systems was used in this catalogue for identification. Approximate colors could oftentimes not be determined with the unaided eye, and a stereo microscope was used. Description was limited to hue, with the values light, medium, and dark.

Nearly one hundred colored fibers were selected for dye analysis for Liliane Masschelein-Kleiner and Luc R. J. Maes at the Institut royal du patrimoine aristique in Brussels (see pp. 52–53). Of these colored fibers, only one, a brown thread of animal fiber (21), did not contain any dye stuff. The rest of the fibers had been dyed before weaving; whether this was done before or after spinning is unknown.

Textiles believed to have been made locally are in many shades of brown and in blue, red, and yellow. The dyes appear to have been available locally. Green-colored threads, introduced as woven stripes in a few of the textiles (35), indicate that dying of blue with yellow was known.

A number of fabrics carry the full range of primary colors, especially the carpets (66, 67, 59, 115, 158), as well as fragment 33, belt 16, and the large cover fragments 85 and 68. Such fabrics were probably imported, as were those that combine purple with colors ranging from yellow to orange. These elaborately colored textiles are also the fabrics whose structures stand out as being different from those of most of the other textiles.[26]

Tyrian purple was discovered in the stripes of one fabric (14), which makes it one of the most significant textiles in the collection.[27] The wool was woven in an extremely fine twill weave, 2:2. However, the textile was subsequently cut in odd dimensions, which indicates that it was reused. It was certainly imported.

PROCEDURES
Spinning

Before the cotton, flax, or wool fibers of either goat, camel, or sheep were transformed into yarn and subsequently woven on looms into fabric, the fibers had to be spun. The specific methods of preparation, although very ancient, are only partially known to us today. The paintings in Egypt at Beni Hasan of the Twelfth Dynasty and at Thebes of Djehutynefer of the Eighteenth Dynasty show clear illustrations of spinning.[28] Crowfoot studied and published in 1931 the hand-spinning methods and processes used in Egypt and the Sudan at that time, and compared them with known ancient methods.[29]

The problem with discerning ancient spinning techniques is that in modern times different spinning techniques are sometimes used even in adjacent villages. From the existing records, it cannot be discovered whether one technique superseded another in the past. Some modern methods that may have been used include: stick with whorl, stick with natural crook at end, stick without whorl, grasped spindle, supported spindle, and suspended spindle. Regardless of the instrument used, spinning resulted in attenuation, twisting, and winding. It twisted the fibers to either the right or the left, wrapping them in either a spiraling "S" or reverse "S" direction (S-spun or Z-spun, fig. 1). The physical properties of different fibers had to favor certain spindle types, though several types may have been appropriate for one fiber. In 1921, Crowfoot recorded three types of spindle

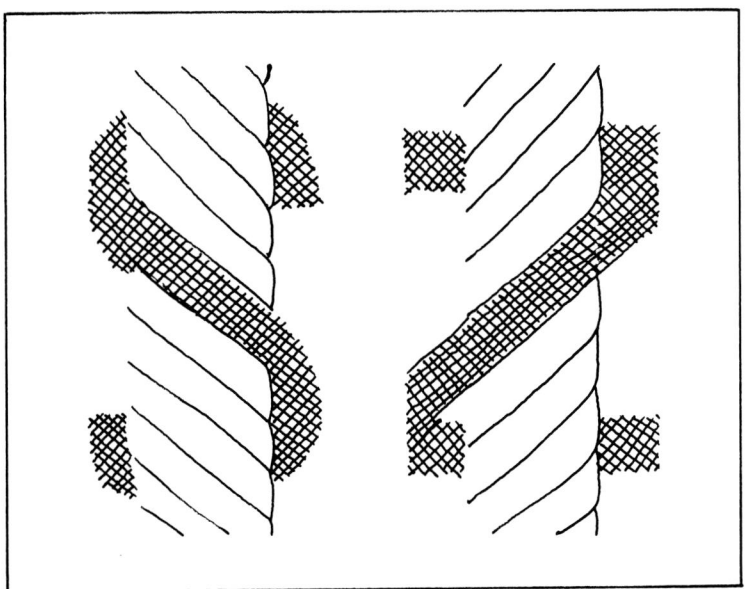

fig. 1

for cotton and one for wool; in 1931 she was able to record six different spindles for cotton, each from a different region of the Sudan.[30] With two exceptions, both of which are carpets (66 and 115), all of the fibers in this collection were twined in the S-direction, as are those known from Egypt.

Weaving

After being spun, the yarn is ready for warping and interlacing, which results in woven fabrics. By Meroitic times the craft of weaving was already ancient and had undergone a number of changes, not the least of which took place in the most important weaving tool, the loom.

Looms are fairly well known from representations in Egypt, primarily from those of the earlier Middle Kingdom and New Kingdom. There are important painted weaving scenes at Beni Hasan[31] and at Bersha,[32] and models, most particularly those of Mekutre, include women operating looms.[33] In all of these scenes the loom used is of the horizontal type. The earliest vertical loom, operated by men, seems to have been introduced just before or during the Eighteenth Dynasty, during which it is represented on tomb walls; it may have been invented in Syria or Palestine.[34] This loom had the warp stretched between two beams rather than weighted from a single beam as in later Greek looms (warp-weighted looms).[35]

In any case, improved loom types must have been introduced into Egypt, perhaps toward the end of Ptolemaic or in Roman times. Archaeological evidence of the more elaborate vertical loom was found by the Metropolitan Museum Expedition at the monastery (laura) of Epiphanius, which is dated to the early seventh century A.D.[36] Eight treadle pits were discovered there,[37] as well as several whorls.[38] Treadle pits imply the existence of floor treadles, which earlier types of looms did not necessarily have. The treadle controlled heddles by means of a harness suspended from the loom frame.[39] The combination of treadle, heddle, and harness is generally found with a more advanced loom, essential for all complex weaving. In the present collection of textiles at least two (83 and 33) and possibly two others (16 and 20) must have been woven on a loom of at least this sophistication.

Simpler looms may have been used to weave most of the other textiles presented here. Judging from some of the complete textiles, which have selvages and head and bottom edges intact, these looms must have had a width of nearly 250 cm (29) or more. It is possible that much larger looms existed, on which more than one piece of fabric could be woven at a time.

In the material excavated by the Scandinavian Joint Expedition, wefts had been turned well within the width of the warp, making fabrics with many wedges. This feature seems to indicate that a complex loom mechanism available for weaving the most elaborate textiles in this collection was not used in Nubia. On the contrary, the warps were often not separated completely to make a complete weft shot possible.[40]

A number of different weaving systems were found in this

collection. The most common was the *plain weave*. In this system, warp and weft elements go over and under one another, and both sides of the fabric are structurally identical.[41] *Weft-faced plain weave* was also often used. In this system weft elements predominate, and cover the warp elements, and the fabric is identical on both sides. In some textiles the entire structure was carried out in this weave (96), and in others only decorations such as stripes were. *Weft-faced plain weave with discontinuous wefts* was used to insert the notched "L" and "H" elements discussed below.

The counterpart of weft-faced plain weave, *warp-faced plain weave,* was also found. Again, the fabric is identical on both sides.

Plain-weave fabrics vary from very dense warp and weft groupings (22) to very open groupings (78) which result in a more open weave.

Fabrics with notched "L" or "H" decorations in the corners have these decorations inserted either by *dovetailing* or *interlocking* (69 and 136). When the method of dovetailing was used in the collection catalogued here, two adjacent color areas were joined to one another through the utilization of a common warp thread. When the method of interlocking was used the two color areas were linked to one another as the weft threads met; this linkage occurred generally in between the warp elements. The weft threads were inserted in weft-faced plain weave with discontinuous wefts. The fabric itself was woven in plain or twill weave. Sometimes both techniques were used on the same textile (172).

Two examples of *twill weave* were found. In this system, warp and weft elements pass in echelon over and under each other so that the points of binding are staggered. Warp and weft occur in a variety of ratios; the staggered diagonals appear in reverse on the opposite side of the fabric and on both sides as floats. The first example is one of the finest ever found (14). The entire fabric is woven in 2:2 twill weave; purple stripes are inserted in discontinuous wefts. The second example is a grass mat with 4:1 twill interlacement (32). As no selvages have survived, it is difficult to determine if the mat was woven on a loom; even the warp and weft direction cannot be identified with certainty.

As expected, *pile weave* is found in all carpet fragments (59, 66, 115, 13, 67, 158). It is impossible to determine whether or not the pile is worn or the present heights of the piles are original.

In all of the examples but one, the pile is made of continuous weft slip loops pulled forward through the warps and held in place by the warp threads.[42] Thereafter the process is repeated until all loops are in place.[43] A series of grouped weft shots follow, used to hold the loops tightly in place. These groupings vary in numbers. Loops are normally cut to form the pile, but since we do not know whether the pile in these carpets is worn by use or was originally cut to its present height, the presence or absence of cutting cannot be determined.

There is one textile with knotted pile (72), which was pro-duced by inserting continuous Sehna knots, forming loops 2.5–4cm long. They were inserted 1.5cm apart and appear uncut. Knots were attached to every other warp thread.[44]

Three fabrics were actually woven to shape on the loom (64, 74, 178). Two of these were shrouds, textiles made to enfold a body and woven in a tapered shape (64, 74). One was an almost triangular piece, which appears to have been a loincloth (178).

Decoration

Most of the textiles in the present collection are undecorated. Such decoration as occurs is usually simple. Only fifteen fabrics have elaborate patterns, including the carpets (59, 66, 67, 115, 155), the large cover (68), fragments of a cover or hanging (85), and smaller pieces believed to have been woven on a loom of more advanced type.

Inserted Decoration

Most decorated pieces have inserted decorations, which consist of stripes, most often inserted by means of weft-faced plain weave (176 and 153, for example). With two exceptions (34 and 71), in which the stripes are shorter, stripes of varying widths run from selvage to selvage.

Three fabrics show more elaborate inserted designs, which resemble those of approximately contemporary fabrics from Egypt (66, 67, 85 and 107).[45] All three of these textiles were constructed in weft-faced plain weave with areas of discontinuous wefts. The inlaid designs are intricate geometric patterns typical of Coptic Egypt. The intricate linear patterns are done in either single purple or light brown yarns. However, the three fabrics differ from Egyptian textiles in that warps and wefts are wool and not a combination of linen warps and wool wefts. To weave entirely in wool results in much finer weaving.

In some cases the differences in weave and color between the basic textile and the inserted decorations are even more distinct, as in the mantles with inserted notched "L" or "H" shapes. The basic textile varies from the insert (69, 108).

Frequently, textiles in this collection were made of unevenly dyed fibers (55). The effect this produced and the juxtaposition of openly and densely woven areas (78) make striking visual impressions.

Needlework and Surface Decoration

Surface decorations were found, but the method of insertion is uncertain (29, and 185). Two clear examples of needlework were found, including one with a little tree (22). Several fabrics had intricate inlaid patterns. These patterns resemble decoration on contemporary textiles from Egypt (85, 68, and 107).

Numerous examples of weft twining and countered weft twining were found in the collection from Ballana and Qustul. This technique is often used for decoration and is done by enclosing warp elements with weft elements. Weft twining has

Q 203 Intact Burial

fig. 2

either tight or open spacing and is chainlike in appearance.[46] In this collection it was primarily done by twining wefts in pairs around single warps. In countered weft twining, the threads can be of two different colors, which alternate. It is not entirely clear how the yarn was inserted. As the wefts do not have to go through a shed no loom is necessary, although the technique is easier to execute if the warp thread is stretched and taut (121, 119). It is for that reason that the technique is also known as finger weaving.

Generally, weft twining appears along the edge of a fabric preceding either tassels (74) or loose-hanging warp threads (99) which are either grouped or have been worked into specific fringes. The threads can be of different colors which alternate as for example red and yellow, yellow and green, or yellow and dark brown. In other instances, weft twining appears in repeated parallel running rows, near the neck opening of a tunic (29) or near the selvages of a sheet (71). In these cases, they appear in the same color as the tunic or sheet and terminate in loose hanging portions that may have been used for tying.

In a few cases, two short parallel lines are inserted near the selvages, either by needlework (73) or by weaving (72, 91). These may be a form of identification, such as a weaver's mark.

Stitching was used not only as decoration or for identification but also to assemble fabrics—apparently at the time of burial—so as to have a textile large enough to make a wrapping (120, 170). Such stitching was often hasty and crude; somewhat more careful was the stitching used to assemble tapes for tying up the body. These were made from torn sheets (123).

In one case, stitches were used to finish the edges of a fabric (14). These stitches were so fine they could just barely be detected by the naked eye.

Edges

If the preserved fabrics are any indication, fabric edges were often given interesting treatment. Often, the warp ends were twisted together to form a cord at the edges of the textile (148). The technique is well illustrated by 71 from Q 68, where the edge has opened up. It shows how the warp ends were originally worked into the cord. In some cases a thread was added to this cord to make the cord thicker (125).[47]

The warp threads were knotted or wrapped near the edges of several fabrics, all of which were of cotton that had undergone extensive fiber degradation. For this reason, specific features of the technique were difficult to identify; individual

40

threads could not be distinguished even under magnification. In several cases, the knotted or wrapped warp threads end in loose-hanging fringe. (1, 2, 15, 20, 25, 106, 162, 168).

TEXTILE OBJECTS AND THEIR USES

Few, if any, of the textiles from Seele's excavation were being used in the way intended by their manufacturer. Most of those that had been undisturbed since they were deposited were last used as various kinds of burial cloths. Often these cloths were originally sheets, or articles of clothing, or fragments that were assembled by careless stitching into a piece large enough for wrapping up a body.

Textiles as Burial Cloths

In Meroitic and X-Group times burial cloths were generally simply wrapped around the body.[48] Because most of the bodies had been disturbed, details of how this wrapping was done are often obscured.

Occasionally a textile was found used as a loincloth (147, 111, 112, 113).[49] It is, however, uncertain whether or not they were originally loincloths as they could also have been reused sheet or tunic fragments.

In Christian times a more elaborate arrangement of wrapping was introduced, paralleling in simpler fashion the mummy-like wrapping of Christian burials in Egypt (fig. 2). The body, on its back with hands over the pubis (in one case with the two big toes tied together), was wrapped in a cloth. The cloth was secured by tapes constructed of fragments torn from sheets, and the edges of the fragments were sewn from end to end to prevent unraveling. The tapes are tied in crisscross fashion from the head to the feet (64).[50]

Only one object (64) was probably originally intended as a burial shroud. Brown to black in color, it has a slightly tapered shape. Two cords are attached to one end and tassels to the other. Although the object was not found in position, the fact that the tasseled end contained hair and the other end was knotted indicates that the tasseled end went over the head, with the tassels apparently arranged around the forehead, and the knotted end went around the feet.

Although almost all of the other fabrics were being used as burial wrappings, they had originally been made for other purposes, particularly for use as mantles, tunics, and sheets. In some cases they had been modified and reused, possibly several times, before they were finally deposited in the tomb. Sheets in particular had been used in burials. In one case, apparently after the worn parts of the sheet had been cut away, the sheet was stitched together again, so that the warp stripes no longer matched (120). In some cases a burial cloth had been made up of various bits of fabric layered and crudely stitched together (113 and 170). Often the burial wrappings were made of garments, some of which were almost intact and therefore complete enough to be identified.

Textiles for Daily Use

Garments that could be identified included mostly tunics (29) and mantles (69). Sheets were also common. Mantles had a relatively open weave and fragments could often be distinguished from those of sheets and tunics by this open weave. Thus a number of fragments of sheets and tunics which could easily be distinguished from mantles are only somewhat provisionally assigned to one or the other of these two groups (Table 3).

Some fragments were so minute that it was not possible to identify the original use of the fabrics. Only one textile was found that had had both ends and selvages completely cut away as part of the preparation for reuse (14). All of the edges were finished with plain stitches or with the stitching used today for reinforcing buttonholes.

One fragment appears to have been from a modern textile, perhaps lost during plundering or the excavations (179). The cotton warps and wefts of this fragment are particularly fine, and the black dye is chromium.

Sheets

Simple fabrics that are of large size are designated as *sheets* in this catalogue. At most, they are decorated with stripes at one end (45) or both ends (48). Fragments with more extensive decoration such as horizontal stripes (21) or countered weft twining (185) are identified as tunics, though the identifications are not certain.

In one case a sheet had been repaired by cutting away damaged or worn areas and sewing the sound portions together, but with the very pronounced warp stripe reversed (120).

Tunics

Garments called tunics are rectangular one-piece fabrics with an opening for the head. These garments are intended to be folded over the shoulders and tied with a separate belt at the waist. Of the total of fifty-six found, four (29, 119, 121, 131) were identified with certainty. If this identification is correct, tunics are the most numerous objects in the collection. The tunics must have been woven on extraordinarily wide looms the long way of the fabric,[51] so that the neck opening was in the warp direction, which made selvaged edges possible (29). In

Table 3

Shrouds	2	Tapes or belts	5
Sheets	24	Balls	2
Tunics	23	Fragments	58
Tunic or sheet fragments	33	Border fragments	2
Mantles	13	Edgings	5
Carpets	6	Not available for study	5
Hangings or covers	3	Nontextiles	
Loincloth	1	Portion of a mat	1
Uncertain	2	Twisted grass or reed	2
		Piece of sheepskin	1

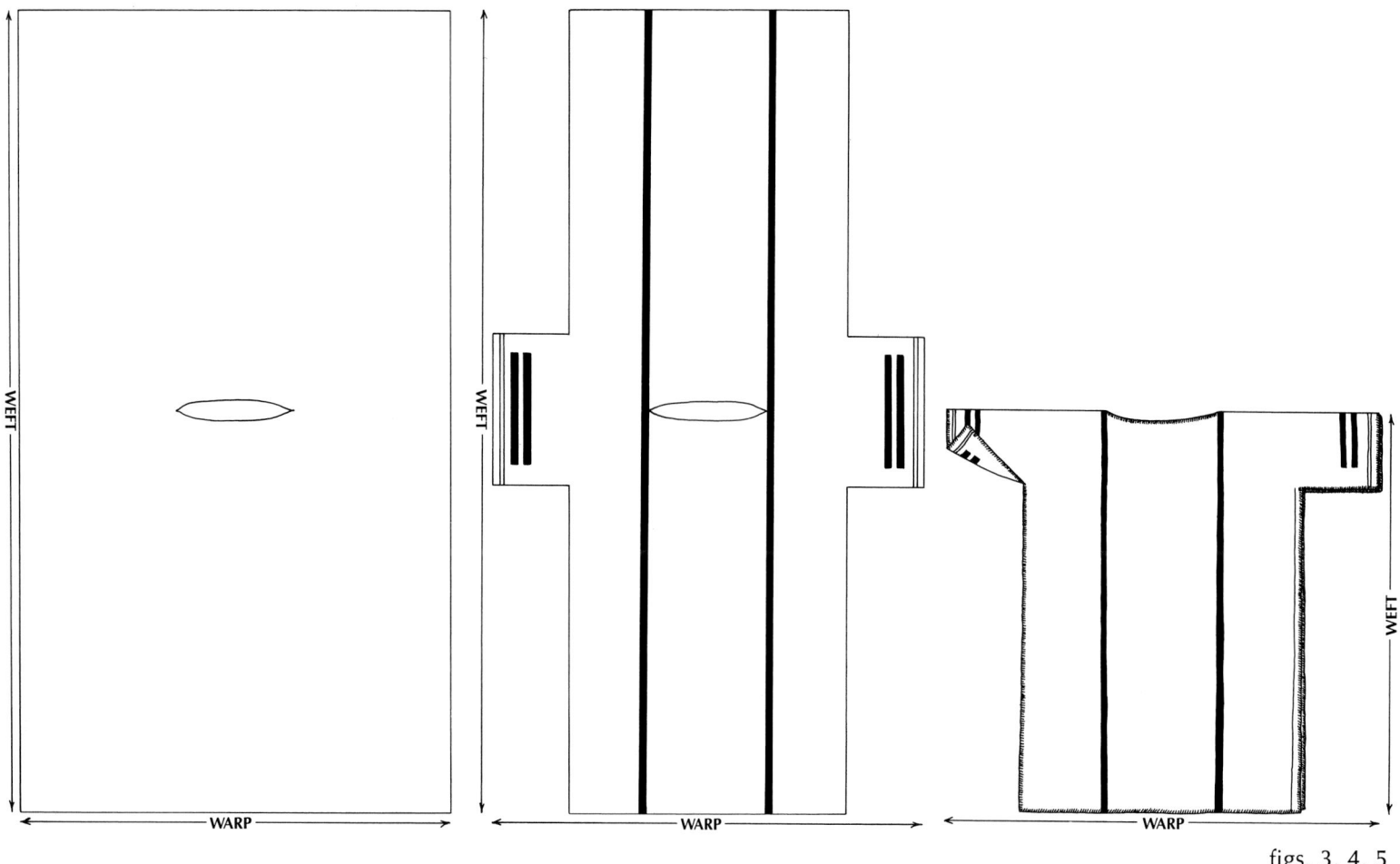

figs. 3, 4, 5

the cases of sleeved tunics, weaving began with one sleeve and ended with the other.

This collection includes both sleeved (131) and unsleeved (29) tunics. Note that the places where the edges of the unsleeved tunic cited would strike the wrists or lower arms are marked by decoration (figs. 3, 4, 5).

In the collection is a tunic sleeve (132) with the typical decoration of wide double stripes woven in purple on medium brown warps in weft-faced plain weave with discontinuous wefts.

One unusually short tunic, which appears to have been woven for a juvenile (121), was found in the grave of a child.

Mantles

Mantles were identified as large rectangular textiles with notched "L" or "H" inlaid decorations in each of the four corners. The use of fabric so decorated is indicated by the occurrence of mantles in the paintings, which are probably of third century date, in the Mithraeum and the Synagogue at Dura Europos (69 and 108).[52] A total of thirteen were found; three were almost complete. (27, 69, 139).[53] Mantles were woven in plain weave with widely spaced warps and wefts. The notched "L" or "H" shape was inserted in weft-faced plain weave with discontinuous wefts, joined through either dovetailing or interlocking[54] and worked into the mantle by the use of dovetailing or interlocking.[55] The colors of the inserts are mainly purple, brown, red, blue, and yellow.

The notched "L" and "H" decoration is often found on ancient textiles. A number were found in Kharga Oasis at the necropolis of el Bagawat, and dated to ca. 300–330 A.D.[56] There, also, the decoration was inserted in weft-faced plain weave with discontinuous wefts (MMA 33.10.49), but other techniques in which pile was formed through loops were also used (MMA 33.10.24). Textiles with this decoration were found at Karanis[57] and Palmyra.[58] One is in the Errera collection in Brussels.[59] The designs are sometimes misunderstood as the endings of bands that run the length of the garment,[60] but they are all in fact isolated decorative elements.

Carpets

Six pieces of carpet in various states of preservation comprise one of the most interesting and important groups of objects in this collection. (59, 66, 67, 115, 155, 13, 158). All textiles constructed primarily of pile were identified as carpets. One small fragment from Q 38[61] was beyond conservation. Since it was made of colored pile, however, it could be identified as a carpet fragment.

In entry 115, a central rectangular panel containing abstract floral shapes has two double borders; the outer border introduces a running key design.

In entry 66, a central square is bordered by a mixture of linear, architectural, and plant motifs. It cannot be determined whether this is the center of the carpet or one unit of a larger design which would have been repeated several times.

The center of entry 59 has a branching plant motif, probably a tree. This is surrounded by a triple border with simple linear and geometric decorations which in turn is surrounded by a border of rectangles containing geometric and linear patterns.

A carpet, or possibly cover, of special interest is the almost complete example from R 113 (155). Its structure is slightly different from that of the elaborately polychrome carpets because its warp and weft threads are both two-ply and Z-spun. The design is simple. In each corner the ancient motif of the *flyflot* or *gammadion* appears.[62] Each end of the carpet has two dark blue stripes, one in the pile area and one in the plain weave area near the edge. These stripes are almost separated into four equal stripes by two brown stripes. The brown stripes do not run the entire width of the fabric. They were inserted in the weft direction and end short of each selvaged edge by 5 to 6 centimeters.

A small fragment, originally part of a large carpet found by the Egypt Exploration Society at Buhen, both of which are now in the British Museum (67073), was made available for examination. The wefts were Z-spun and grouped generally in bundles of four that alternate with bundles of three. The warps were S-spun. The colored yarns, as in all of the carpets, were inserted —slip loops through a light to medium brown ground.[63]

A second carpet in the British Museum (66708), excavated by the Egypt Exploration Society at Qasr Ibrim, has an overall pattern of small scale in the center field, a design that is closely related to that of a carpet found by the Scandinavian Joint Expedition in Cemetery 25 (tomb 131:2).[64] The latter carpet has a border resembling the one on a carpet believed to have been found at Antinoe, which is now in the Metropolitan Museum.[65]

It seems clear that in technique, color, and decoration these carpets belong to a common tradition of manufacture, which is thought to have originated either in Egypt or in Anatolia. In any case, they must have been exported to Nubia.[66] The carpets may have been deposited as grave goods, as they were too cumbersome to have easily been used as wrappings for the body.

Hangings and Covers

Three elaborately constructed fabrics were identified as parts of hangings or covers. One fabric, a hanging (85), was constructed in weft-faced plain weave with areas of discontinuous wefts. These areas include stripes of color as well as intricate linear and geometric decorations of types common in contemporary fabrics from Egypt.

The other two objects combine relatively large areas of pile and areas constructed in weft-faced plain weave with discontinuous wefts (68 and 70). Because the pile is long and the areas of weft-faced plain weave with discontinuous wefts are relatively flat, these textiles could not conveniently have been used as carpets. They have therefore been identified as hangings or covers.

Entries 68 and 85 show large circular areas filled with intricate curvilinear and geometric designs. In addition, the hanging (85) has narrow borders that contain leaf motifs. The intricate designs relate to the large circular areas. The other object (68) is patterned with stripes that contain complex curvilinear and geometric designs.

Loincloth

A textile with tapered shape was constructed in plain weave with increasing or decreasing wefts and warps (178). It is identified as a loincloth on the basis of an example found on a body by the Scandinavian Joint Expedition in Sudanese Nubia.[67]

Identification Uncertain

One fabric, less than half the size of a sheet or mantle, has a series of special features. It must have been some sort of garment for the mature person with whom it was buried (71). A series of loose, hanging twisted cords appear in staggered arrangements on both sides near the left selvage. Two rows of weft shots in purple stop 14.5cm short of the left selvage. Finally, a small glass bead is attached to a group of opened-up warp threads, which had once been worked into a twisted cord.

No special purpose could be inferred for the cloth from entry 34. The textile has two weft stripes which do not run from selvage to selvage and there is a single warp stripe near one selvage. These haphazardly placed stripes may indicate that the weaver was using up odd lots of yarns.

Tapes or Belts

Five long narrow textiles were designated tapes or belts (16, 20, 28, 89, 124). Two of these (16 and 20) are of special interest, because they must have been woven on a more advanced type of loom. They are decorated with small-scale geometric designs.

Balls

One tomb and a burial pit filled with animals contained balls made of fiber. The burial pit Q 5 contained 27 balls or fragments of balls (36). Since the pit contained many horses, donkeys, and camels, these balls were undoubtedly attached to animal trappings.

Tomb Q 600 contained a ball made of pile (146). Its use is uncertain.

Fragments

Fifty-eight fragments were so small that their identification was uncertain. For that reason they could not be placed in a specific category. Two additional fragments were from borders and five more were possibly from edgings.

Not Available for Study

Five entries in the catalogue cover textiles that were too poorly preserved to be conserved and studied effectively. At a later date it may be possible to attempt conservation and study.

Nontextiles

Four objects are not constructed of either animal or twisted vegetable fibers. One is a small piece of sheepskin (173). Two are cords (10 and 109), made of twisted or braided coarse grass or reeds.

One mat, also of coarse grass or reed (32), is part of this collection. It had been used to cover the ground below a corpse.

The nontextile objects were discovered in the course of the treatment of the textiles. They do not represent the entire range of such objects that the expedition excavated at Qustul and

CONCLUSION

The textiles in this collection made by the Oriental Institute are closely related to those found by the Scandinavian Joint Expedition in Sudanese Nubia just to the south of the Oriental Institute's Nubian Expedition concession, though the present collection is somewhat smaller. (Because the Scandinavian Joint Expedition textiles were discussed only as fragments and not grouped as textile objects the number of objects represented in that collection cannot be discerned.)

The largest number of identifiable textiles are sheets and tunics, followed by mantles and carpets. Culturally, these objects can be divided into two groups, local and imported. Although these groups could not be distinguished with confidence in all cases, the simpler fabrics in plain weave were certainly made locally while the elaborate pieces, especially the carpets (pp. 42–43) and hangings or covers (p. 43), were imported. In some cases, local fabrics imitated imported fashions, as in the cases of locally woven mantles with notched "L" or "H" decorations, which imitate Egyptian and Near Eastern styles, especially the examples cited from Kharga Oasis and Dura Europos (see p. 42). The textiles discussed here are later than the paintings at Dura and may thus indicate that mantles of this type were made for a fairly long time.

The imported textiles, especially the carpets and carpet fragments, are intrinsically the most unusual objects in the collection. Comparisons with examples found elsewhere in Nubia have broadened our knowledge of the types in use there at this time (pp. 42–43).

A number of technical details are of special interest. Although various colors occur in this material, most fabrics are in varying shades of brown. The discovery that the stripes on one fabric are actually Tyrian purple is therefore all the more remarkable (14).

One of the textiles woven in weft-faced plain weave has loose-hanging warp threads on one of its sides (21). The warp, in cotton, is arranged in groups; double warp threads alternate with single ones. Every fourth warp is left hanging free at the point where a stripe of blue-green color is introduced.

Long, plied, loose-hanging weft threads were introduced into parts of two fabrics (70 and 68). Up to 6cm in length, they appear after 17 or 18 weft shots and are inserted after each ninth warp thread. These threads overlap the three that follow.

Two fabrics decorated with stripes are unusual. In one case, four light-blue cotton wefts were introduced, juxtaposed to four medium-brown weft shots (145 and 100). In the second case, very narrow weft stripes of dark blue interlace with light brown warps in such a way as to produce the effect of tiny squares in blue and brown.

Two features of textile construction are to be especially noted, the shaping on the loom of cloth, as seen in entries 178, 64, and 74 and the construction of both sleeved (131) and unsleeved tunics (29).

One of the most interesting aspects of this collection is the change that occurred in the fiber materials used during Meroitic and X-Group periods. At Qustul and Ballana, cotton and linen almost ceased to be used and their place was taken by animal fibers, which until then had been used much less frequently.[68] This is a major transition and must indicate a change in trade relations or a preference for fabrics made out of one or the other fibers. Early in the Christian period there was another and less important change. Vegetable fibers became common again, though they hardly dominated the textiles of that period.

NOTES:

1. Carl E. DeVries, "The Nubian Publication Project," *Annual Report 1973/74, The Oriental Institute of the University of Chicago* (1974): 39–40; idem, "Communication concerning the Work of the Oriental Institute Nubian Expedition," in *Actes du Colloque nubiologique international au Musée national de Varsovie, 19–22 Juin 1972,* ed. Kazimierz Michalowski (Warsaw: Musée national, 1975), pp. 18–21; and Christa Mayer-Thurman, "Textile Findings from the Aswan Region," in *Irene Emery Roundtable of Museum Textiles, 1974 Proceedings,* ed. Patricia L. Fiske (Washington: Textile Museum, 1975), pp. 207–8.

2. A great variety of specimen sizes are to be noted (see entries 90 and 91). This variety reflects the inconsistency with which the fabrics were selected and taken, often only as a sample of a specific textile and for the purpose of recording as many different types or structures as were obvious.

   The samples were removed from the sites and put into polyethelene bags for safekeeping until treatment became possible. A field number and an Oriental Institute number were recorded on a slip of paper, which was placed on the inside of the bag or taped to the outside. The bags were closed with tape and packed into cardboard boxes. The collection was kept in this way until work on the fabrics was started in 1972. Not all textiles originally discovered were kept. A great many were discarded in the field (for a complete listing of those textiles, see p. 148). A few were beyond conservation or else they totally disintegrated in their bags. Such instances are recorded under the specific entries.

3. Joanna Brandford to Thurman, pers. comm., 1976, 1979. Prof. Louis V. Zabkar, pers. comm., 1979; these textiles were excavated in 1966–67 and 1967–68. They were taken from Meroitic and X-Group cemeteries.

4. I am grateful to Prof. Nicholas Millet, Royal Ontario Museum, who permitted me to see the National Geographic Society's collection in October 1975.

5. Ingrid Bergman, *Late Nubian Textiles*, contributions by Hans-Åke Nordström and Torgny Säve-Söderbergh, The Scandinavian Joint Expedition to Sudanese Nubia, vol. 8 (Stockholm: Scandinavian University Books, 1975), pp. 7–9. About 10 tombs were either definitely or probably Meroitic. There were approximately 72 Meroitic–X-Group, 46 X-Group, 9 X-Group–early Christian, and 5 Christian tombs.

6. Identifications attempted for the Scandinavian Joint Expedition textiles were more specific. Testing by one method identified 28 fabrics that were all or partly camel, 4 that were all or partly sheep (2 of which were also possibly partly camel), and 1 that was possibly goat. In six cases these findings were checked by another method: one identification was in agreement; four were in disagreement; and one fabric could not be identified. See Bergman, *Late Nubian Textiles*, p. 11.

7. Camels were sacrificed in the royal tombs. Walter B. Emery and L. P. Kirwan, *The Royal Tombs of Ballana and Qustul*, vol. 1, Service des antiquités de l'Egypte, Mission archéologique de Nubie, 1929–34 (Cairo: Government Press, Bulaq, 1938), p. 26.

8. H. Epstein, *The Origin of Domestic Animals in Africa*, vol. 2 (New York: Africana Publishing Corp., 1971), pp. 56–62. For the question of the derivation and date of introduction into Africa of the hairy thin-tailed sheep, see ibid., pp. 71–79. The wooled thin-tailed sheep were apparently introduced later and were of much less importance (ibid., pp. 99–100). Fat-tailed (wooled) sheep, which were more diverse and important, were also imported into Egypt (after the Twelfth Dynasty; see ibid., pp. 110, 117–18). Wild-type sheep of the mouflon and Argali groups were unavailable as were the domestic fat-rumped types.

9. H. Idris Bell, *Egypt from Alexander the Great to the Arab Conquest* (Oxford: At the Clarendon Press, 1948), pp. 47, 49. However, Bell's statement that wool was a royal monopoly is disproved by M. Rostovtzeff (*A Social and Economic History of the Hellenistic World* [Oxford: Oxford University Press, 1941]; for the wool industry see pp. 307–8, 358, 377–80, 1164).

10. A. Lucas, *Ancient Egyptian Materials and Industries*, 4th ed., rev. and enl. by J. R. Harris (London: Edward Arnold, 1962), pp. 146–47. The situation with wool is reviewed: some evidence for goat can be noted but none for camel or antelopes. Epstein, *The Origin of Domestic Animals*, pp. 266–71. For a general review of the occurrence of camels before A.D. 1, see ibid., pp. 558–76. For commercial use in Egypt see Williams, this volume, n. 114.

11. Lucas (*Ancient Egyptian Materials and Industries*, p. 143) cites Badarian examples from Mostagedda and Badari. For Neolithic examples of the use of flax from Fayum see G. Caton-Thompson and E. W. Gardner, *The Desert Fayum* (London: Royal Anthropological Institute, 1934), p. 46. The earliest occurrence of flax in the Near East is at Tepe Sabz in Iran, ca. 5500-5000 B.C. (Peter J. Ucko and G. W. Dimbleby, *The Domestication and Exploitation of Plants and Animals* [London: Duckworth, 1969], p. 168, Table 1).

12. Rostovtzeff, *A Social and Economic History of the Hellenistic World*. On p. 1277 flax traders are mentioned; see also Index under flax and linen.

13. George Steindorff, *Aniba*, vol. 2, Service des antiquités de l'Egypte, Mission archéologique de Nubie, 1929–34 (Glückstadt, Hamburg, New York, 1937), pl. 101 and p. 243.

14. Ernest J. H. MacKay, *Early Indus Civilization*, 2nd ed. (London: Luzac, 1948), pp. 82, 105, 131, 133.

15. Lucas, *Ancient Egyptian Materials and Industries*, pp. 147–48; F. Ll. Griffith and G. M. Crowfoot, "On the Early Use of Cotton in the Nile Valley," *JEA* 20 (1934): 7.

16. Pliny *Natural History* 19. 2. 14–15.

17. C. L. Woolley and D. Randall-MacIver, *Karanog: The Romano-Nubian Cemetery*, Eckley B. Coxe Junior Expedition to Nubia, vol. 4 (Philadelphia: University Museum, 1910), pp. 27–28, 245; R. E. Massey, "A Note on the Early History of Cotton," *Sudan Notes and Records* 6 (1923): 231–33; Dows Dunham, *The West and South Cemeteries at Meroe*, The Royal Cemeteries of Kush, vol. 5 (Boston: Museum of Fine Arts, 1963), pp. 143, 146. At least some of these textiles from Meroe are from W 308, which contained glass vessels and millefiore plaques and beads, dated 50–60 in Dunham's sequence, or Roman. The Karanog speciments were first identified as linen but this was corrected by Griffith and Crowfoot, "Early Use of Cotton." It could as well be Sudanese cotton (Lucas, *Ancient Egyptian Materials and Industries*, p. 148).

18. Griffith and Crowfoot, "Early Use of Cotton," pp. 5–12.

19. Ibid., p. 7.

20. K. A. Chowdhury and G. M. Buth, "4,500 Year Old Seeds Suggest that True Cotton is Indigenous to Nubia," *Nature: International Journal of Science* 227, no. 5253 (July 4, 1970): 85–86. See Williams, this volume, pp. 12–13 for the date of A-Group.

21. R. J. Forbes, *Studies in Ancient Technology*, vol. 4, 2nd ed. rev. (Leiden: E. J. Brill, 1964), p. 50.

22. Ibid., p. 53.

23. Emery and Kirwan, *Royal Tombs of Ballana and Qustul*, vol. 1, p. 385; vol. 2, pl. 110C.

24. Lucas, *Ancient Egyptian Materials and Industries*, p. 149.

25. Pers. comm., Millet to Thurman, March 1979.

26. These structural features include tapestry weaving with inlaid single thread decoration and carpet techniques. Pierre du Bourguet, *Musée national du Louvre: catalogue des étoffes coptes I* (Paris: Editions des Musées nationaux, 1964); M. S. Dimand and J. Mailey, *Oriental Rugs in the Metropolitan Museum of Art* (New York: Metropolitan Museum of Art, 1973), pp. 8–9 and fig. 12.

27. Liliane Masschelein-Kleiner and Luc R. J. Maes, this volume, pp. 52–53.

28. Percy E. Newberry, *Beni Hasan*, 2 pts., Egypt Exploration Fund–Archaeological Survey Publications, vols. 1–2 (London: 1893), 2: pls. IV, XIII; N. de G. Davies, "The Town House in Ancient Egypt," *Metropolitan Museum Studies* 1, pt. 2 (May 1929): 234, fig. 1.

29. G. M. Crowfoot, *Methods of Handspinning in Egypt and the Sudan*, Bankfield Museum Notes, 2nd ser., no. 12 (Halifax: Bankfield Museum, 1931).

30. G. M. Crowfoot, "Spinning and Weaving in the Sudan," *Sudan Notes and Records* 4 (April 1921): 21, 39; idem, *Methods of Handspinning in Egypt and the Sudan*, pl. 38.

31. Newberry, *Beni Hasan*, pt. 1, pls. XI, XXIX; pt. 2, pls. IV, XIII.

32. Percy E. Newberry, *El Bersheh*, 2 pts., Egypt Exploration Fund-Archaeological Survey Publications, vols. 3–4 (London, 1892–94), 1: pl. XXVI.

33. Herbert E. Winlock, *Models of Daily Life in Ancient Egypt*, Publications of the Metropolitan Museum of Art Egyptian Expedition, vol. 18 (Cambridge, Mass.: Harvard University Press, 1950), pp. 29–33, pls. 25–27, 66–67.

34. N. de Garis Davies, *Five Theban Tombs*, Egypt Exploration Fund–Archaeological Survey Publications, vol. 21 (London, 1913), pl. XXXVII; Lucas, *Ancient Egyptian Materials and Industries*, p. 142; H. Ling Roth, *Ancient Egyptian and Greek Looms*, Bankfield Museum Notes, 2nd ser., no. 2 (Halifax: Bankfield Museum, n.d.), pp. 14–18, figs. 9, 13, 14, 16. These include representations from the tombs of Djehutynefer, Neferhotep, and Neferrenput. See also C. H. Johl, *Altägyptische Webestühle und Brettchenweberei in Altägypten* (Leipzig: J. C. Hinrichs'sche Buchhandlung, 1924), pp. 49–58; Aug. Braulik, *Altägyptische Gewebe* (Stuttgart: Arnold Bergstrassen Verlagsbuchhandlung, 1900), pp. 57–73. In the earlier weaving scenes, women are shown working the horizontal looms; the vertical looms are worked by men.

35. Ling Roth, *Ancient Egyptian and Greek Looms*, p. 30.

36. H. E. Winlock and W. E. Crum, *The Monastery of Epiphanius at Thebes*, Metropolitan Museum of Art Egyptian Expedition, vol. 3 (New York, 1926), pp. 220–31.

37. Ibid., pp. 68–69, pl. XXI.

38. Ibid., pl. XX.

39. Ibid., p. 69. See also Crowfoot, "Spinning and Weaving in the Sudan," p. 30 and diagram. At Omdurman, Crowfoot found the more advanced loom without the rectangular frame. This is most unusual, for the loom needs a frame to maintain its rigidity. The Sudanese loom described by Crowfoot had the following parts: batten and treadles are hung from a rod; the rod is attached to the beams of the roof; in place of the frame two short front posts are introduced. They support the cloth beam. A third, somewhat taller, post is also mentioned; Crowfoot calls it a warp post. The weaver sits on the floor and works the treadles in the pit.

40. Bergman, *Late Nubian Textiles*, p. 21.

41. For more elaborate explanation of weaving terminology and diagrams see Irene Emery, *The Primary Structures of Fabrics* (Washington: Textile Museum, 1966), *plain weave*: p. 76; *weft-faced plain weave*: p. 77; *warp-faced plain weave*: p. 76; *dovetailing*: p. 80; *interlocking*: pp. 80–81; *twill weave*: pp. 92–98; *pile*: pp. 148–49.

42. Charles Grant Ellis, "Garden 'Carpets' from Upper Egypt," in *Irene Emery Roundtable on Museum Textiles, 1974 Proceedings*, ed. Patricia L. Fiske (Washington: Textile Museum, 1975), pp. 209–11.

43. For detailed information on pile see Louisa Bellinger, *Textile Analysis: Pile Techniques in Egypt and the Near East*, pt. 4, Workshop Notes, paper no. 12 (Washington: Textile Museum, 1955); and Emery, *Primary Structures of Fabrics*, pp. 148–49.

44. Ellis to Thurman, pers. comm., March 1979. Also Emery, *Primary Structures of Fabrics*, pp. 222–23.

45. Deborah Thompson, *Coptic Textiles in The Brooklyn Museum* (Brooklyn: Brooklyn Museum, 1971). These textiles date approximately from Roman to Islamic times and are usually called Coptic.

46. Emery, *Primary Structures of Fabrics*, pp. 196–200; Bergman, *Late Nubian Textiles*, pp. 25–27.

47. For elaborate technical analyses and drawings of cords and edges see Bergman, *Late Nubian Textiles*, pp. 26–38. See also Braulik, *Altägyptische Gewebe*, pp. 8–25.

48. Bergman, *Late Nubian Textiles*, pls. 5:3–4, 6:1–3.

49. Ibid., pl. 5:2.

50. Winlock and Crum, *Monastery of Epiphanius at Thebes*, pls. XI:C, XII. The wrapping procedures used at Qustul are much simpler than those used in Egypt. Tying of limbs is noted both at Thebes and at Kharga.

51. Laura E. Start, *Coptic Cloths*, Notes from Bankfield Museum, 2nd ser., no. 4 (n.p., 1914), pp. 33–35.

52. R. Pfister and Louisa Bellinger, *The Excavations at Dura-Europos*, pt. 2: *The Textiles*, ed. M. I. Rostovtzeff (New Haven: Yale University Press, 1945), p. 10; figs. 3–6. The term *Mantle* appears throughout the publication. The date is given on ibid., p. 1.

53. If traces of selvages and endings for top and bottom are present in spite of losses in the center portion of a given item, it can be considered complete from a technical point of view.

54. See p. 39; for fuller information see Emery, *Primary Structures of Fabrics*, pp. 76ff.

55. Ibid., pp. 80–81.

56. Bruce Williams, "An Overview of Roman Kharga in The Metropolitan Museum of Art" (New York, 1976).

57. Lillian M. Wilson, *Ancient Textiles from Egypt in the University of Michigan Collection* (Ann Arbor: University of Michigan Press, 1933), no. 77; pl. IV. (The piece is illustrated incorrectly. It should be turned so that the protruding prong points to the left.)

58. See R. Pfister, *Textiles de Palmyre*, vol. 3 (Paris: Les Editions d'art et d'histoiré, 1934–40), frontispiece.

59. Isabelle Errera, *Collection d'anciennes étoffes égyptiennes*, Musées royaux des arts décoratifs (Brussels: Imprimerie J.-E. Goossens; Librairie Henri Lamertin, 1916), cat. no. 19; see p. 6. Errera describes the fragment as "a portion of a burial shroud made of linen" and dates it tentatively to the first century A.D.

60. Wilson, *Ancient Textiles from Egypt*, p. 33.

61. In one additional instance (entry 60), the remnants were so heavily encrusted that no conservation work could be attempted at all. They were left as they were originally found and are not included in this publication.

62. *Webster's New International Dictionary*, s.v. "swastika, swastica." This very ancient design relates to the Greek meander or fret. It has association with ancient Persia, India, China, and Japan as well as with South, Central, and North America.

63. Carpets #67073 (1968) Buhen and #66708 (1962) Qasr Ibrim. I am grateful for this information to Professor I. E. S. Edwards, Keeper, Department of Egyptian Antiquities, The British Museum (Edwards to Thurman, pers. comm., 20 August 1973). In a follow-up visit in May of 1977, I was able to study a fragment of the Buhen Carpet (#67073) in the Department of Egyptian Antiquities.

64. Bergman, *Late Nubian Textiles*, p. 66; pls. 16, 72. The pottery associated with the tomb was dated 300–500 A.D.

65. M. S. Dimand; "An Early Cut-Pile Rug from Egypt," *Metropolitan Museum Studies* 4 (1932–33): 151–62; H. E. Winlock, "A Roman Tapestry and a Roman Rug," *Bulletin of The Metropolitan Museum of Art* 27 (1932): 157–59 (acc. no. 31.1.1); and Dimand and Mailey, *Oriental Rugs in The Metropolitan Museum of Art*, p. 9.

66. Ellis to Thurman, pers. comm., March 1979. In 1974 he delivered a preliminary report on these carpets entitled "Garden 'Carpets' from Upper Egypt." (Summary in *Irene Emery Roundtable on Museum Textiles*, pp. 209–11.)

67. Bergman, *Late Nubian Textiles*, p. 23; pls. 5:1 and XX.

68. See ibid., pp. 11–13. No significant body of Meroitic textiles was found; vegetable fiber was somewhat more common in the X-Group material, but textiles made of it were still only a very small fraction of the total.

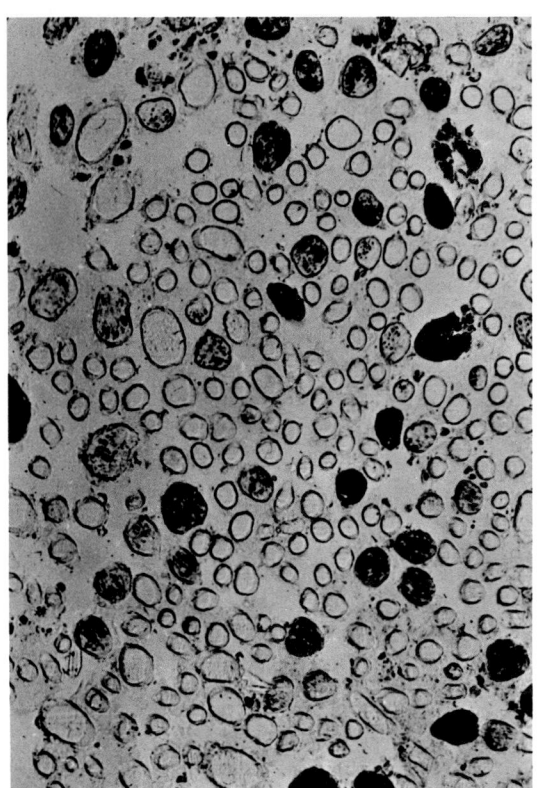

Microscopic Cross Section, 180:1, entry no. 34
CIBA photo no. 1 (Norbert Bigler), CIBA-GEIGY AG, Basel

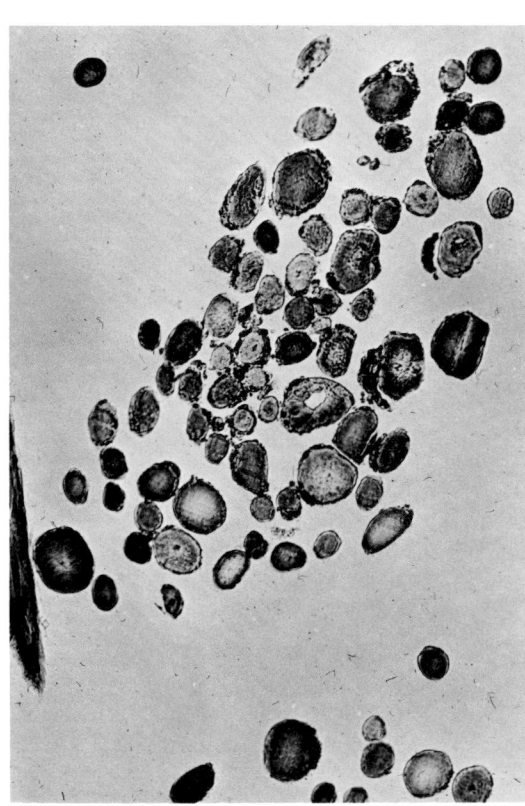

Microscopic Cross Section, 180:1, entry no. 161
CIBA photo no. 2 (Norbert Bigler), CIBA-GEIGY AG, Basel

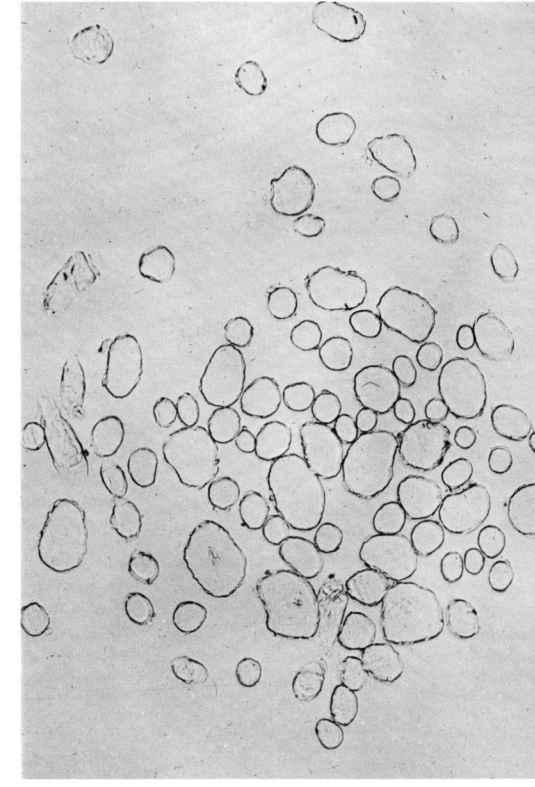

Microscopic Cross Section, 180:1, entry no. 48
CIBA photo no. 3 (Norbert Bigler), CIBA-GEIGY AG, Basel

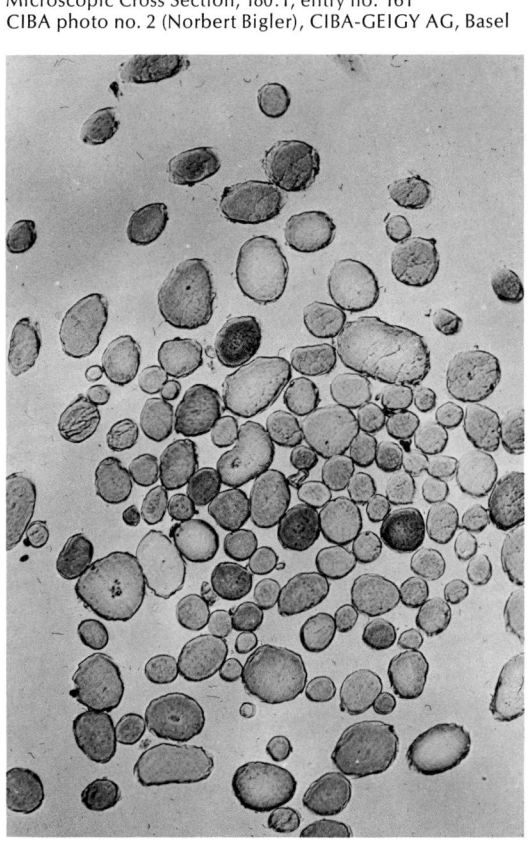

Microscopic Cross Section, 180:1, entry no. 54
CIBA photo no. 4 (Norbert Bigler), CIBA-GEIGY AG, Basel

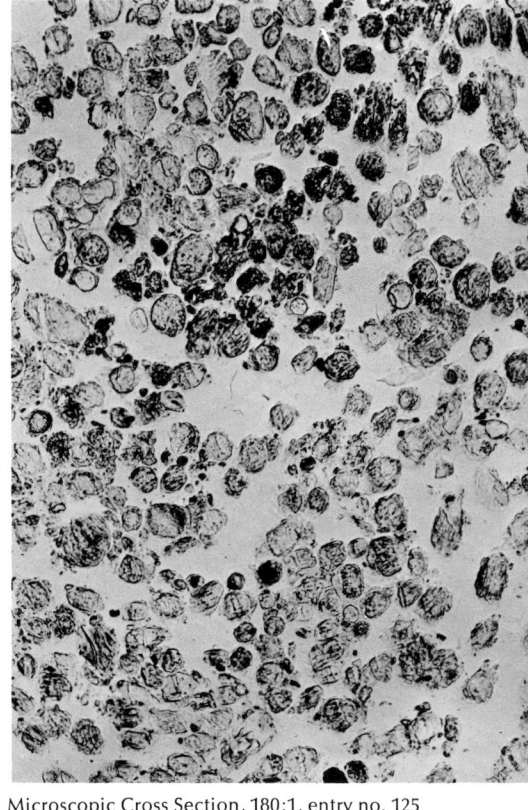

Microscopic Cross Section, 180:1, entry no. 125
CIBA photo no. 5 (Norbert Bigler), CIBA-GEIGY AG, Basel

THE FIBERS

Inge Fiedler
Painting Conservation Department
The Art Institute of Chicago

A representative group of fibers from the burial wrappings was studied by both optical and scanning electron microscopy to determine the identity of the various types of materials used in Nubia during the Meroitic, X-Group and Christian periods. Three materials were analyzed—wool, cotton and linen. The wool can further be classified as camel, sheep, and, possibly, goat. Effort was concentrated on the wool samples, since these proved the most difficult to identify positively. One of the main reasons for this difficulty is that the standards available are of modern origin. Unfortunately there is very little known about the changes in fiber morphology of the animals in question during this time span, especially when one considers the breeding which went into producing a creature as tailored to man's ideas as the modern sheep.

Another complication was the fact that some of the fabrics were more or less degraded by the passage of time and the degree of this degradation was determined by the individual history of a given sample; i.e., conditions in the burial environment as to temperature, moisture, chemical agents such as decomposition products from the body, etc., and storage conditions after the material was collected. The rigors which the wrappings underwent are in general unknown; furthermore, it is assumed that they were used in life as well as for burial. As the degree of use and wear through life is equally uncertain, it is no wonder that there is a wide latitude of fabric condition ranging from barely perceptible changes seen by microscopy to cases where many if not most identification details have been eradicated. The deterioration is not easily subject to quantification, though categories of none, slight, moderate, and severe were subjectively established during microscopic examination. The category of "none" only refers to the appearance when examined optically with no regard to chemical changes which were not visible. In extreme cases much of the cuticle of the animal fibers was missing and some of the underlying core of the fiber was severely pitted, with the diameter varying from point to point. In addition, some samples were very brittle and would invariably break apart during preparation.

A polarizing light microscope was used to identify fibers teased out from the bulk material and mounted in Aroclor 5442[1], a thermoplastic resin with a refractive index of 1.66. The properties noted were: overall morphology, birefringence, scale pattern, scale relief, pigmentation, medulla, ranges in fiber diameter, degree of degradation and whether or not the sample was dyed. Comparisons were made with available present-day standards. Replicas using cellulose acetate were made of some of the fibers to get a better idea of cuticle structure. While the replicas showed enhanced contrast, the degradation and consequent brittleness of some of the fibers made replication difficult.

In addition to the optical work, samples and standards were examined with a scanning electron microscope. In this case preparation consisted of mounting the fibers on double-sided tape and then coating with a conductive layer of about 100Å[2] of gold-palladium alloy. The electron microscope was used in hope that the increased resolution and depth of field would clarify surface detail, though any internal structure such as pigmentation or medulla was not revealed by the SEM. Even with the 100Å or better resolution available the alteration with time of some of the fibers gave problems with positive identification.

Present-day sheep wool can be characterized as a non-pigmented, usually non-medullated fiber with very distinct relief of the scale pattern, and a size range of 10–70 micrometers[3] with an average of about 20. Common goat has a similar size range and good scale relief but with the possibility of pigmentation which is usually concentrated near the center of the fiber. A medulla can be present, though this is somewhat rare. Cashmere goat is also very similar, though less likely to be pigmented. Camel fibers occur in two forms; one consists of the finer "wool" hair which are usually lightly pigmented, though some can be clear, and have a size range of 5–20 micrometers, while the coarser ones are more deeply pigmented and can range up to 120 micrometers in diameter, with values around 40 the most common. The pigmentation pattern is generally linear and oriented along the length of the fiber. This pigment arrangement is distinctive enough to aid in identification. The medulla is very rarely present in the finer fibers, though sometimes present in discontinuous form in the coarse

hair. One of the main differentiations between camel and the sheep/goat types is the lack of relief of the scales in the case of the camel. Both camel and sheep have coronal and imbricate geometry of the cuticle with smooth, nonserrated margins. The pattern can vary not only from fiber to fiber in a given sample but also along the length of some individual fibers.[4]

The cotton used in these textiles was similar though not identical to the modern variety. The fibers were coarser, thicker, had non-uniform spiral spacing and many of them were immature fibers which tended to be cylindrical rather than the flattened ribbons normally associated with cotton.[5] Because of larger dimensions the birefringence colors were higher than those of modern cotton, though the general morphology and lack of extinction normally seen were evident. Additionally, there were many of the double twisted fibers which are used by the plant to aid in seed dispersion.

The linen or flax samples had characteristic individual fibers as well as bundles of fibers, with distinct nodes or cross-markings similar to an "X" at intervals. Extinction was parallel and complete and birefringence measured 0.6 to 0.7. The diameter range of the fibers is approximately 6–30 micrometers.

Ancillary material found with the fabrics was also examined microscopically. A piece of sheepskin (173) was identified from the characteristics of the attached hair. This was an ideal sample with the coarse kemp hair and the finer "wool" fibers in a good state of preservation. The confidence in this identification is high and lends credence to the presence of sheep in the area. A mat sample (32) of twisted pieces of coarse grass or reed which were interleaved. This material is of plant origin, and a plant of the grass type (epithelium with evenly distributed stomates on both sides, coarse reticulated structure of the epidermis, linear structure of the underlying cells, etc.), but no further identification was attempted. Two other pieces of similar plant material (9) and (109) were taken from individual non-interleaved strands. Finally, entry 61 was characterized as being horsehair based on size and morphology.

As noted under entries 34, 161, 48, 54, and 125 CIBA-GEIGY AG, Basel,[5] in Switzerland did fiber identification in June, 1974. Their methods involved gelatin impressions and cross sections as well as morphological analysis. Their results were also based on the fact that camel hair tends to be finer than sheep wool. Enzymatic degradation tests usually performed to determine the difference between sheep and camel wool were not attempted since these samples had already undergone degradation with time. (Camel normally disintegrates at a faster rate than sheep.)[6]

The exact identity of entries 34 (CIBA #1) and 161 (CIBA #2) is uncertain. Optically the first has pronounced scales, very little pigmentation, and a size range which overlaps with the finer sheep wools used as standards. Unfortunately, the morphology is very similar to cashmere goat or a genetic precursor of the species. In entry 161 the intense blue dye which extended throughout the fiber diameter masked much of the detail. The scale relief was almost nonexistent; the fibers appeared to have natural pigmentation in linear orientation characteristic of camel, and the smaller fibers which were not as intensely dyed showed a distinct light brown color at the edges where the least amount of dye influenced the coloration. However, because of degradation and the subtlety of morphological characteristics it was not possible to positively identify these samples.

NOTES:

1. Aroclor 5442 trade name of Monsanto Chemical Company for their chlorinated polyphenyl. Distributed by McCrone Associates, Chicago, Illinois.
2. 1 angstrom = 0.0001 μm (1/254,000,000 inch)
3. 1 micrometer = 0.001 mm (1/25,400 inch)
4. For a more detailed discussion of fiber analysis the reader is referred to the following: A. B. Wildman, *The Microscopy of Animal Textile Fibres* (Leeds, England: Wool Industrial Research Association, 1954); Herbert R. Mauersberger, ed., *Matthew's Textile Fibres*, 5th ed. (New York: John Wiley and Sons, Inc., 1947); Milton Harris, ed., *Handbook of Textile Fibers* (Washington: Harris Research Laboratories, 1954); and American Association of Textile Chemists and Colorists, Test Method 20–1973, "Fibers in Textiles: Identification," *AATCC Technical Manual* (Research Triangle Park, N.C.: American Association, 1973), pp. 49–64.
5. Several cotton samples, entries 16, 17, 18, 19 and 179 were also analyzed by Nobuko Kajitani, The Metropolitan Museum of Art, New York; Kajitani to Thurman, pers. comm., December 1978.
6. Professor Dr. W. Jenny, CIBA-GEIGY AG, Basel, Switzerland to Thurman, pers. comm., September 1974 and June 1975. The fibers were analyzed by Mr. Norbert Bigler.

1. Standard 11-E: Wool sample from Cargille Laboratories, Inc., Cedar Grove, N.J., at 132× magnification (Mike Bayard)

3. Standard: Kashmir Goat from Merrimack Valley Textile Museum, Mass., at 332× magnification (M.B.)

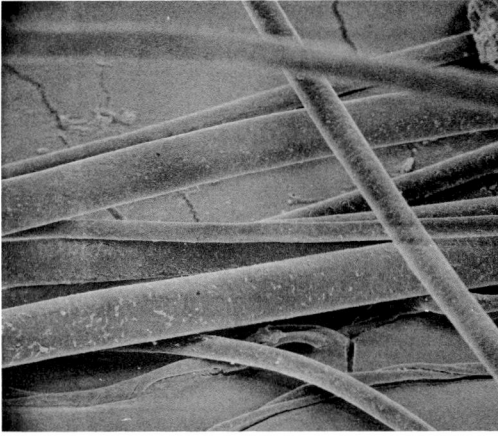

5. Standard: Camel Hair (fine) from Merrimack Valley Textile Museum, Mass., at 332× magnification (M.B.)

2. Standard no. 47: Wool-Merino Sheep from McCrone's Fiber Reference Set, England, at 660× magnification (M.B.)

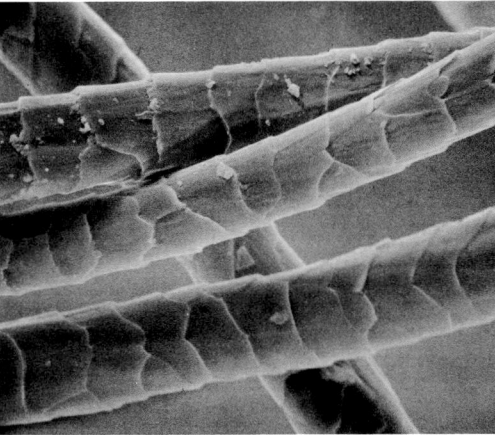

4. Standard: Camelus Dromedarian-Egyptian Camel from Lincoln Park Zoo, Chicago, Ill. at 132× magnification (M.B.)

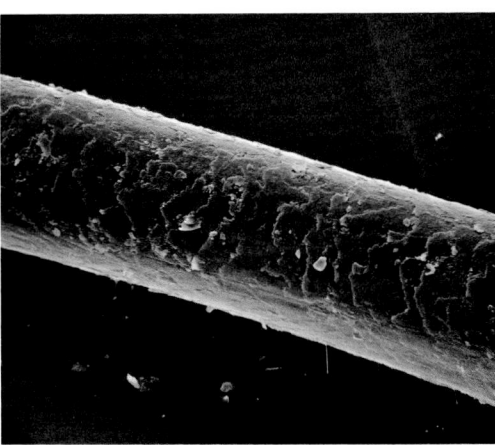

6. Standard: Camel Hair (coarse) from Merrimack Valley Textile Museum, Mass., at 332× magnification (M.B.)

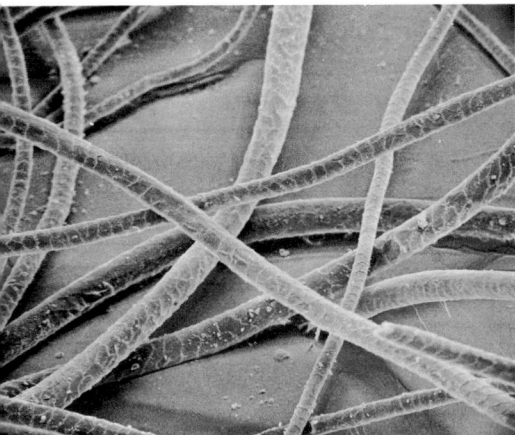

Sample: Entry no. 54, Sheep wool, at 132× magnification (Mike Bayard)

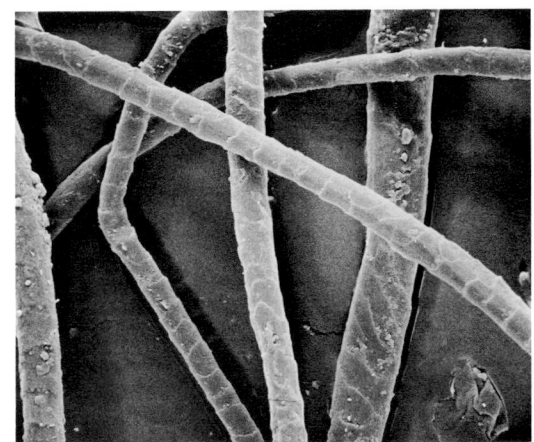

8. Sample: Entry no. 34, Wool, exact identity uncertain, at 332× magnification (M.B.)

9. Sample: Entry no. 125, Very badly degraded Camel Hair, at 66× magnification (M.B.)

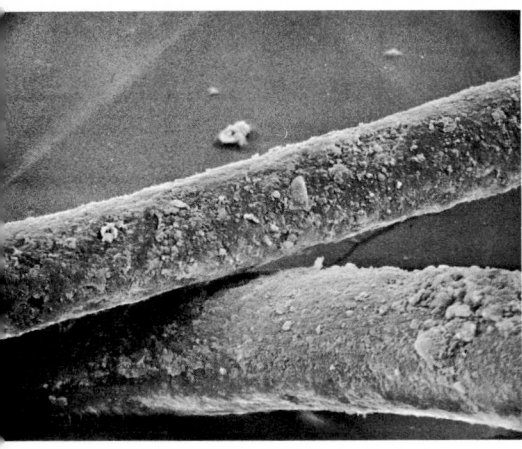

Sample: Entry no. 161. Very degraded wool fibers, possibly camel or sheep, at 660× magnification (M.B.)

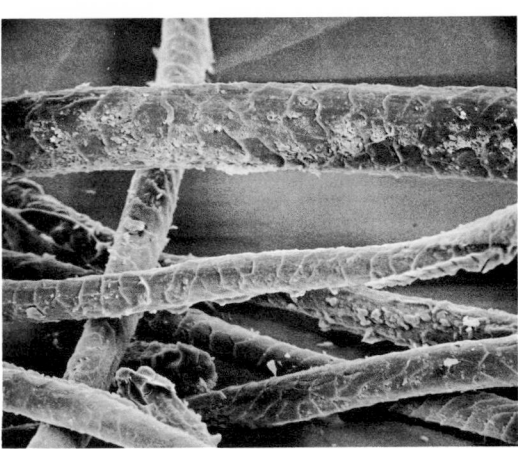

11. Sample: Entry no. 48, Sheep wool, 332× magnification (M.B.)

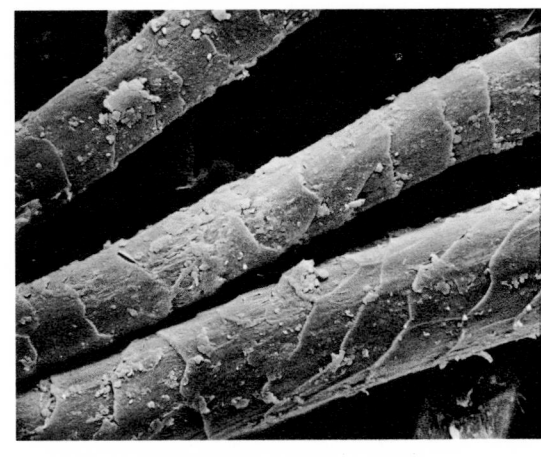

12. Sample: Entry no. 77, Sheep wool, at 660× magnification (M.B.)

13. Sample: Entry no. 17, Cotton fibers, at 74× magnification (M.B.)

14. Sample: Entry no. 37, Linen fibers, at 332× magnification (M.B.)

THE DYES

Liliane Masschelein-Kleiner, Dr. Sc.
and Luc R. J. Maes
Institut Royal du Patriomoine
Artistique, Brussels, Belgium

The dyestuffs and the metallic mordant were determined in about one hundred samples taken from the Nubian textiles belonging to The Oriental Institute, The University of Chicago. The individual results are to be found under the specific entries in the catalogue.

RED, ORANGE AND PURPLE SHADES

One chief constituent, *purpurin*, was found in most red threads. This red dyestuff was found together with *alizarin* in the madder (*Rubia tinctorum*). The Nubian dyers probably used another plant since the samples contain very little alizarin. Several kinds of Rubia, such as *Rubia munjista*, *Rubia cordifolia*, and *Rubia peregrina* are known sources of *purpurin*. Other plants, i.e. the *Relbunium* species also contain this red pigment.[11] They are reported to have been used in Peru some 2000 years ago.

Another explanation could be that the dyers were able to extract *purpurin* in order to get a more carmine shade than with the complete madder.

Another red dyestuff was found in a carpet. It contains five components one of them being carminic acid (66). This unknown dye is likely to be an insect dye.[1] We often find it in Coptic textiles.[10]

The famous *Purple*[2] was identified in textile entry 14. This dye was known as far back as 1500 B.C. It was no doubt the most highly-prized dye of antiquity because more than 12,000 molluscs, usually murex, were needed to extract only 1.5g of the dye. The use of purple garments was therefore limited to only a few privileged people.

YELLOW, GREEN AND BROWN SHADES

The Nubian yellow dyeings were also quite surprising. Until now, we have usually found *Weld* (Reseda luteola), in most yellow threads dating since antiquity till the 20th century, in Europe, Northern Africa and Western Asia.[3,4,5,6,7] We were therefore very astonished to find it in only one yellow sample, 66. We did, however, find it in some green shades, mixed with indigo and in olive tones where it was mordanted by iron.

The ultraviolet absorption spectrum shows the presence of luteoline without genistein. This proves the use of weld and not of broom, (Genista tinctoria).

The other yellow samples present a difficult problem. They are no doubt different from the most common sources of yellow dyes, such as safflower, (Carthamus tinctorius), saffron, (Crocus sativus), turmeric, (Curcuma longa), Persian berries (Rhamnus infectorius).

The Nubian yellow shows some similarity with only one known dye: *Orlean* (rocou or annatto). This coloring matter is produced from the seeds of a small tree (Bixa orellana). It yields a bright orange color.

Forbes[1] reports that *orlean* was known during antiquity but its use is seldom mentioned.

The dye contains a carotenoid, *Bixin*, which has an infrared and an ultraviolet absorption spectrum very similar to those of the Nubian yellow. Unfortunately, none of these spectra are sufficiently characteristic to allow a definitive identification. We cannot exclude the possibility for the dyeing to be due to some kind of tanin.

This is certainly the case for a series of beige and brown shades in which we found traces of *gallic acid*. This gallotanin was found alone or mixed with weld, indigo or purpurin. It was frequently mordanted with iron.

A brown thread from textile entry 21 does not contain any dyestuff: it must be a naturally brown colored wool.

BLUE SHADES

The blue tones were achieved with indigo. They often contain traces of weld, purpurin and tanins.

METALLIC MORDANTS

Aluminum was probably used with most mordant dyes but it is difficult to identify it with certainty in very little samples. Iron was found in about 50% of the samples. It was used not only with tanins but also with mordant dyes.

Traces of zinc were found in most samples taken from carpet entry 59. We often identified this metal in Egyptian and Hebrew textiles.[10]

The most amazing result was the presence of tin in both a blue and a brown thread, entry 70 also found as traces in three others (red, blue and brown). In Europe, its use as mordant occurs only from the 17th century on.

EXPERIMENTAL

Analysis of the mordants: X-ray fluorescence

The analysis of dyeings begins with the determination of the mordants by X-ray fluorescence spectrometry. This method is not destructive and enables further analysis of the dyestuffs to be carried out on the same thread.

The samples are washed in order to remove metallic soils, especially iron. The metallic elements are determined on threads about 1 cm long by comparison with an undyed woolen thread and another one which was mordanted by a known metal. Tin, zinc; copper and chromium are easily detected in this way. Aluminum requires a larger amount of a sample: at least 5 cm.

Experimental conditions

Generator: Kristalloflex 4 —Siemens S.R.S.
Tube: Tungsten—40 kV, 30 mA
Crystal: LiF

For the determination of aluminum: Helium flow, crystal AdP.

Analysis of the dyestuffs

1. Thin-layer chromatography

We used conditions as described in 1967:[8] thin-layers of 10% acetylated cellulose powder (Macherey, Nagel and Co-MN 300 AC); solvent: ethyl acetate tetrahydrofuran water (5/35/45); detection reagent: 2-aminoethyl diphenylborate (Fluka AG-Duchs SG, Switzerland-n^r· 42810) 1% in methanol.

2. Ultraviolet and visible spectra[9]

Apparatus: Beckman, model DB
The dyestuff was extracted from the wool sample by hydrolysis with diluted HCl (1/1). After evaporation, the dye was dissolved in methanol. Another way of extraction is to treat the wool sample with concentrated sulfuric acid and to take the spectrum of the resulting solution.

3. Infrared absorption spectra[9]

Apparatus: Perkin-Elmer, model 221
The hydrolysed dyes extracted from the samples are diluted in amyl alcohol, washed twice with water and evaporated till dry. The solid thus obtained is pressed into a micro palette of potassium bromide (diameter 1 mm) and examined by means of a beam condenser (6x).

CONCLUSIONS

In surveying the dyeings of these Nubian textiles, it clearly appears that the dyers had reached a high level in the art of dyeing. They were able to select a series of local plants and were able to achieve the very sophisticated vat dyeing process with indigo and purple.

We hope, one day, to extend our knowledge by further comparisons with the dyeing techniques of the surrounding civilizations.

NOTES:

1. R[obert] J[ames] Forbes, *Studies in Ancient Technology*, 9 vols. (Leiden: E. J. Brill, 1956), 4: 98–148.
2. J. T. Baker, "La Pourpre de Tyr: colorant ancien, problème moderne," *Endeavour* 33 (1974): 11–17.
3. Liliane Masschelein-Kleiner, Nicole Znamenski-Festraets, and Luc Maes, "Les Colorants des tapisseries tournaisiennes au XVe siècle," *Bulletin de l'Institut Royal du Patrimoine Artistique* 10 (1967–1968): 126–140 (hereafter cited as *Bulletin de l'IRPA*).
4. Liliane Masschelein-Kleiner, Nicole Znamenski-Festraets, and Luc Maes, "Etude technique de la tapisserie tournaisienne au XVe siècle. Les Colorants." *Bulletin de l'IRPA* 11 (1969): 34–41.
5. Liliane Masschelein-Kleiner and Luc Maes, "Etude technique de la tapisserie tournaisienne au XVe et XVIe siècles. Les Colorants," *Bulletin de l'IRPA* 12 (1970): 269–279.
6. Liliane Masschelein-Kleiner and Luc Maes, "Etude technique de la tapisserie des Pays-Bas Méridionaux aux XVe et XVIe siècles," *Bulletin de l'IRPA* 14 (1973–1974): 193–195.
7. Liliane Masschelein-Kleiner and Luc Maes, "Etude technique de la tapisserie des Pays-Bas Méridion-

aux. Les Tapisseries anversoises des XVIe et XVIIe siècles. Les Teintures," *Bulletin de l'IRPA* **16** (1976–1977): 143–147.

8. Liliane Masschelein-Kleiner, "Microanalysis of Hydroxyquinones in Red Lakes," *Mikrochimoca Acta* 6 (1967): 1080–1085.

9. L. Masschelein-Kleiner and J. B. Heylen, "Analyse des laques rouges anciennes," *Studies in Conservation* 13 (1968): 87–97.

10. Liliane Masschelein-Kleiner and Luc Maes, "Ancient Dyeing Techniques in Eastern Mediterranean Regions," ICOM Committee for Conservation, 5th Triennial Meeting, Zagreb, 1978 (Paris: International Council of Museums, 1978), no. 78–9–3.

11. R. H. Thomson, *Naturally Occurring Quinones* (London: Butterworth, 1957).

THE DATING OF THE GRAVES

The assignment of dates (see catalogue) was based first on the study of the tombs' architecture. Some features, such as the tumulus of the X-Group, the rectangular bench, or the lamp niche of the Christian period were clearly indicative of date by themselves, as were the foundations for the brick pyramids of the Meroitic period.

The elaborate wrapping of the body for a Christian burial served to distinguish Christian burials from those of the late X-Group and of Meroitic tradition. The semicontracted position distinguished adult burials of the X-Group from those of Meroitic and Christian times.

Because the distinctions between the tombs of the Meroitic period and those of the X-Group of the Meroitic tradition cannot be made on the basis of the type of burial or architecture, only the objects found in the tombs were used for this purpose. In some cases, distinctions could not be made with certainty because the graves contained very few objects or other distinctive features. Graves that contained no distinctive pottery were the most difficult to date, and the reader is warned that the dates assigned to some tombs are tentative and may be changed in the final publication of the complete tomb material.

B.W.

The material is divided as to the time periods of *Meroitic, Meroitic-X-Group, X-Group, X-Group-Christian, Christian* and *Questionable*. Within these divisions it is subsequently grouped in numerical order by grave numbers. Within each entry *Grave, Burial,* and *Body* are briefly described (if the information was available), followed by a listing of all objects found within that particular grave (see entry 1). This information was compiled by Bruce Williams. The textiles are included in these listings, followed by *Oriental Institute Museum numbers* as well as *A's* and *B's* if applicable; if the textile is listed in the object column as *3.* (see entry 1), it is *3.* which is fully catalogued, analysed and illustrated. In instances where the fabric has three major pieces (see entry 64), small letters of *a, b* and *c* have been assigned in descending order: *a* to the largest, etc.; if their decorations differ they were individually described; in those instances their dimensions were treated separately as well; in all other cases when it could be clearly established that the many separate pieces were from one and the same piece it lists them as *Fragments* followed in parentheses ( ) by a count of the number of scraps there are, i.e., *18 pieces* (see entry 1).

Designations such as *Mantle, Tunic* and *Sheet* are fully described on pages 41–42.

The numbers listed in connection with warp and weft elements, such as 8 warps per cm, and 8 wefts per cm, record the actual warp or weft elements counted that fall within one centimeter; the count is established by placing a thread counter on top of the fabric and by counting the threads at right angles as they occur; frequently, these countings were taken at more than one location in a fabric and if they varied, two numbers rather than one is given: example: 10/14 wefts per cm:

In spinning yarn a twist is being inserted generally analysed by the angle formed in relation to the center portion of either the letter S or Z; therefore, one distinguishes either S or Z spun yarn; (see fig. 1 page 38).

Unless otherwise stated all fibers are single ply. For information on the *Structures* see page 38. For information on the *Materials* see page 36. For information on the *Dyes* see pages 52–53.

As far as color terminology is concerned the variations of light, medium or dark have been used in connection with basic colors such as red, blue, green, etc. For more information on the colors see page 37.

In instances where *Fiber and Dye Analyses* were carried out the results are listed at the end of the entry (see entry 21).

In all instances the placement of the fragments must be looked upon as being arbitrary. All identifying markings such as beginning or finishing edges, selvages, decorations, density or openness of weave, coloration or discoloration were, however, taken into account. (See entry 47).

As it was impossible to provide individual measurements for each tiny scrap the dimensions are grouped and listed as *all-over*.

Sometimes where there were no selvages or any other identifying features to determine warp and weft directions, a *(?)* follows in both the analytical portion of the entry as well as under the dimensions. (See entry 15).

The illustrations and details are all printed in the *warp* direction; they may occasionally be upside down as it was impossible to determine without heading or finishing edges which way the piece was originally woven.

Even if the warp dimensions are smaller than those of the wefts, all warp measurements come first.

C.C.M.T.

1

Grave Q 251   Meroitic Tomb

Shaft with ramp and end-chamber, stone blocking
Burials: Disturbed
Bodies:
A. Mature, male?
B. Adult, female?
Objects:
1. Sherds of painted cup
2. Lamp
3. Textile (see entry below) 20552
4. Beads
5. Jug
6. Fragments of palm-wood

3. Fragments (18 pieces)

Material: Vegetable (Cotton)
Structure:
Plain weave in dark brown, 9 warps per cm, S-spun;
11/12 wefts per cm, S-spun
Decoration:
Twining ending in knotted or wrapped border
terminating in fringe
Dimensions: All-over: 18cm (warp) x 27cm (weft)

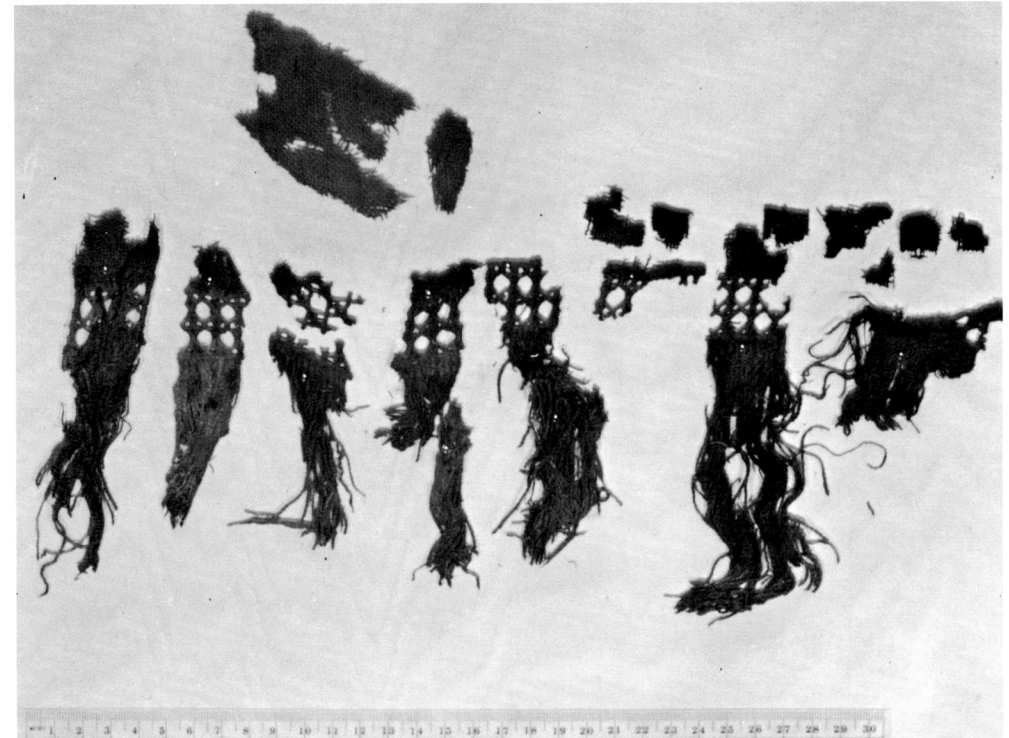

2

Grave Q 254   Meroitic Tomb

Shaft, ramp and end chamber, stone blocking
Burials:
a. In chamber:
A. Head east, extended on back, hands above pelvis
B. Same
C. Same, shrouded
b. In shaft:
D–F. Three skulls
Bodies:
A. Mature
B. Infant
C. Child
D–F. Adults
Objects:
1. Bowl at entrance to tomb
2. Bends at neck of C
3. Textile (see entry below) 20590

3. Fragments (21 pieces)

Material: Vegetable (Cotton)*
Structure:
Plain weave in dark brown, 11/12 warps per cm,
S-spun; 8/9 wefts per cm, S-spun; one selvage
present
Decoration:
One crudely stitched edge present; finished edge
with knotted or wrapped border terminating in
fringe; broken into ten parts
Dimensions: All-over: 39cm (warp) x 40cm (weft)

Fiber Analysis:
Cotton; *Degradation:* Severe

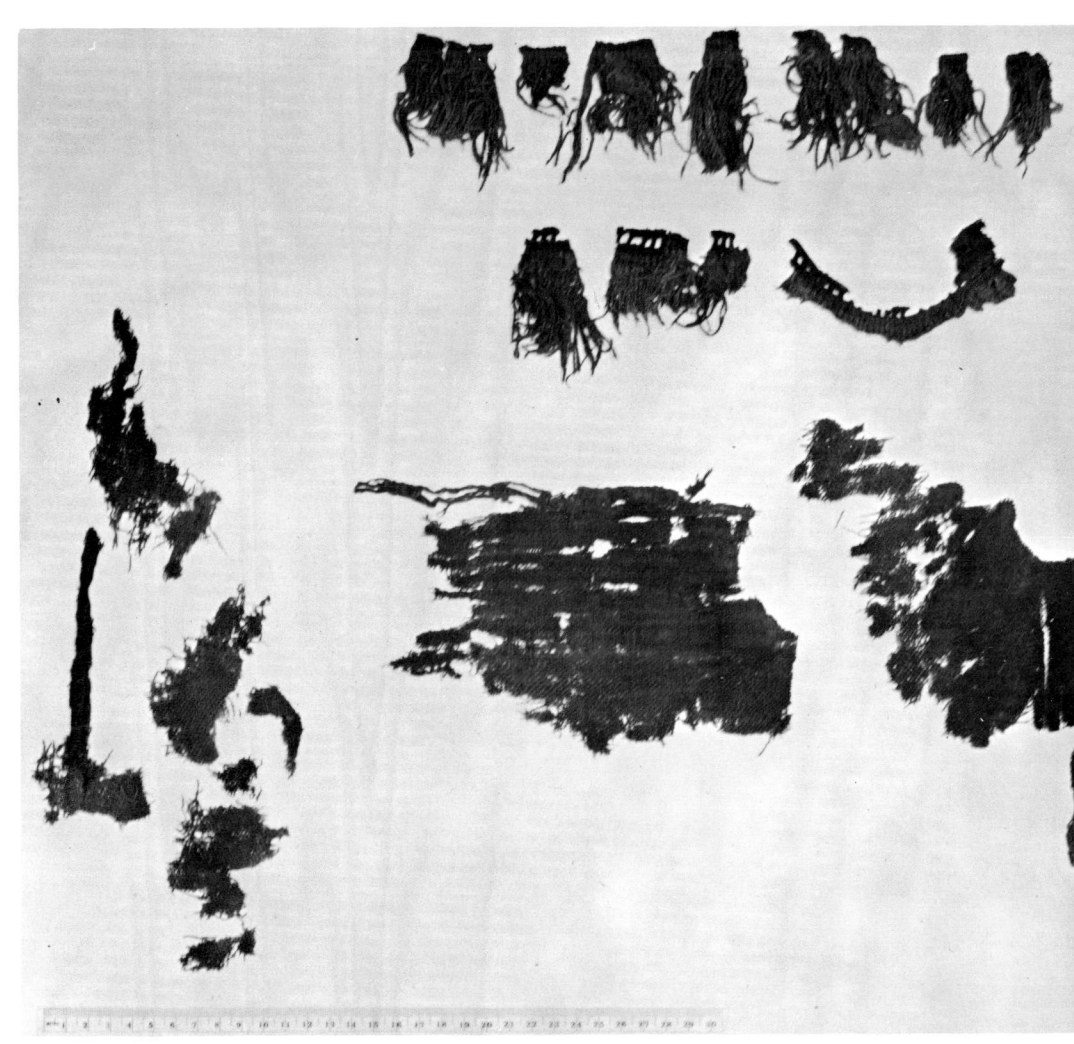

3

Grave Q 306   Meroitic or Earlier

Square brick superstructure, like a pyramid-chapel,
   shaft with end-chamber under chapel
Burial: Extended in coffin, head to left, hands resting
   on either side of pelvis and fingers on pubis
Body: Senile, female
Objects:
1. Bottom of coffin with slots for tongues
2. Sandals, tooled, one against each wrist
3. Textile (see entry below) 20921
4. Necklaces and loose beads

3. Fragments (30 pieces)

Material: Vegetable (Linen)
Structure:
Warp-faced plain weave in light brown,* 20/21
warps per cm, S-spun; 8 wefts per cm, S-spun; one
fragment shows grouped wefts of 5/6 with warp
floats
Dimensions: All-over: 88cm (warp) x 61cm (weft)

* *Dye Analysis:* Brown—tanin

4

Grave Q 528   Meroitic

Shaft and end-chamber, one large stone for blocking
Burial: Disturbed
Body: Juvenile, female?
Object:
1. Textiles (see entry below) 21735 A–B

1A. Tunic (?) Fragment

Material: Vegetable (Linen)
Structure:
Plain weave in medium brown,* 8 warps per cm,
some 2 ply, S-spun; 5 wefts per cm, some 2 ply,
S-spun
Decoration:
Extended and twisted warp threads along one side
Dimensions: All-over: 34cm (warp) x 26cm (weft)

* *Dye Analysis:* Brown—gallotanin

5

1B. Fragments (14 pieces)

Material: Vegetable (Cotton)
Structure:
Weft-faced plain weave in medium brown,* 6/8
warps per cm, S-spun; 8 wefts per cm, S-spun; one
selvage present
Dimensions: All-over: 48cm (warp) x 24cm (weft)

* *Dye Analysis:* Brown—tanin

6

Grave Q 560   Meroitic

Shaft and end-chamber, side-chamber added later,
    brick blocking
Burials:
A. Head west, extended on right side, head turned
    to right, disturbed
B. Head west, extended on back, head turned to
    right in remains of coffin
Bodies:
A. No information
B. No information
Objects:
a. With A:
1, 3. Jars
2. Painted cup with handles
b. With B:
5. Jar near head
6. Leather fragment
7. Coffin
4. Barbotine cup—originally with A
c. Uncertain location:
8. Textile—Not available for study
    Beyond restoration

7

Grave Q 563   Meroitic

Shaft with end-chamber
Burial: In coffin, extended on back, hands at pubis
Body: Senile male
Objects:
1.   Remains of coffin
2.   Textile (see entry below) 21787 A–B

2A. Tunic Fragment

Material: Vegetable (Linen)
Structure:
Weft-faced plain weave in dark brown, 5/6 warps
per cm, S-spun; 14/15 wefts per cm, S-spun; uneven
weave in both directions with occasional double
warps and wefts
Decoration:
Overlapping areas and stitching in warp direction
Dimensions: 15cm (warp) x 19cm (weft)

8

2B. Sheet or Tunic (?) Fragment

Material: Vegetable (Linen)
Structure:
Plain weave in medium brown,* 6 warps per cm, (2-
ply), S-spun; 5 wefts per cm, (2-ply), S-spun
Dimensions: 17cm (warp) x 11cm (weft)

* *Dye Analysis:* Brown—gallotanin

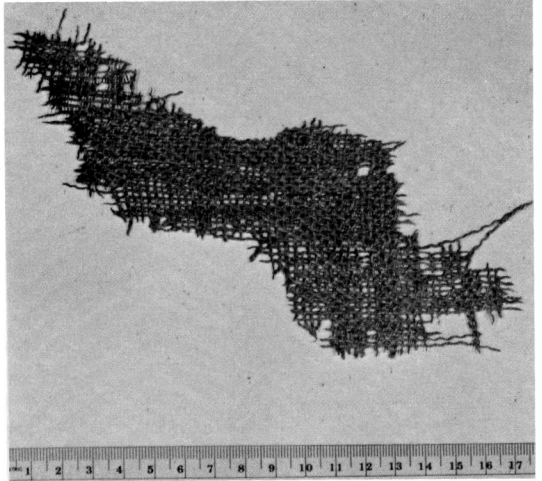

9

Grave Q 572   Meroitic

Shaft with end-chamber
Burial: Disturbed in coffin
Body: Adult
Objects:
1.   Textiles, partially wrapping scattered remains
     (see entry below) 21790 A–B
2.   Twisted straw cord
3.   Remains of coffin

1A. Fragment (8 pieces)

Material: Vegetable (Linen)*
Structure:
Plain weave in medium brown, 9 warps per cm,
S-spun; 5/6 wefts per cm, S-spun; warp heading and
selvage present
Decoration:
Weft groupings of 3/8 occur near heading
Dimensions: All-over: 25cm (warp) x 18.5cm (weft)

* *Fiber Analysis:* Linen; *Degradation:* None

10

Grave Q 572   Meroitic

1B. Fragments

Material: Coarse grass or reed
Construction:
Twisted cords
Dimensions:
Fragment a: 17cm x 2cm
Fragment b: 17cm x 1.5cm

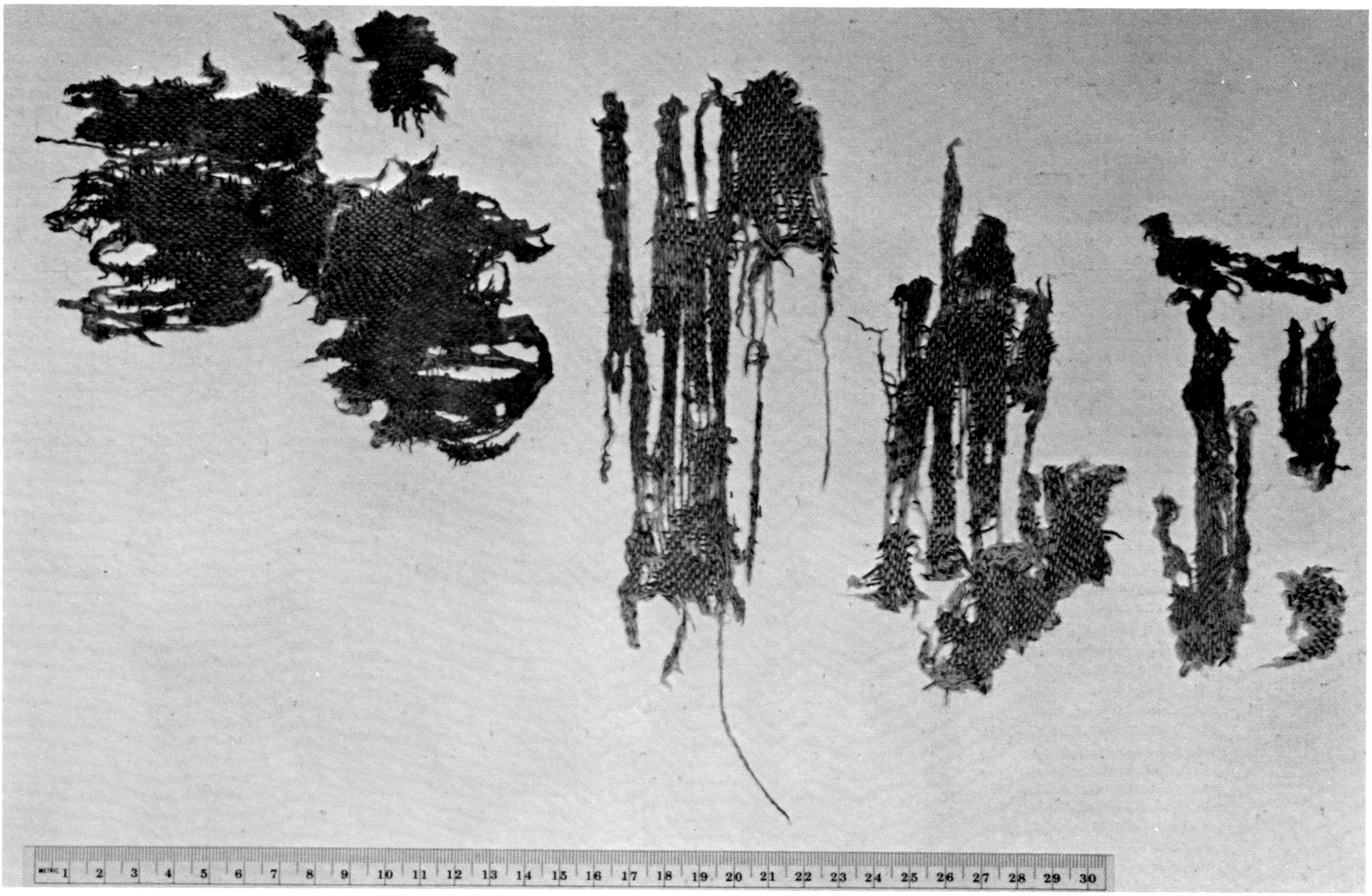

11

Grave Q 636   Meroitic

Shaft and side-chamber, stone blocking
Burial:
A. Head west, in coffin, extended on back, head
   slightly left, one hand at side, the other on pelvis
B. Disturbed in shaft, uncertain date, two or more
   bodies
Bodies:
A. Senile, female?
B. Mature, male?

Objects:
a. In shaft:
1. Sherds of several vessels
2. Cup
3. Bowl
4. Textile (see entry below) 22019
b. In chamber:
5. Coffin remains
6. Painted cup inverted over no. 7
7. Jug
8. Sherds, of same vessels as found in shaft

4. Fragments (7 pieces)

Material: Animal
Structure:
Plain weave, 8/9 warps per cm, S-spun, in dark
brown; 8/9 wefts per cm, S-spun, in light brown
Dimensions: All-over: 19.5cm (warp) x 30cm (weft)

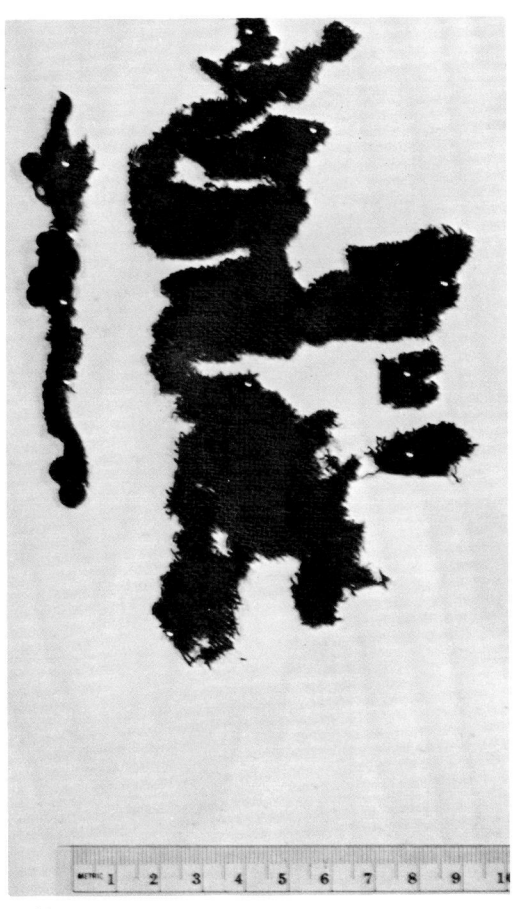

12

Grave B 32   Meroitic

Brick vaulted chamber built in shaft
Burial: Extended on back, hands at sides?, disturbed
Body: Mature, female
Objects:
1, 2, 9. Painted cups
3, 4. Bottles
5. Cup
6. Jug
7, 8. Bottles
10. Textile (see entry below) 22502

10. Fragments (4 pieces)

Material: Animal
Structure:
Plain weave in medium brown, 15 warps per cm,
S-spun; 10 wefts per cm, S-spun
Decoration:
Tiny pom-poms attached to the finishing edge;
(most of them are loose now)
Dimensions: All-over: 16cm (warp) x 10cm (weft)

13

Grave B 187   Meroitic

Vault built into walls of shaft
Burials: Two, Disturbed
Bodies: Both Adult, females
Objects:
1. Fragments of wooden box
2. Textile (see entry below) 22721

2. Fragments (7 pieces)

Material: Vegetable (Cotton)
Structure:
Plain weave of double warps and double wefts in
medium brown extensively stained; ca. 10 warps
per cm, S-spun; ca. 10/12 wefts per cm, S-spun
Decoration:
Weft forms pattern through uncut pile; pile not
separately inserted but formed by pulling up weft
threads where needed
Dimensions: 25cm (warp) x 27cm (weft)

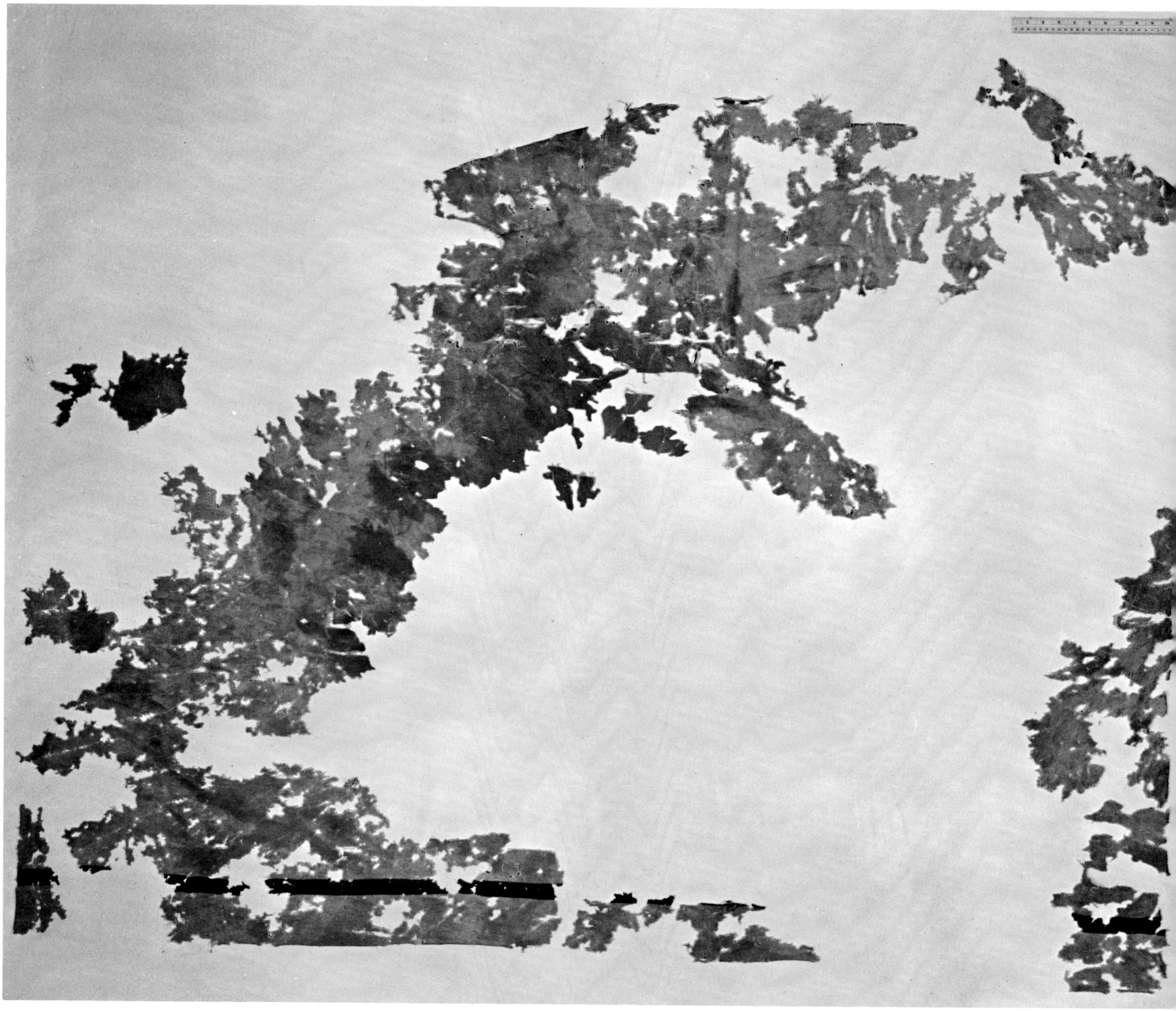

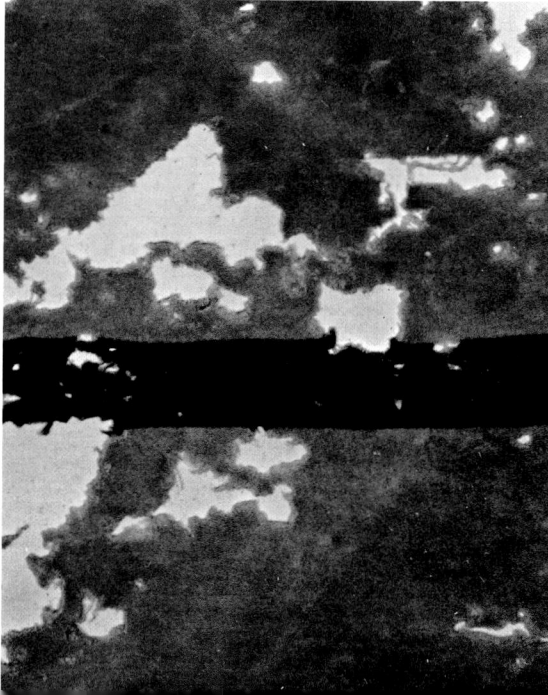

Fragment Aa

14

Grave B 188   Meroitic

Vaulted chamber built in shaft
Burial: Disturbed
Body: Adult, female
Objects:
1. Textiles, above fill (see entry below) 22730 A–B
2. Cup
3. Amphora

**1A. Sheet or Mantle and Tunic (?) Fragments
(Aa 9 pieces) (Ab 12 pieces)**

Material: Animal
Structure:
Very fine weft-faced twill weave 2:2, 17 warps per
cm, S-spun; 56 wefts per cm, S-spun
Decoration:
Purple* stripe, 2.5 cm in width, 36 weft shots, S-spun
Fragment Aa: edges finished with buttonhole stitches
Fragment Ab: purple stripe terminating in corners

Dimensions:
Fragment Aa: All-over: 83cm (warp) x 100cm (weft)
Fragment Ab: All-over: 140cm (warp) x 195cm (weft)
Remarks:
Although Fragments Aa and Ab give the appearance
of having once been part of the same piece, this
theory has to be disputed the moment one analyzes
all the remaining fragments, the directions of warps
and wefts and the position of the weft inserted
stripes of purple, as well as remnants of sewn edges.
The two corner sections cannot be brought within
correct weaving context within piece Aa. Therefore,
one must be dealing with two separate larger pieces
of the above mentioned approximate dimensions.

* *Dye Analysis:* Real Purple

Fragment Ab

15

Grave B 188   Meroitic

1B. Fragments (12 pieces)

Material: Vegetable (Cotton)
Structure:
Plain weave in dark brown, 22 warps(?) per cm,
S-spun; 8/9 wefts(?) per cm, S-spun
Decoration:
At one edge warp threads wrapped or knotted and
fringed; additional pieces in either warp-faced plain
weave or weft-faced plain weave
Dimensions: All-over: 17cm (warp) (?) x 21cm
(weft) (?)

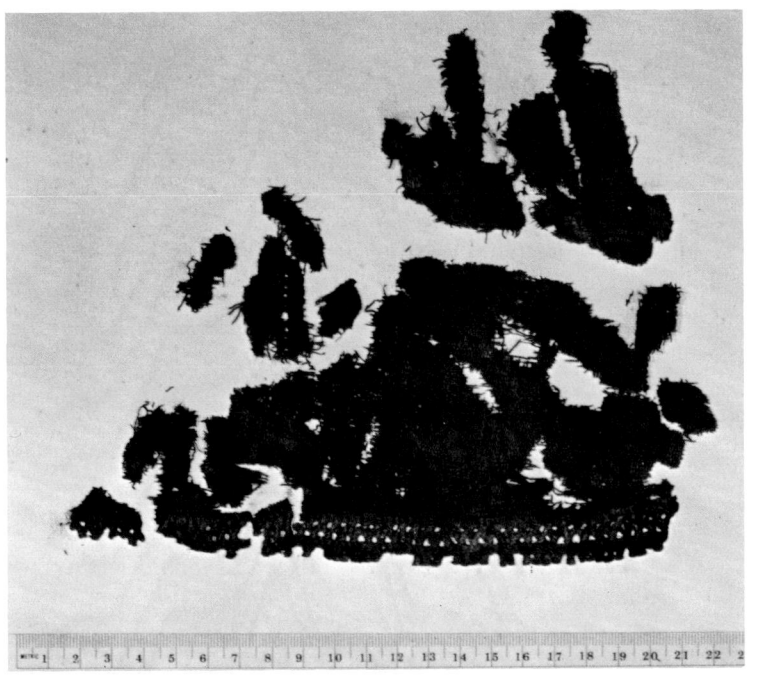

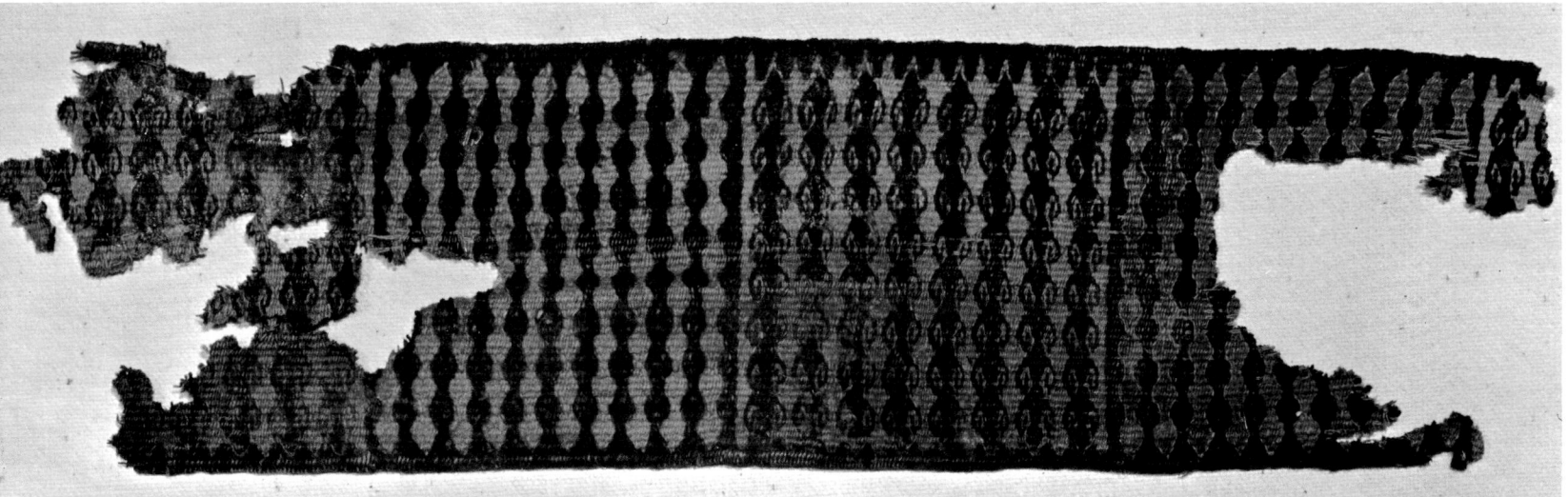

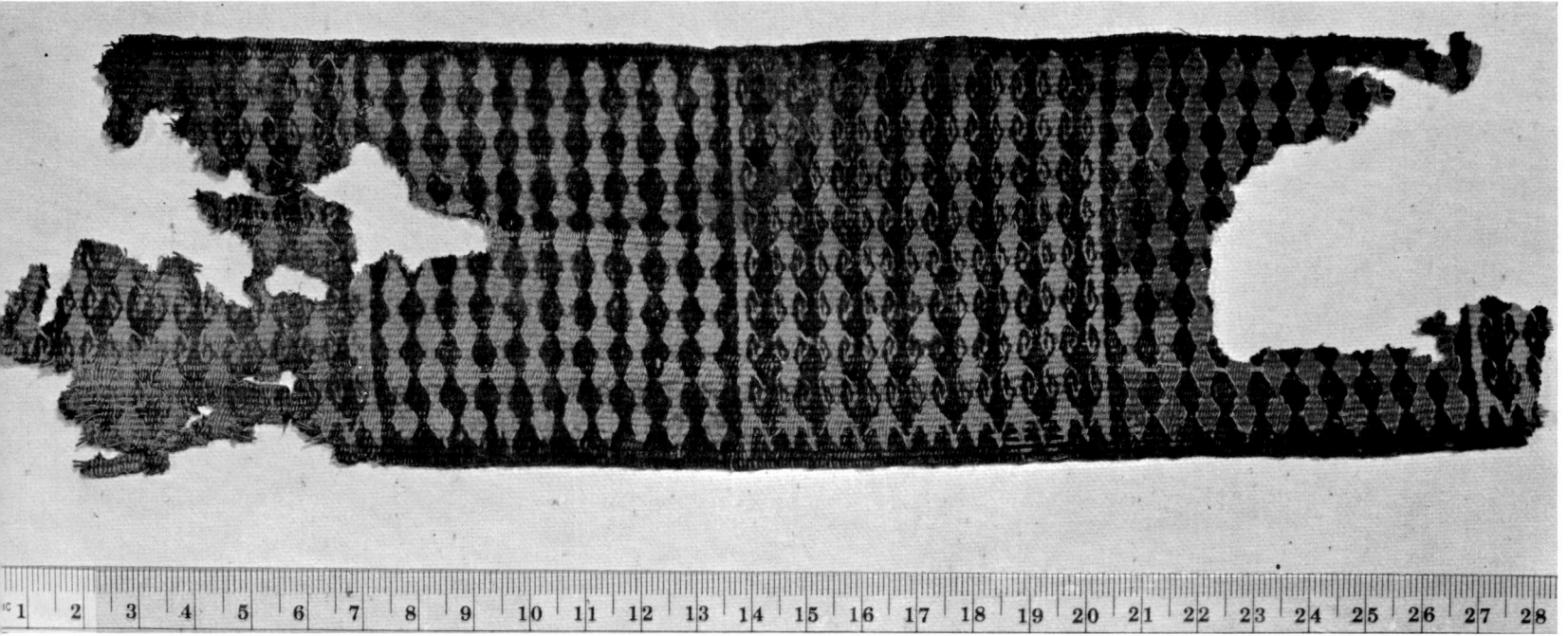

Side 2

16

Grave B 213   Meroitic, but possibly reused

Vault built into sides of shaft
Burial: Disturbed
Body: Adult, male
Objects:
1. Quiver
2. Cup
3. Belt
4. Textile (see entry below) 22769
5. Textiles (see entry below) 22770 A–C
6. Head of ba-statuette in fill

4. Portion of a Belt

Material: Vegetable (Cotton)*
Structure:
Weft-faced plain weave (reversible), with double warps, 18/19 warps per cm, S-spun (individually counted), approximately 28 wefts per cm, S-spun; two selvages present
Decoration:
Small scaled pattern of two different kinds in rows of 8 and 10 respectively contained in squares of 7cm (warp) x 7cm (weft) in dark blue, green and light brown
Dimensions: 28cm (warp) x 7cm (weft)

* *Fiber Analysis:* Cotton; *Degradation:* Slight

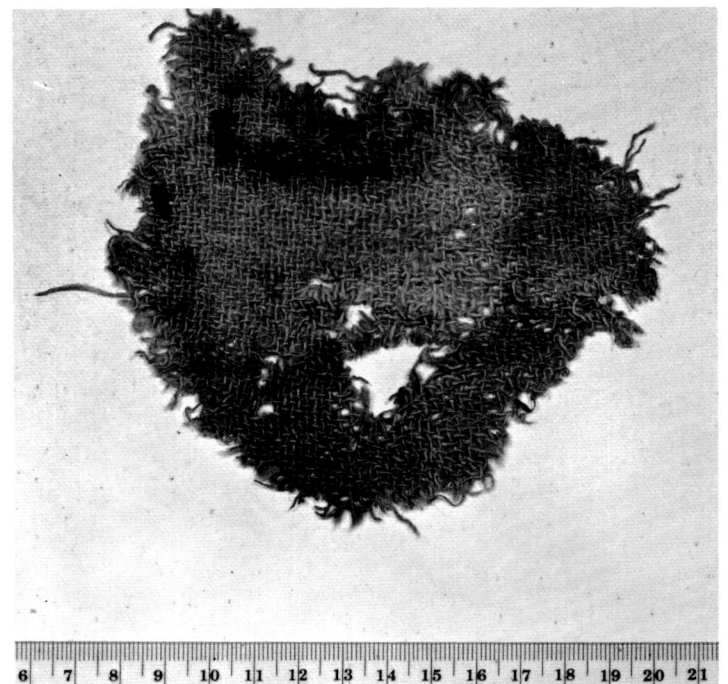

17

Grave B 213

5A. Sheet or Tunic (?) Fragment

Material: Vegetable (Cotton)*
Structure:
Plain weave in light brown, 6 warps (?) per cm,
S-spun; 9 wefts (?) per cm, S-spun
Decoration:
Stain in dark brown
Dimensions: 13cm (warp) (?) x 11cm (weft) (?)

* *Fiber Analysis:* Cotton; *Degradation:* Slight

18

Grave B 213

5B. Sheet (?) Fragment

Material: Vegetable (Cotton)*
Structure:
Warp-faced plain weave in light brown, 25 warps
per cm, S-spun; 6 wefts per cm, S-spun
Decoration:
Ridges formed by grouping 8 weft threads through-
out which are introduced at every 3rd weft shot;
ridges are separated by 2 weft shots in plain weave
Dimensions: 8.5cm (warp) x 14cm (weft)

* *Fiber Analysis:* Cotton; *Degradation:* Slight

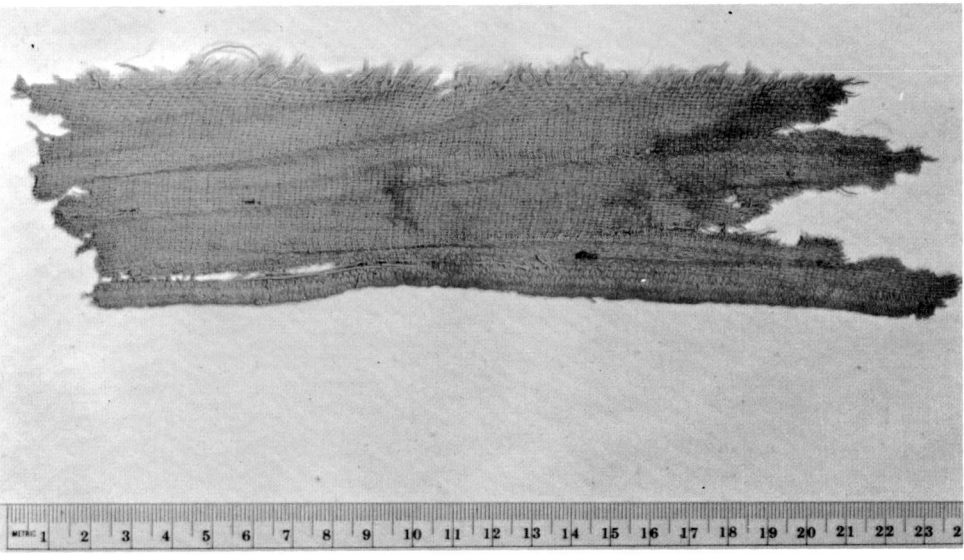

19

Grave B 213

5C. Sheet or Tunic (?) Fragment

Material: Vegetable (Cotton)*
Structure:
Plain weave with double wefts in light brown; 14
warps per cm, S-spun; 14 wefts per cm (individually
counted), S-spun; one selvage present
Dimensions: 24cm (warp) x 5.5cm (weft)

* *Fiber Analysis:* Cotton; *Degradation:* Slight

Side 2

Side 1

20

Grave B 236 Meroitic

Vault built into sides of shaft
Burials:
A–E. In vault, disturbed
F–G. On vault, extended on back, heads west
Bodies:
F. Juvenile, female
G. Adult, male
Objects with F and G above vault:
1. Bottle
2, 3. Cups, one painted
4. Bowl
5, 6. Jugs
7. Beads, from G
8. Leather loincloth from F
9. Rings, iron, on each hand of G
10. Textile (see entry below) 22762

10. Belt (?) Fragments (11 pieces)

Material: Vegetable (Cotton)
Structure:
Weft-faced plain weave; (reversible); in medium
brown, blue and green, 11 warps per cm, S-spun;
20/21 wefts per cm, S-spun; two selvages present
Decoration:
Narrow bands of blue of 1.5/2cm in width, 20 wefts
per cm, S-spun on medium brown warps; in some
of the stripes two different small patterns occur;
finished edge on one side in weft direction in combination of medium brown wrapped warp threads
worked into loops
Dimensions: All-over: 32cm (warp) x 8cm (weft)

21

Grave B 251 Meroitic

Vault built into sides of shaft
Burial: Disturbed
Body: Adult, female
Objects:
1. Sherds from fill
2. Textile (see entry below) 22800
3. Lead bowl

2. Tunic or Sheet Fragments (12 pieces)

Material: Vegetable (Cotton)*
Structure:
Plain weave in light brown, 9/11 warps per cm,
S-spun; 8/12 wefts per cm, S-spun; with weft-faced
insertions in blue-green,** 10/12 warps per cm,
S-spun; 20/22 wefts per cm, S-spun; every fourth
warp was left loose on the one side of the fabric
while the weft-faced plain weave portion was
woven; the other warps appear in a double and
single arrangement; one selvage present
Decoration:
Blue-green stripes of varying widths
Dimensions: All-over: 43cm (warp) x 92cm (weft)

* *Fiber Analysis:*
Blue-Green Cotton; *Degradation:* Moderate
Light Brown Cotton; *Degradation:* Severe

** *Dye Analysis:* Green—weld, indigo

22

Grave B 310 Meroitic

Vault built into sides of shaft
Burials:
A. Extended on back in vault
B. Disturbed in fill
Bodies:
A. Senile, male
B. Juvenile, male
Objects:
1, 3, 5. Bottles
2, 4, 8. Cups
6. Bronze or copper bowl
7. Bottle
9. Textile (see entry below) 22810

9. Center Portion of a Tunic, Neck Area (?)

Material: Vegetable (Cotton)
Structure:
Plain weave with grouped weft threads (four threads
per grouping, separated by three single weft shots);
these groupings create two stripes formed by four
groupings each; 14/16 warps per cm, S-spun; warps
float over grouped weft threads; 11/12 wefts per
cm; S-spun
Decoration:
Two stripes formed by grouping of weft threads;
these stripes are toward the top portion of the
fragment; twisted cord stitched to heading forming
wrapped cord at one corner; use of brown and blue
threads; in blue cotton thread an embroidered
motif of a small tree appears in the center of the
neck
Dimensions: 31cm (warp) x 37cm (weft)

Side 1

Side 2

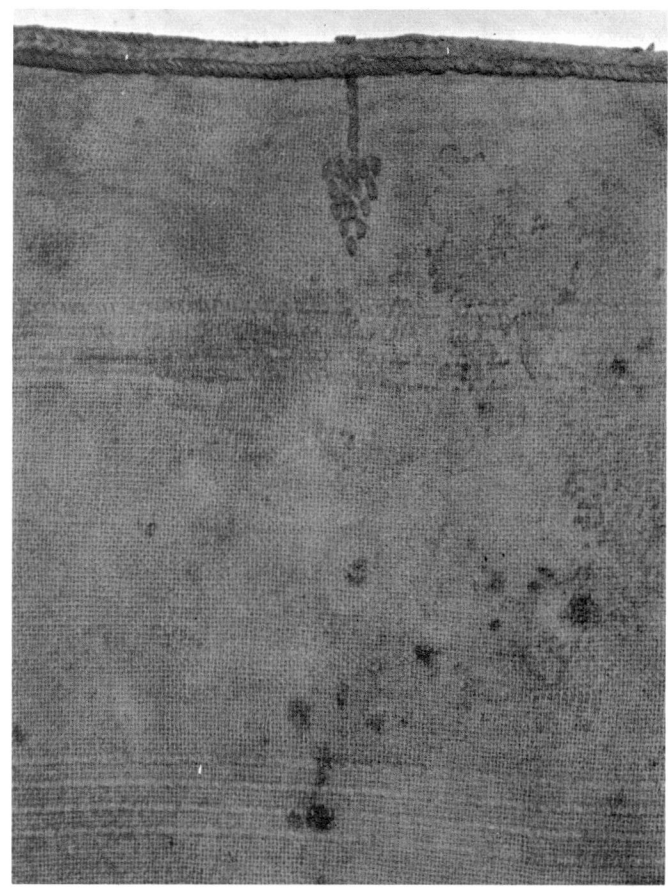

23

Grave B 320   Meroitic (?)

Vault built into sides of shaft
Burial: Disturbed
Body: Adult, female
Object:
1.   Textiles (see entry below) 22926 A–C

1A. Fragments (2 pieces)

Material: Vegetable (Cotton)
Structure:
Plain weave in medium brown,* 10 warps per cm,
S-spun; 11 wefts per cm, S-spun; one selvage
present
Dimensions: All-over: 57cm (warp) x 33cm (weft)

* *Dye Analysis:* Brown—iron, tanin

24

Grave B 320

1B. Tunic (?) Fragment

Material: Vegetable (Cotton)
Structure:
Plain weave in medium brown,* 11 warps per cm,
S-spun, (double warps throughout; individually
counted); 13 wefts per cm, S-spun, (double wefts
throughout; individually counted)
Decoration:
Narrow stripe of 22/23 weft shots in blue, followed
by 2 medium brown weft shots, 2 blue weft shots, 2
medium brown weft shots and 5 blue weft shots
Dimensions: 36cm (warp) x 29cm (weft)

* *Dye Analysis:* Brown—orlean?

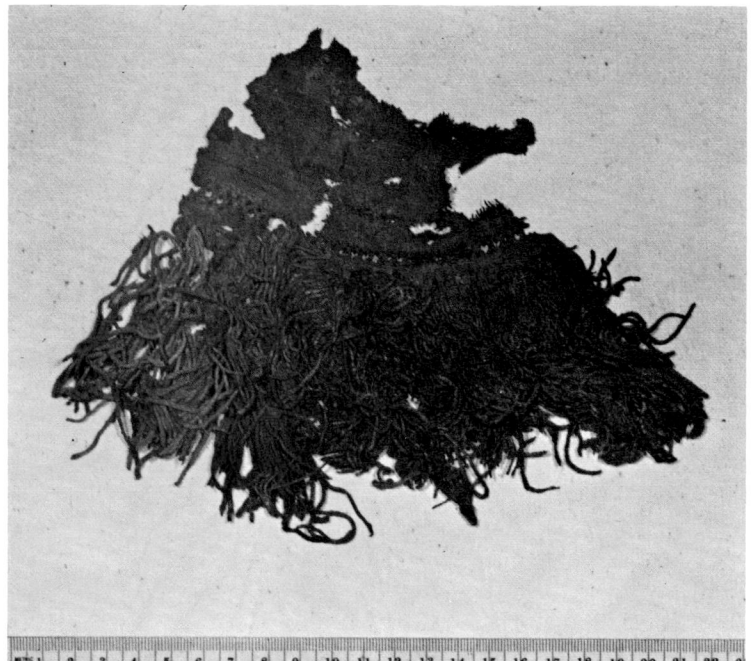

25

Grave B 320

1C. Fragment

Material: Vegetable (Cotton)
Structure:
Plain weave in medium brown, 13 warps per cm,
S-spun; 13 wefts per cm, S-spun
Decoration:
Occasionally grouped wefts of 4; wrapped or
knotted edge with ends
Dimensions: 15cm (warp) x 18cm (weft)

26

**Grave R 12   Tomb Meroitic, Burial? (Intrusive
Christian ?)**

Rectangular superstructure of brick, brick vaulted
    chamber built in shaft, entry at end, ramp
Burial: Head west, extended on back, hands at pubis
Body: Mature, female
Objects:
1.   Textiles (see entry below) 20922 A–C

1A. Tunic (?) Fragments (7 pieces)

Material: Animal*
Structure:
Plain weave in dark brown, 9/10 warps per cm,
S-spun; 20/21 wefts per cm, S-spun; one selvage
present
Decoration:
Narrow red braid which has been worked into warp
threads and along one corner where selvage is
present
Dimensions: All-over: 35cm (warp) x 40cm (weft)

* *Fiber Analysis:* Wool—Camel; *Degradation:* Slight

27

Grave R 12

1B. Mantle (?) Fragments (5 pieces)

Material: Animal
Structure:
Plain weave in dark brown, 8 warps per cm, S-spun;
8/9 wefts per cm, S-spun
Decoration:
Probably notched "L" shape in purple in weft-faced
plain weave on dark brown warps, 18 wefts per cm,
S-spun
Dimensions: All-over: 22cm (warp) x 21cm (weft)

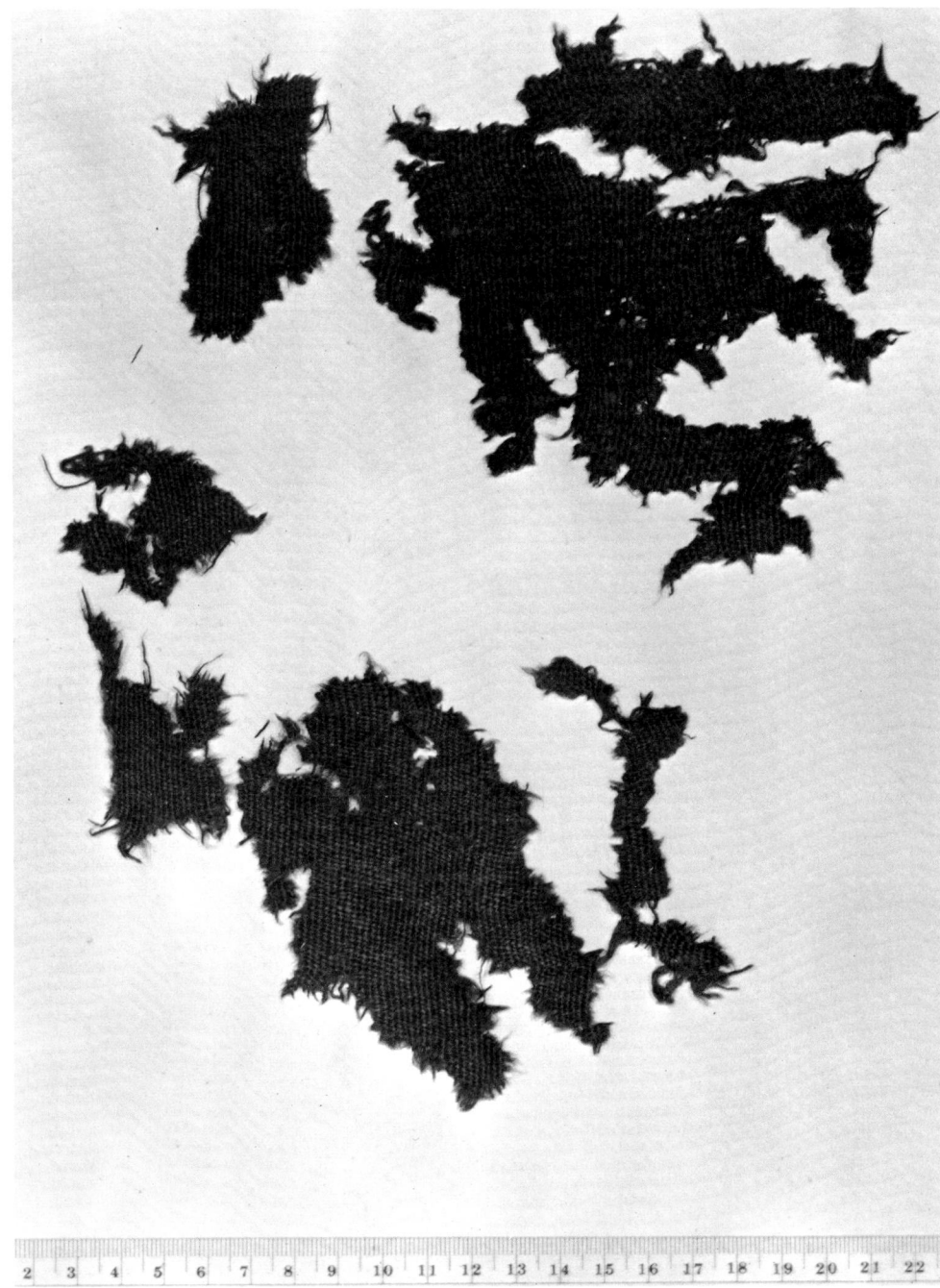

28

Grave R 12

1C. Tape or Belt (?) Fragments (2 pieces)

Material: Animal
Structure:
Four dark brown warps per cm (grouped in 3's) with
countered weft twining in red and yellow; all fibers
S-spun
Dimensions: All-over: 13.5cm (warp) x 4cm (weft)

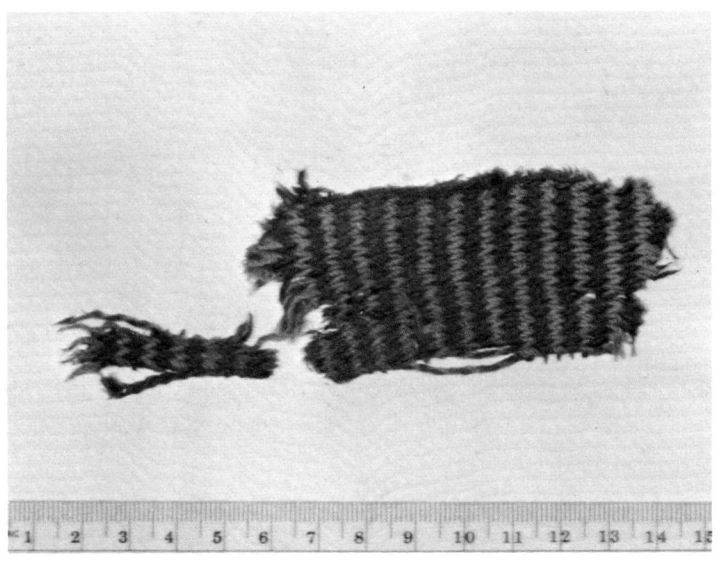

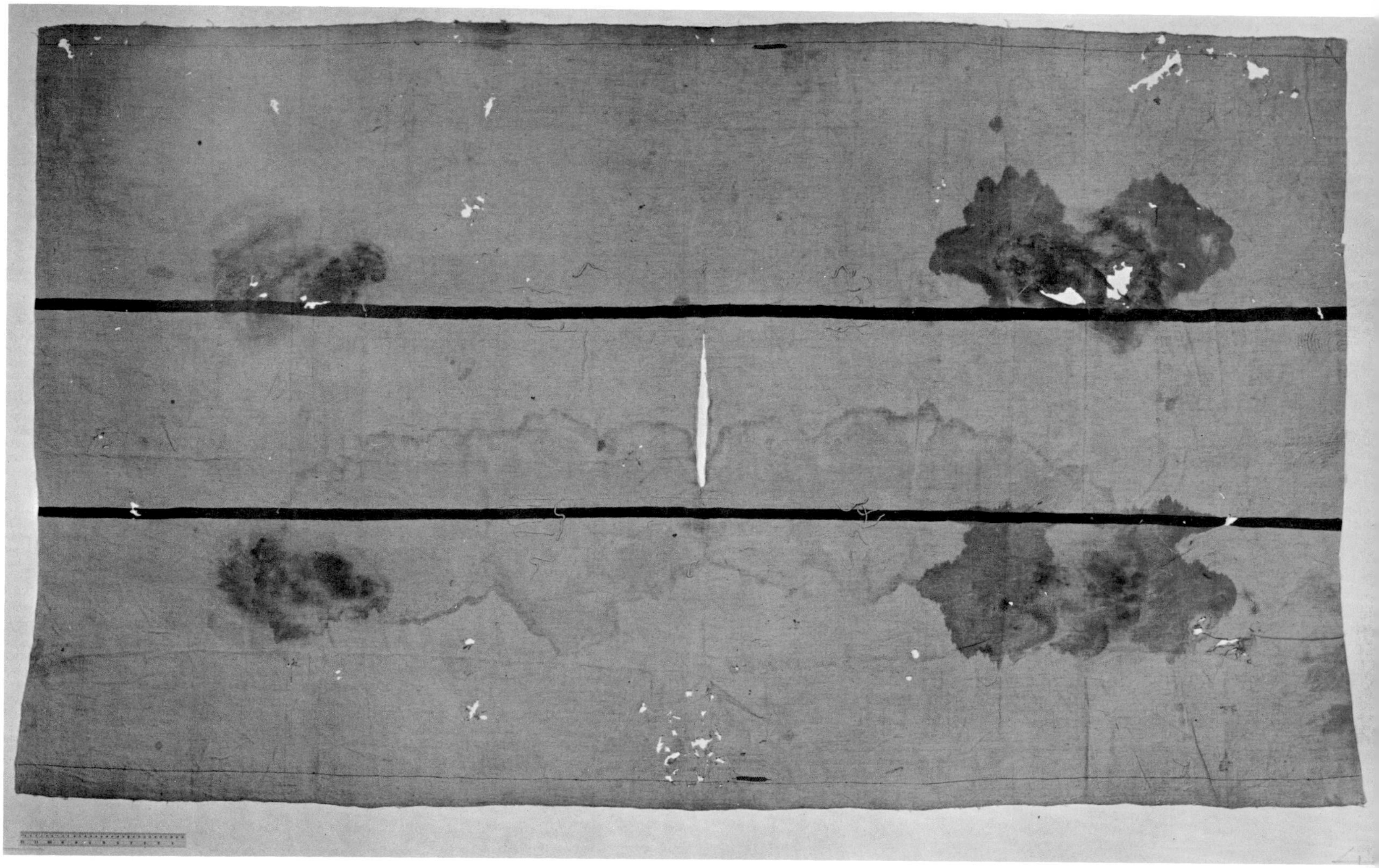

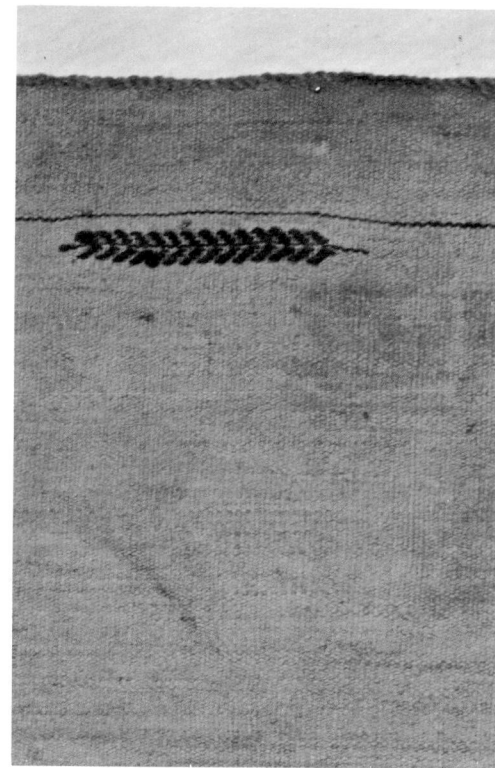

29

Grave Q 150   Meroitic or Later

Rectangular shaft; intrusive pit at south-west corner
Burials:
A. In shaft: Extended on back, head north, hands at pubis
B. In shaft: Extended on back, head north, hands at pubis
C. In pit: Wrapped in textile
Bodies:
A. Child
B. Mature, female?
C. Infant
Objects:
a. In shaft:
1. Small amphora
2. Painted cup
b. In pit:
3. Textile (see entry below) 20349

3. Tunic (Complete)

Material: Animal
Structure:
Plain weave in light brown, 11/12 warps per cm,
S-spun; 28 wefts per cm, S-spun; two selvages
present; warp threads worked into twisted cord
at both ends; two selvages along neck opening;
badly stained in four corresponding areas
Decoration:
Two purple stripes of 2/2.5cm in width inserted in
weft-faced plain weave, 36 wefts per cm, S-spun;
35/36.5cm apart; at both ends two weft shots in
purple, 1.5/2cm above twisted warp thread cord;
at both ends in warp direction rows of sewing
visible due to remaining hanging sewing threads,
33/35cm and 63.5/66cm from selvages respectively;
slit of 31cm in warp direction left for neck opening;
to either side of the neck opening five rows of weft
twining of 49/53cm centered on neck opening and
1.5/3.5cm apart; weft twining cord left hanging at
both ends of 4.5/9cm in length; inserted in weft
direction; two additional cords left to either side
in warp direction and neck opening of 5/6cm in
length; additional decoration of 8cm in length in
weft direction in purple, inserted through needlework or brocading in staggered rows forming grain
motif
Dimensions: 140/141cm (warp) x 248cm (weft)

30

Grave Q 240   Meroitic or Later

Rectangular pit with sunken sub-pit to the north,
  stone covering
Burials: Disturbed
Bodies:
A. Infant
B. Child (above)
Objects:
1. Remains of coffin made from palm log, from
   upper burial
2. Beads
3. Twisted straw
4. Textiles (see entry below) 20563 A–B

4A. Fragment

Material: Animal
Structure:
Plain weave in dark brown, 9 warps (?) per cm,
S-spun, 18/19 wefts (?) per cm, S-spun
Dimensions: 5.5cm (warp) (?) x 8cm (weft) (?)

31

Grave Q 240

4B. Fragment

Material: Vegetable (Linen)
Structure:
Plain weave (irregular) in medium brown, 6 warps
(?) per cm, S-spun; 8 wefts (?) per cm, S-spun
Dimensions: 9cm (warp) (?) x 13cm (weft) (?)

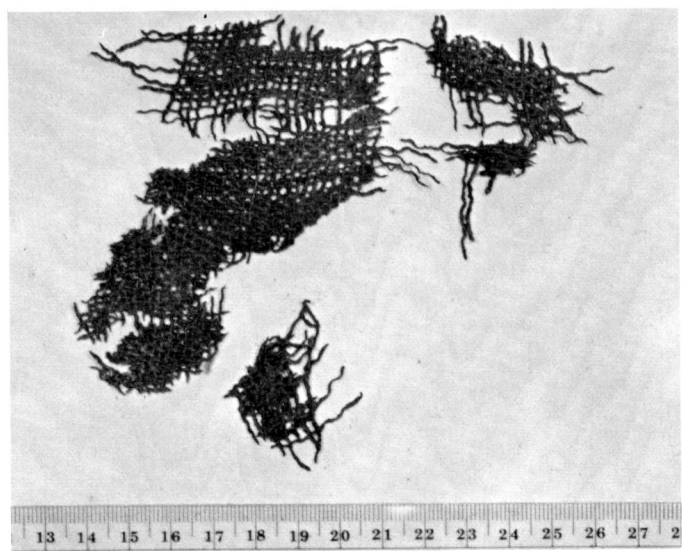

32

Grave B 156 Meroitic—X-Group

Shaft with side-chamber, brick blocking
Burial and body: Infant with mat underneath
Objects:
1. Mat of halfa grass under part of body
   (see entry below) 22764
2. Feeding cup

1. Portion of a Mat

Material: Coarse grass or reed*
Structure:
Twill weave, 1:4, in medium brown, 3 warps per cm;
3 wefts per cm
Dimensions: 62cm (warp) x 71cm (weft)

Fiber Analysis:
Plant—Coarse Grass or Reed
Degradation: Moderate
Remarks: It is not known as to whether or not this
mat was constructed on a loom

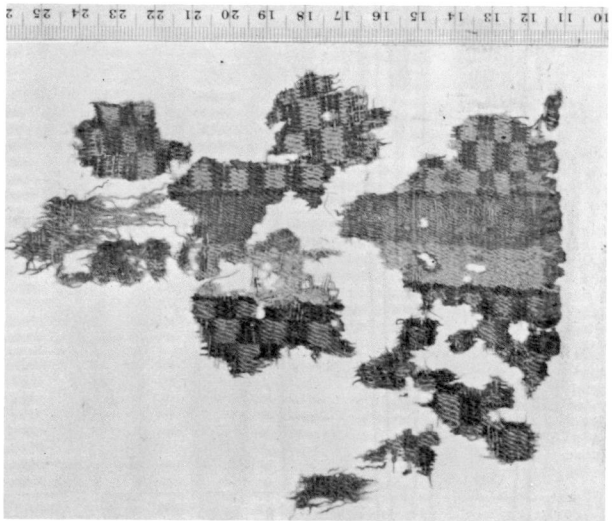

33

Grave B 259 Meroitic Tomb, Burial?

Vault built into sides of shaft
Burials: Disturbed
Bodies:
A. Juvenile, male
B. Infant
C. Adult, female
Objects:
1. Textile (see entry below) 22766
2. Glass Sherd

1. Tunic (?) Fragments (9-10 pieces)

Material: Animal
Structure:
Weft-faced plain weave formed by complementary
wefts and inner warps in red, blue, green and
yellow, 11 warps per cm, of yellow and red, S-spun;
20 wefts per cm, S-spun; one selvage present
Decoration:
Small checkerboard pattern in yellow and green, as
well as in red and blue, separated by two narrow
stripes of yellow and red weft-faced plain weave of
1 cm and 1.5cm respectively
Dimensions: All-over: 10.5cm (warp) x 15cm (weft)

34

Grave B 284   Meroitic or Later

Vault built into sides of shaft
Burials: Disturbed
Body: Adult, female
Objects:
1. Textile (see entry below) 22807

1. Sheet or Cloth (?) Fragments (2 pieces)

Material: Animal*
Structure:
Plain weave in light grey and shades of light brown,
7 warps per cm, S-spun; 15 wefts per cm, S-spun;
selvages, heading and finishing edges present
Decoration:
Weft stripes in varying widths from 0.5cm to 3cm;
in two instances the stripes do not run the entire
loom width; near one selvage warp stripe of
0.5cm present
Dimensions: All-over: 134cm (warp) x 150cm (weft)

* *Fiber Analysis:*
Wool—Sheep or Goat; *Degradation:* Moderate
Wool—Camel (CIBA no. 1)

***Dye Analysis:*
Brown—purpurin (alizarin)
Grey-Brown—purpurin (alizarin)

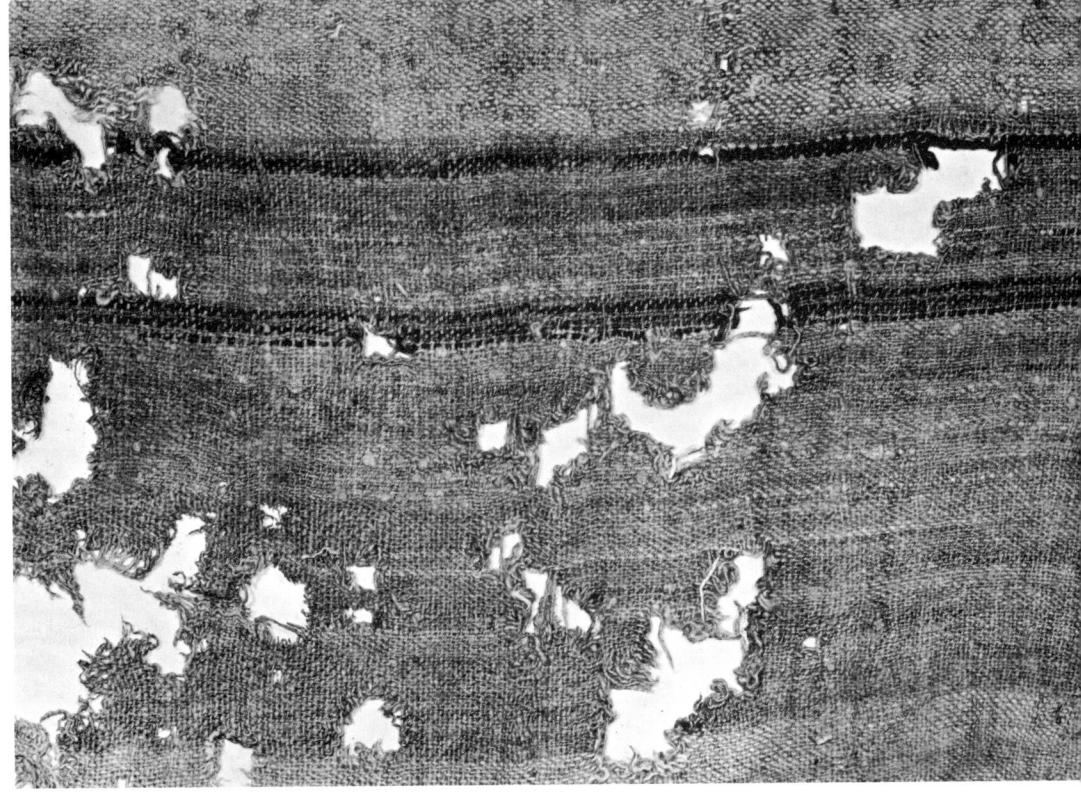

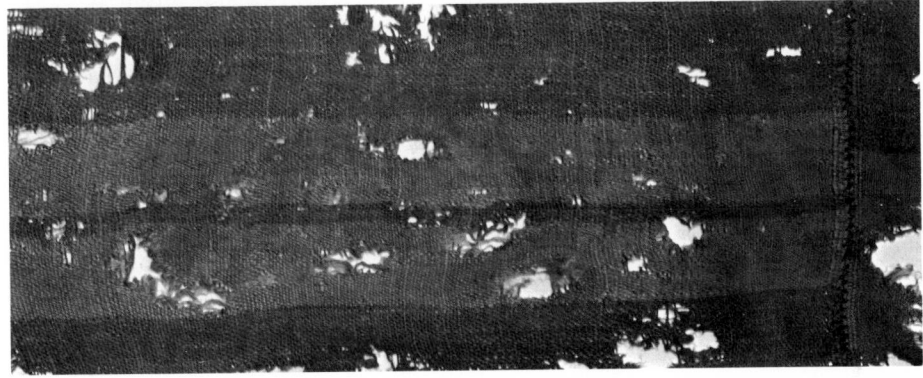

35

Grave Q 2   X-Group

Tumulus, shaft and side-chamber, stone blocking
Burial: Head west?
Body: Adult, female?
Objects:
1–8. Pottery
9. Textile (see entry below) 19941
10. Beads
11. Date pits
12. Leather sandal fragments
13. Leather wrist guard
14. Copper wire ring with tweezers and needle

9. Sheet Fragments (9 pieces)

Material: Animal*
Structure:
Plain weave in medium brown, 9 warps per cm,
S-spun; 11/15 wefts per cm, S-spun; two stitched
together selvages present
Decoration:
Two green** stripes of 19/20 wefts per cm in a total
of 65 and 62 weft shots respectively, separated by
a narrow stripe of medium brown of 9 weft shots;
warp threads worked together into twisted cord at
one end; one sewn edge
Dimensions: All-over: 135cm (warp) x 146cm (weft)

Fiber Analysis:
Wool, probably Camel; *Degradation:* Moderate

** *Dye Analysis:* Green—indigo, weld

36

Grave Q 5   X-Group Animal Sacrifice Burial

Rectangular shaft
Burial:
Bodies scattered in two layers with sand between,
scattering due either to plundering or to the
deposition of disarticulated bones
Bodies: 7–9 horses, 4–5 donkeys, 3 camels
Objects:
1. Textile—Not available for study
2, 13, 15. Bronze vessels and fragments
3. Textile (see entry below) 19898
4, 19. Rope fragments
5. Silver studs
6. Copper pendant on ring
7. Iron knife blade
8, 17. Iron rings and fragments
9. Iron fragments
10. Textile (see entry below) 19987
11. Stomach contents
12. Carved wood, yoke?
14, 18. Wood fragments
16. Silver pendant

3. Balls (originally part of horse-trappings)

Material: Animal
Structure:
About 27 (or parts thereof) balls in dark brown;
seem to have been made of a center fiber ball
covered with two "lids" with hole in upper portion
Dimensions: Diameter varying from 4cm to 2cm

37

Grave Q 5

10. Fragment

Material: Vegetable (Linen)*
Structure:
Plain weave in dark brown, 7 warps per cm, S-spun;
15 wefts per cm, S-spun
Dimensions: 33cm (warp) x 37cm (weft)

* *Fiber Analysis:* Linen; *Degradation:* None

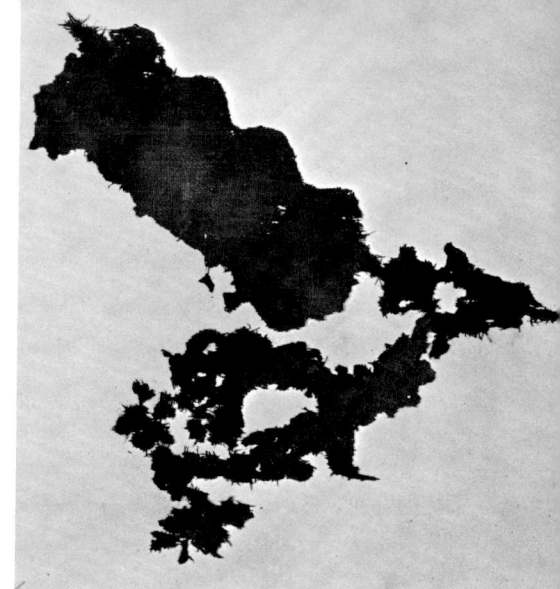

38

Grave Q 6   X-Group

Tumulus, shaft and side-chamber
Burial: Head south, disturbed
Body: Mature, male?
Objects:
1, 2. Jars
3. Bowl
4. Spouted jar
5. Axe-head
6. Textile fragment found at surface (see entry
   below) 19936
7. Leather quiver fragment

6. Fragments (6 pieces)

Material: Animal
Structure:
Plain weave (irregular) with some double threads in
both weft and warp direction; in dark blue; 14
warps (?) per cm, S-spun; 10 wefts (?) per cm,
S-spun; (individually counted where double)
Dimensions: All-over: 16cm (warp) (?) x 11cm (?)
(weft) (?)

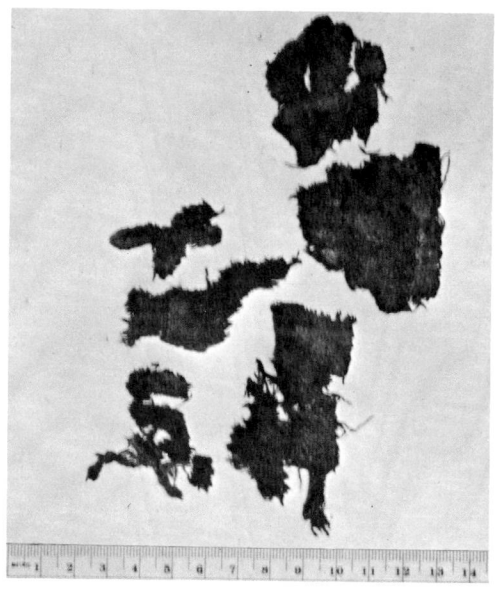

39

Grave Q 7   X-Group

Tumulus, shaft and side-chamber
Burial: Disturbed
Bodies:
A. Adult, male?
B. Infant
Objects:
1. Textile near adult (see entry below) 19956 A–B
2. Small leather bag
3. Matting fragment

1A. Tunic Fragments (10 pieces)

Material: Animal
Structure:
Open plain weave in dark brown,* 5/8 warps per
cm, S-spun; 9/10 wefts per cm, S-spun; portions of
selvages present
Decoration:
One sewn edge; joining of areas through sewing
with horsehair
Dimensions: All-over: 129cm (warp) x 162cm (weft)

* *Dye Analysis:*
Lighter Brown—orlean?, iron
Darker Brown—gallotanin, iron

1B. Textile—Not available for study

40

Grave Q 9   X-Group

Tumulus, shaft and side-chamber with stone
  blocking
Burial: Disturbed in chamber, head south
Body: Mature, male?
Objects:
a. From burial chamber:
1, 3. Cups
4. Jar
b. In shaft:
5, 7. Cups
6. Jar
c. From fill and surface:
8. Three arrowheads
9. Dates
10. Beads
11. Leather fragment
12. Cup
d. Bottom of shaft:
13. Textile (see entry below) 19896
14. Twisted hair

13. Fragment

Material: Silk
Structure:
Plain weave in polychrome, 44/46 warps (?) per cm,
48 wefts (?) per cm
Decoration:
Traces of a plaid and striped pattern in red, blue,
green and yellow
Dimensions: 3cm (warp) (?) x 6cm (weft) (?)
Remarks: This is the only silk fragment found among
the excavated fabrics from Ballana and Qustul.

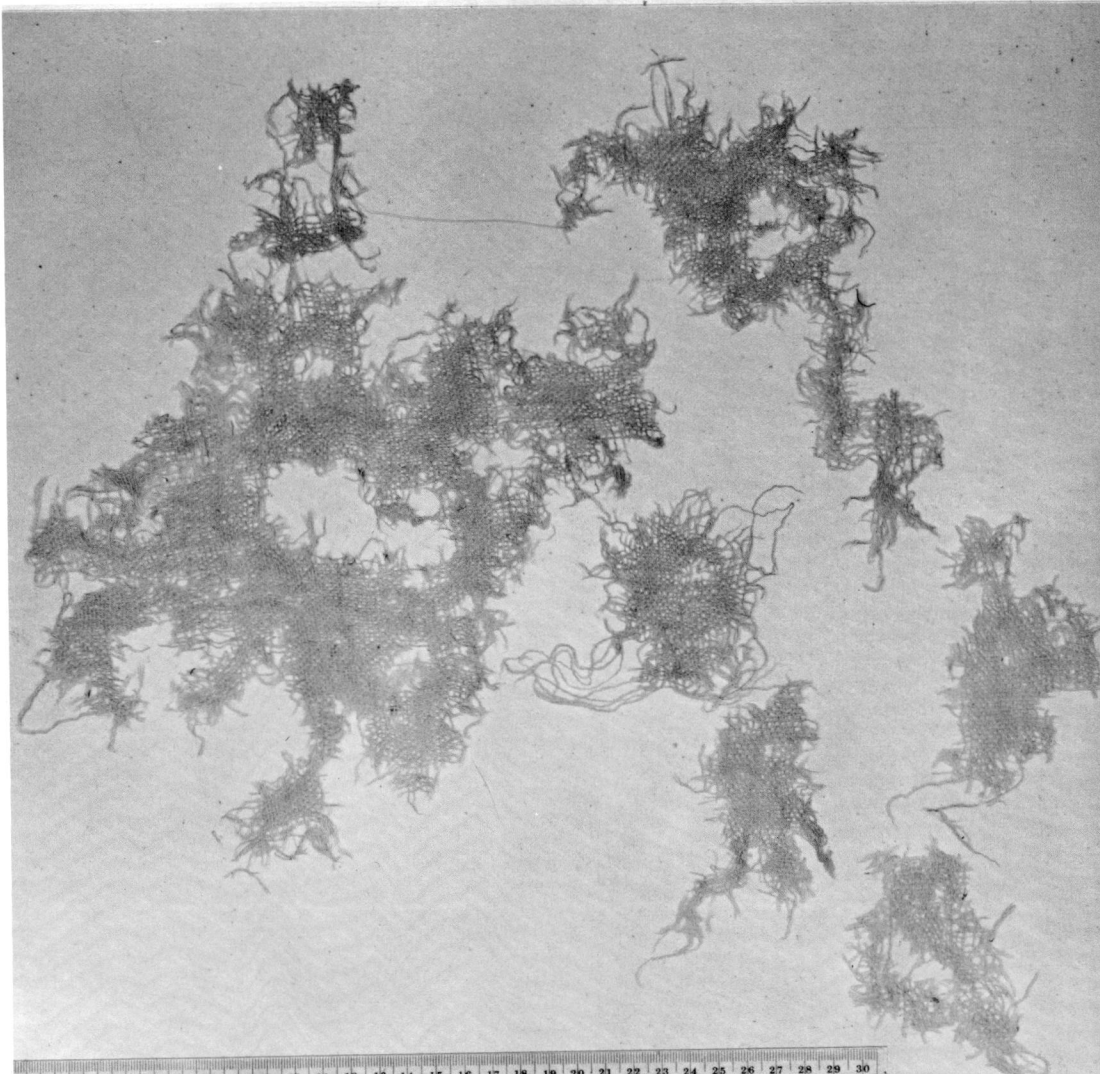

41

Grave Q 10   X-Group

Tumulus, shaft and side-chamber with stone
  blocking
Burial: Slightly disturbed, head north,
  semi-contracted on left side
Body: —
Objects:
a. From shaft:
1. Fragment of decorated leather bag
2. Textiles (see entry below) 19958 A–C
3. Textiles (see entry below) 19965 A–B
b. From burial chamber:
4. Four arrowheads
5. Carnelian pendant

2A. Sheet (?) Fragments (7 pieces)

Material: Animal
Structure:
Plain weave in light brown,* 8 warps per cm,
S-spun; 8/10 wefts per cm, S-spun
Dimensions: All-over: 36cm (warp) x 36cm (weft)

* *Dye Analysis:* Brown—tanin

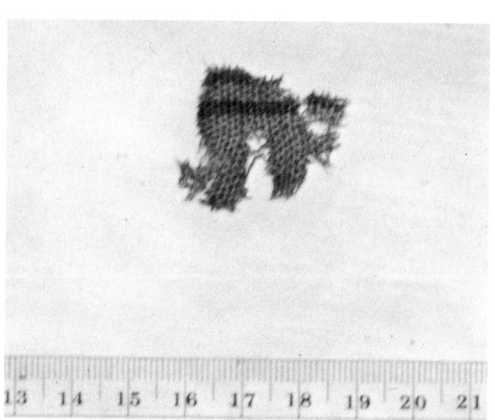

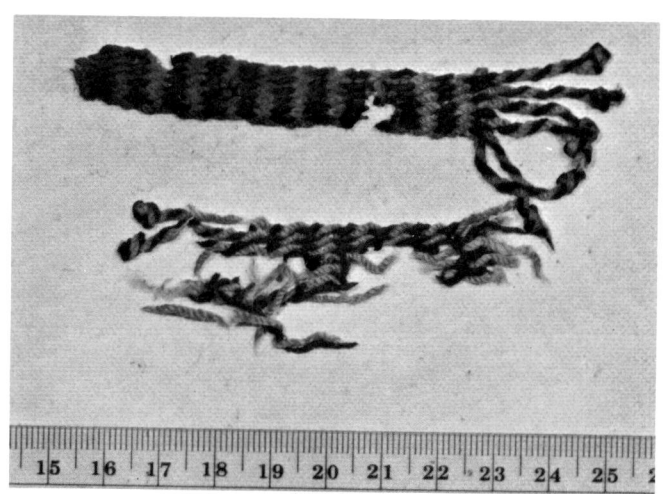

42

Grave Q 10

2B. Fragment

Material: Animal
Structure:
Plain weave in medium brown, 10 warps per cm,
S-spun; 19/20 wefts per cm, S-spun
Decoration:
Two narrow stripes of dark brown of 5 and 6 weft
shots respectively, separated by 5 light brown weft
shots
Dimensions: 2.5cm (warp) x 2.5cm (weft)

43

Grave Q 10

2C. Edging for Sheet or Tunic (2 pieces)

Material: Animal
Structure:
Warp twining in dark brown and yellow; S-spun;
(probably done with fingers)
Dimensions:
Fragment a: 10cm x 3cm
Fragment b: 7.5cm x 1.5cm

44

Grave Q 10

3A. Sheet Fragments (6 pieces)

Material: Animal
Structure:
Open plain weave in medium brown,* 7/9 warps
per cm, S-spun; 7 wefts per cm, S-spun; portions of
one selvage present, including the corner
Decoration:
Top of sheet finished by working warp threads into
twisted cord
Dimensions: All-over: 71cm (warp) x 101cm (weft)

* *Dye Analysis:* Brown—tanin, iron

45

Grave Q 10

3B. Sheet Fragments (2 pieces)

Material: Animal
Structure:
Plain weave in light brown,* 11 warps per cm,
S-spun; 8 wefts per cm, S-spun

Decoration:
Two stripes of weft-faced plain weave in purple of
1.5cm respectively of 28/32 weft shots
Dimensions: All-over: 70cm (warp) x 132cm (weft)

* *Dye Analysis:* Brown—tanin, iron

46

Grave Q 11   X-Group

Tumulus, shaft and side-chamber; two round shafts
  dug in tumulus to southeast of shaft
Burial: Disturbed
Body: Mature, male?
Objects in shaft and disturbed:
1. Leather quiver
2. Textile (see entry below) 19959
3. Faience bead
4. Textile 19951 A–B
5. Textile 19952

2. Tunic (?) Fragment (3 pieces)

Material: Animal
Structure:
Plain weave in variegated shades of dark brown,
9/12 warps per cm, S-spun; 7 wefts per cm, S-spun
Decoration:
Warp threads worked into twisted fringe, held in
place with countered weft twining of alternating
yellow and brown threads, S-spun
Dimensions: All-over: 59cm (warp) x 29cm (weft)

47

Grave Q 11

4A. Fragment of Sheet (12 pieces)

Material: Animal
Structure:
Plain weave in medium brown, 9 warps per cm,
S-spun; 8 wefts per cm, S-spun; selvages present
Decoration:
Grouped warps and wefts worked into twisted cord
of dark brown and medium brown; areas of
weft-faced plain weave of 18 weft shots in dark
brown, S-spun and 2/4 weft shots in dark brown,
S-spun, in other areas
Dimensions: 145cm (warp) x 202cm (weft)

4B. Small Fragments (2 pieces)

Material: Animal
Structure:
Plain weave in medium brown, 9 warps per cm,
S-spun; 8 wefts per cm, S-spun
Decoration:
Countered weft twining
Dimensions: All-over: 14cm (warp) x 24cm (weft)

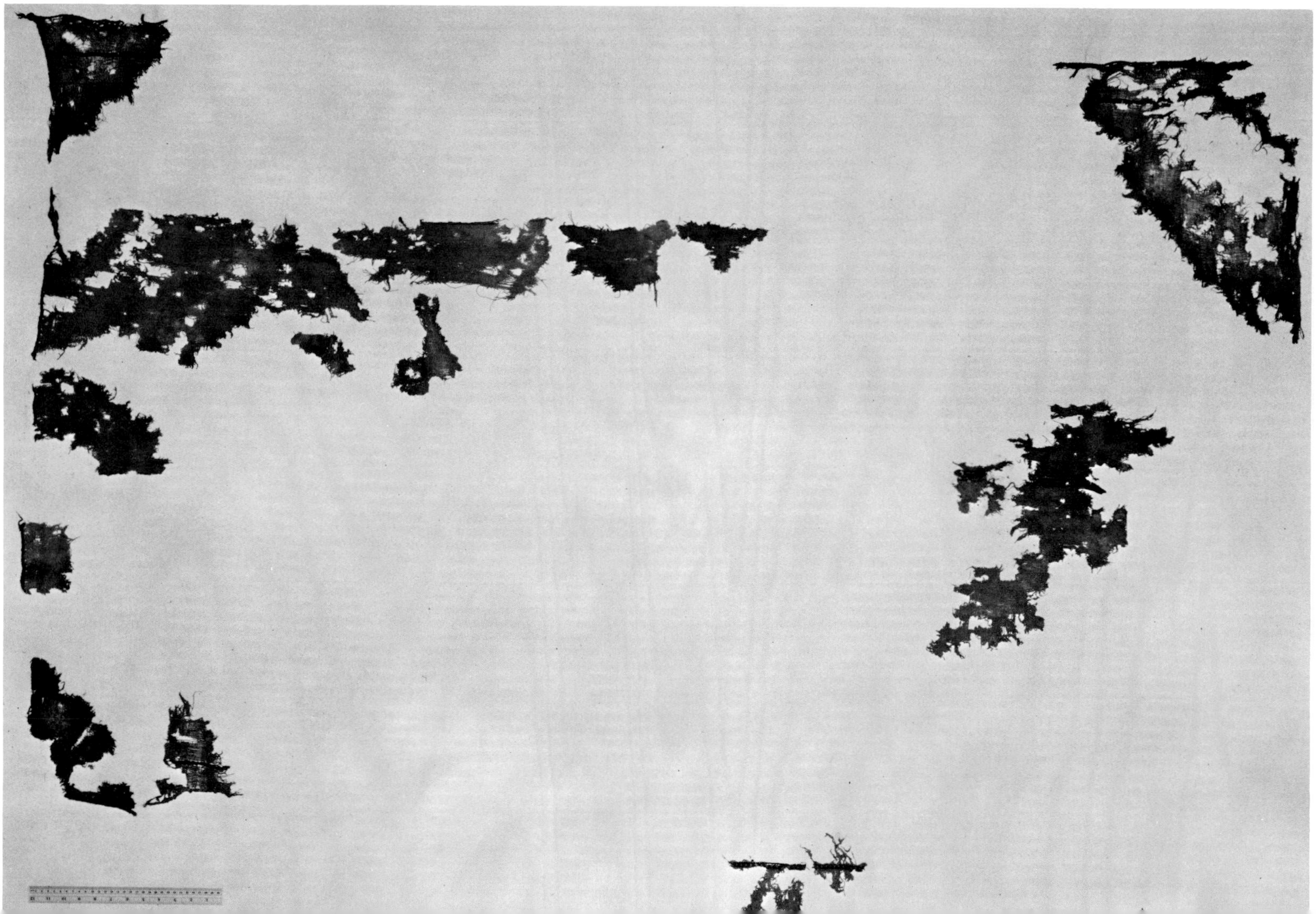

48

Grave Q 11

5. Sheet Fragments (5 pieces)

Material: Animal*
Structure:
Plain weave in light brown, 11 warps per cm,
S-spun; 8 wefts per cm, S-spun; selvages present

Decoration:
Two parallel running stripes in red in weft-faced
plain weave inserted in weft direction at both top
and bottom; 1.5–2cm in width of 27/34 weft shots,
separated by 4 weft shots in plain weave in light
brown; warp threads grouped in 6 at one end
forming fringe

Dimensions: All-over: 155cm (warp) x 240cm (weft)
* *Fiber Analysis:*
Wool—Sheep; *Degradation:* Slight
Wool—Sheep (CIBA no. 3)

49

Grave Q 13   X-Group

Tumulus, shaft and side-chamber with stone
    blocking
Burial: Disturbed
Body: Adult, female?
Objects:
1. Beads
2. Horn
3. Textile 19948—Not available for study
    Beyond restoration

50

Grave Q 15   X-Group

Tumulus, shaft with vault built into the walls, ramp
    to surface brick and stone blocking
Burial: Disturbed
Body: Adult, female?
Objects:
1. Beads
2. Textile (see entry below) 19926

2. Fragment

Material: Animal
Structure:
Plain weave in dark brown, 10/11 warps per cm,
S-spun; 12/13 wefts per cm, S-spun
Dimensions: 35cm (warp) x 30cm (weft)

51

Grave Q 17   X-Group

Tumulus, shaft with vault built into walls, ramp and
    brick blocking
Burial: Disturbed, head south, semicontracted
Body: Adult, female?
Objects:
1. Hair sample
2. Textile (see entry below) 19945

2. Fragment

Material: Animal*
Structure:
Weft-faced plain weave in medium brown,**
3 warps per cm, S-spun; 10 wefts per cm, S-spun
Dimensions: 15.5cm (warp) x 24.5cm (weft)

* *Fiber Analysis:*
Wool—Sheep; *Degradation:* None

** *Dye Analysis:*
Darker brown—gallotanin, iron, tin
Lighter brown—gallotanin, iron

52

Grave Q 18   X-Group

Tumulus, shaft with steps down to side-chamber
Burial: Disturbed, head south?
Body: Juvenile, female?
Objects:
a. In chamber:
1, 5, 6. Cups
2, 7. Jars
3. Jug
b. In shaft:
8. Textile—Discarded
9. Hair sample
10. Textile (see entry below) 19923
11. Date pits
12. Beads

10. Tunic (?) Fragments (3 pieces)

Material: Animal
Structure:
Plain weave in dark brown, 10 warps per cm,
S-spun; 7 wefts per cm, S-spun; dark brown warps
throughout; portion of selvage present
Decoration:
Two narrow stripes in red, S-spun of 13 and 17 weft
shots; the latter in weft-faced plain weave; traces
of a yellow stripe present
Dimensions: All-over: 29cm (warp) x 13cm (weft)

53

Grave Q 19   X-Group

Tumulus, vault built into walls of shaft, ramp, brick
  blocking
Burial: Disturbed
Body: Adult
Objects:
1. Small bowl
2–6. Cups
7. Fragment of iron blade
8. Pottery vessel
9. Textile (see entry below) 20015

9. Tunic (?) Fragment

Material: Animal
Structure:
Plain weave in dark brown, 8 warps per cm, S-spun;
13/14 wefts per cm, S-spun; section from a selvage
present
Decoration:
Wide stripe in weft-faced plain weave in medium
brown; 24 warps per cm, S-spun
Dimensions: 13.5cm (warp) x 28cm (weft)

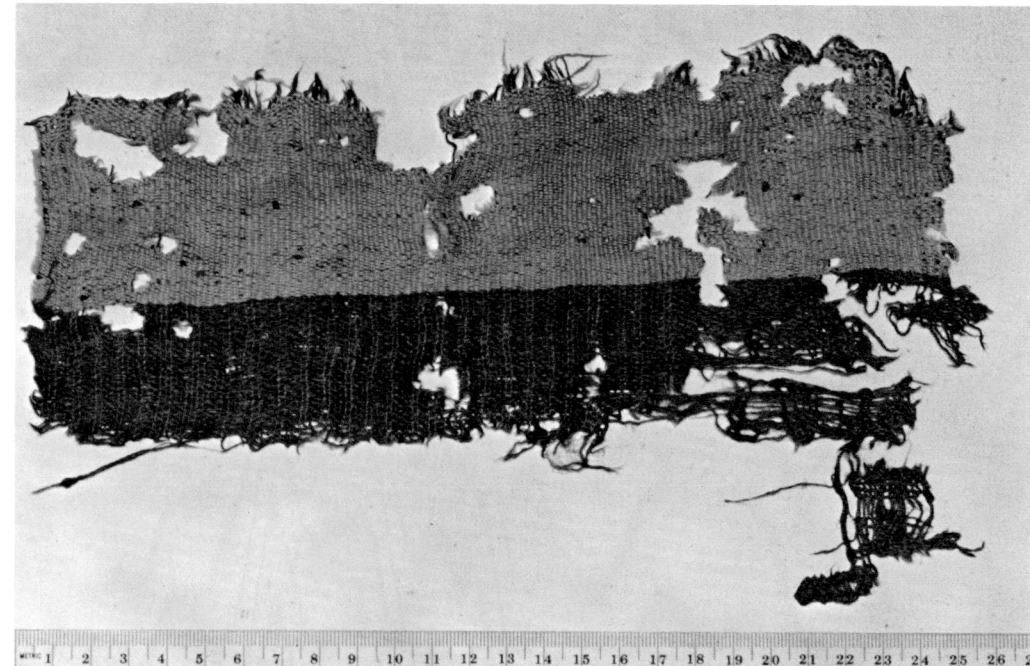

54

Grave Q 22   X-Group

Tumulus?, shaft with side-chamber
Burial: Disturbed, partly wrapped in textile
Body: Juvenile, female?
Objects:
1. Textiles (see entry below) 20003 A–B
2. Cup

1A. Mantle Fragments (12 pieces)

Material: Animal*
Structure:
Open plain weave in dark blue,** 7 warps per cm,
S-spun; 4 wefts per cm, S-spun; portions of selvages
present
Decoration:
Remnants of four large notched "L" shaped
elements at bottom and top in light blue, in
weft-faced plain weave inserted with discontinuous
wefts, 7 warps per cm, S-spun; 9/10 wefts per cm,
S-spun; at bottom one narrow stripe in yellow, 5
weft shots, S-spun
Dimensions: All-over: 147cm (warp) x 139cm (weft)

Fiber Analysis:
Blue—Wool, Sheep; *Degradation:* None
      Wool, Sheep (CIBA no. 4)

**Dye Analysis:* Blue—indigo

55

Grave Q 22

1B. Tunic or Sheet (?) Fragments (2 pieces)

Material: Animal
Structure:
Plain weave in medium and slightly darker brown,
5 warps per cm, S-spun; 10/11 wefts per cm, S-spun
Decoration:
Unevenly striped in weft direction in three different
shades of medium brown
Dimensions: All-over: 47cm (warp) x 52cm (weft)

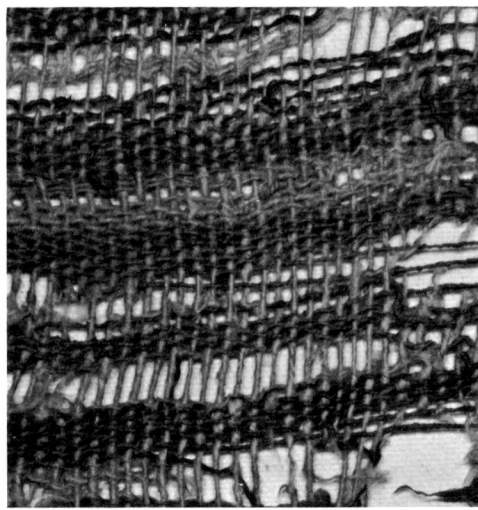

56

Grave Q 27   X-Group

Tumulus, shaft and side-chamber
Burial: Head south, semicontracted on the right side
Body: Adult
Objects:
1.   Beads
2.   Textiles (see entry below) 20005 A–C
3.   Jug
4.   Jar

2A. Textile—Not available for study
Totally disintegrated

2B. Fragment

Material: Animal
Structure:
Originally weft-faced plain weave in red; warps
totally worn away; no count possible
Dimensions: 1cm (warp) x 4cm (weft)

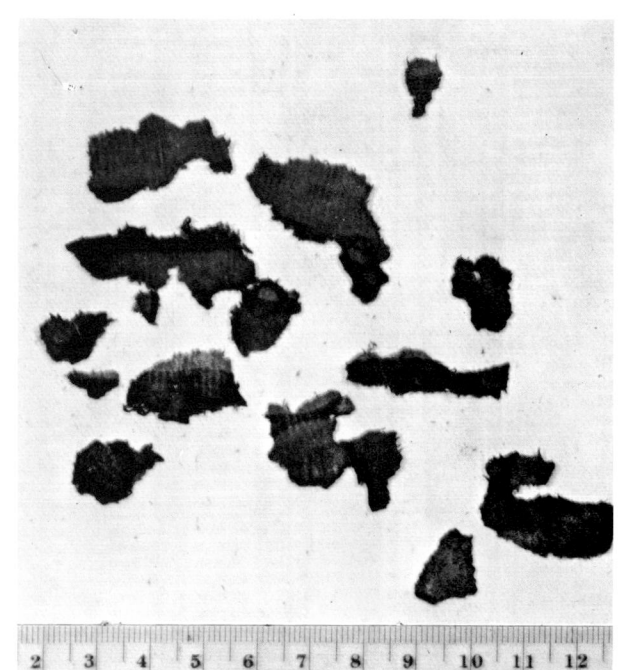

57

Grave Q 27

2C. Fragments (13 pieces)

Material: Animal
Structure:
Weft-faced plain weave in red, blue, light brown
and green on light brown double warps, 14 warps
per cm, S-spun; wefts too disintegrated to get
accurate count, S-spun
Decoration:
Stripes too disintegrated to get accurate count
and sequence, S-spun
Dimensions: All-over: 13cm (warp) x 8cm (weft)

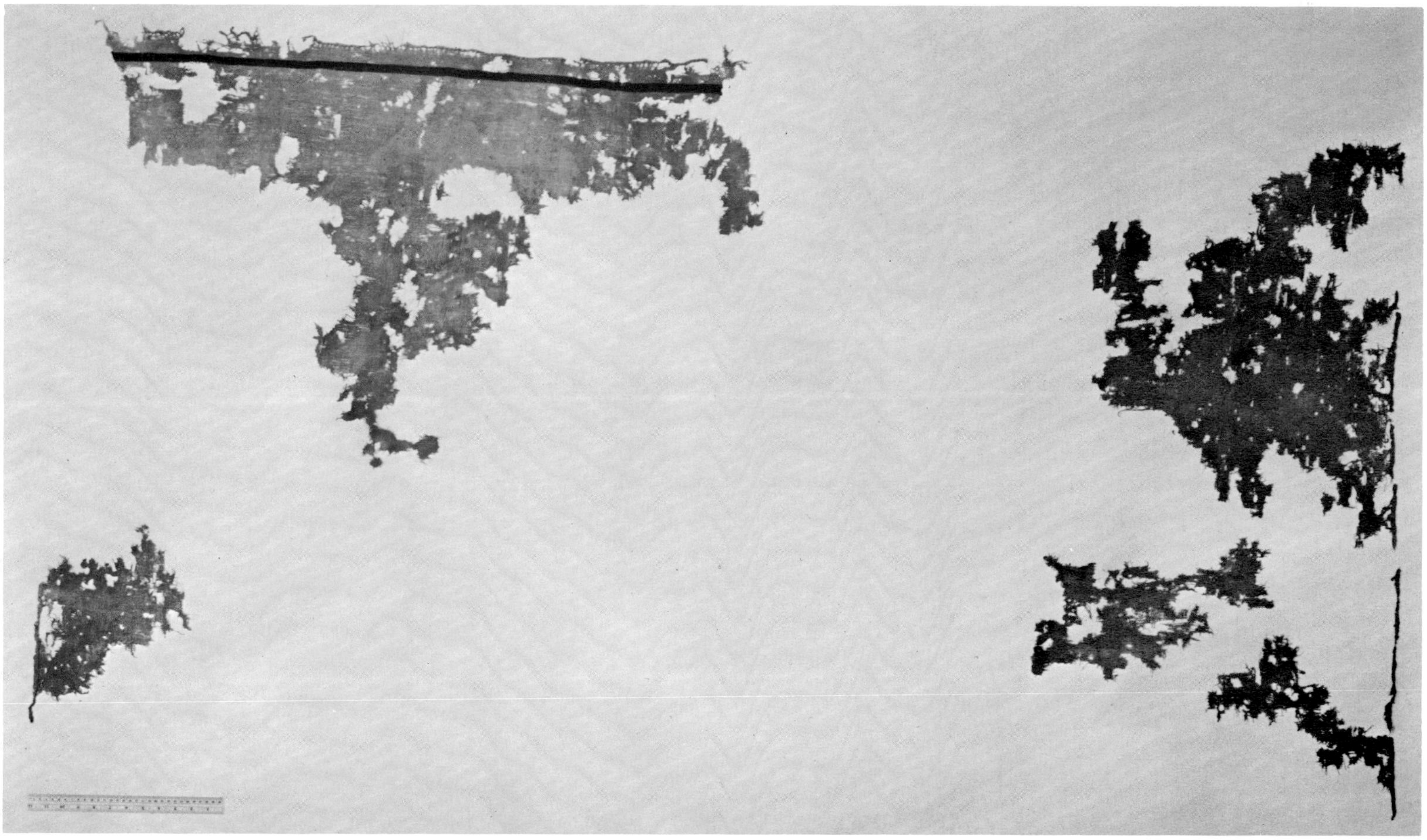

58

Grave Q 30 X-Group

Tumulus, shaft with side-chamber blocked with
stone flags
Burial: Disturbed
Body: Adult, male?

Objects:
1. Leather fragments, of sandal?
2. Beads
3. Textiles (see entry below) 20031 A–B
4. Potsherds

3A. Sheet (?) Fragments (5 pieces)

Material: Animal
Structure:
Plain weave in medium brown, 9 warps per cm,
S-spun; 10 wefts per cm, S-spun; selvages present
Decoration:
One stripe of 16 weft shots in plain weave in
purple, S-spun; warps worked into twisted cord
Dimensions: All-over: 116cm (warp) x 209cm (weft)

59

Grave Q 30

3B. Carpet Fragments (3 major pieces)

Material: Animal
Structure:
Plain weave, 8 warps per cm (2-ply), S-spun;
grouped wefts of 4 each, 10 wefts per cm, S-spun,
with slip loops inserted after each fourth weft shed
opening, S-spun; multicolored*
Decoration:
Remnants of geometric border patterns occur in
four areas of varying dimensions; center field gives
indication of a branching all-over design
Dimensions: All-over: 52cm (warp) x 106cm (weft)

Dye Analysis:
Yellow—orlean?, iron, (zinc)?
Orange—purpurin (alizarin), iron
Red—purpurin (alizarin), iron
Brown—purpurin (alizarin), iron, (zinc)?
Blue—purpurin (alizarin), iron, weld, indigo
Green—indigo, weld, (zinc)?

60

Grave Q 38   X-Group

Tumulus?, shaft with side-chamber, mud-brick
   blocking; impressions for prepared bed-burial at
   corners of chamber
Burial: Disturbed
Body: Adult
Objects:
1. Textile 20084—Not available for study
   Beyond restoration
2. Iron fragments—arrowheads
3. Jar
4. Jar
5. Beads
6. Bronze ring
7. Leather fragments, animals?
8. Potsherds

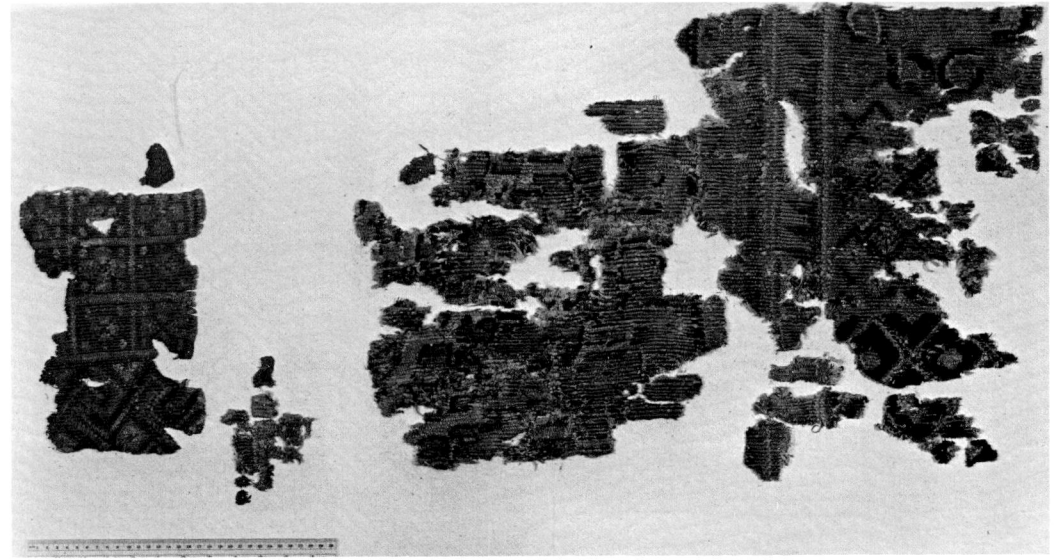

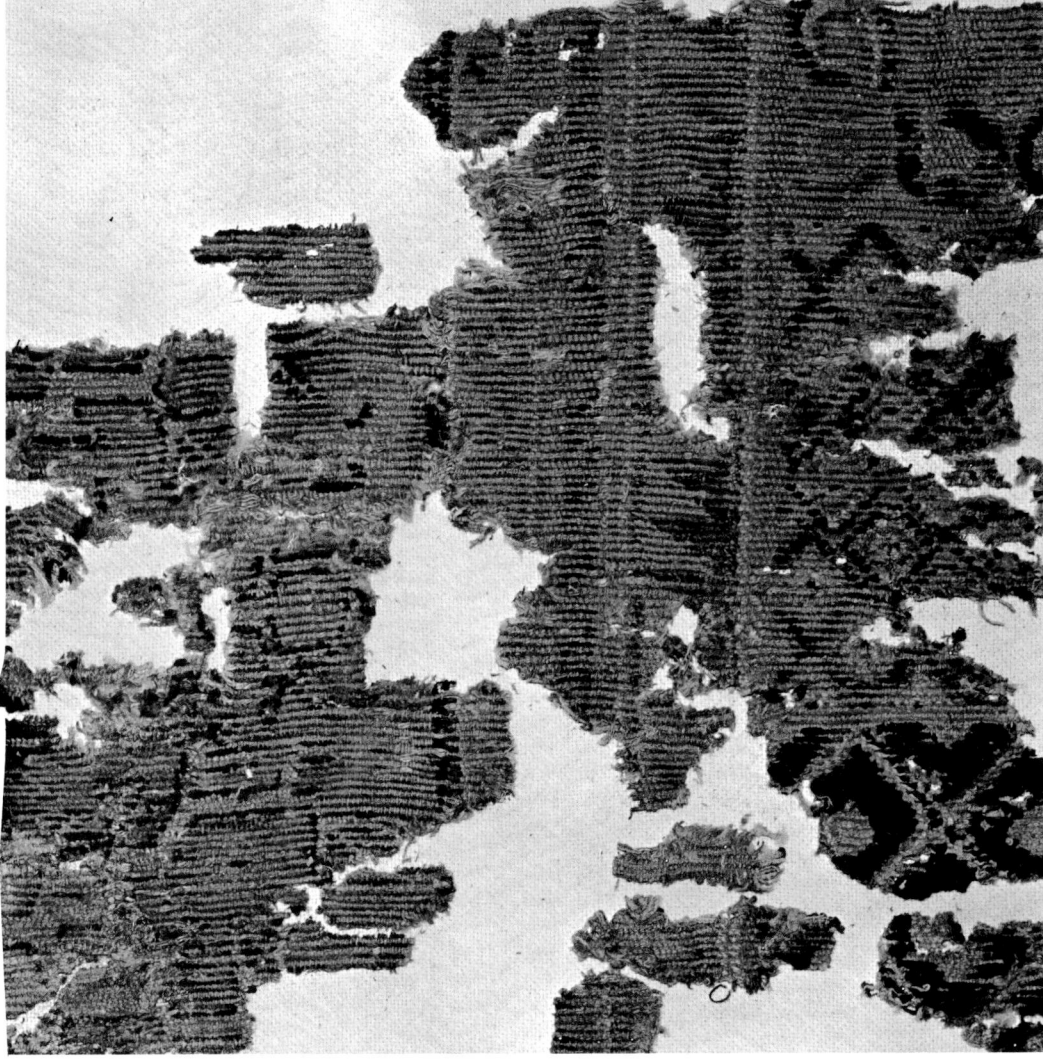

61

Grave Q 39   X-Group Animal Sacrifices

Rectangular shaft
Burials: Disturbed
Bodies: One horse?, one donkey?, two camels?,
   others?
Objects:
1. Textiles (horse trappings) (see entry below)
   20098 A–C
2. Textile 20480—Not available for study—Beyond
   restoration
3. Horse trappings of leather, horsehair with wood
   and iron fittings
4. Animal horns
5. Saddle
6. Stomach contents
7. Leather bag

1 A–C. Fragments (19 pieces; all three lots together)

Material: Horsehair*
Structure:
Plain weave in black, 5 warps per cm; 6 wefts
per cm
Decoration:
Needlework in animal fiber thread in light brown,
with leather (?) decoration, S-spun; twisted and
braided cords and tassels; one finished edge in
horsehair
Dimensions: All-over: 46cm (warp) x 29cm (weft)

* *Fiber Analysis:* Horsehair; *Degradation:* None

62

Grave Q 44   X-Group

Tumulus, remains of single-course stone circle,
  shaft and side-chamber, brick blocking filled shaft
Burial: Disturbed
Body: Juvenile, female
Objects:
a. From shaft:
1. Textile (see entry below) 20040
2. Beads
b. In chamber:
3. Jar
4. Bowl
5. Textile wrapped around body (see entry below)
    20051

1. Sheet or Tunic (?) Fragment

Material: Animal
Structure:
Open plain weave in medium brown, 9 warps per
cm, S-spun, 5/6 wefts per cm, S-spun; one selvage
present
Decoration:
Two narrow stripes in plain weave in orange of 16
weft shots, 12 wefts per cm, S-spun, separated by
narrow yellow stripe of 6 weft shots, in plain
weave, S-spun; another white stripe of 8/9 weft
shots occurs running parallel, plain weave, S-spun;
exposed warp threads at one end, occasionally
three twisted together
Dimensions: 26cm (warp) x 42cm (weft)

63

Grave Q 44

5. Sheet or Tunic (?) Fragment

Material: Animal
Structure:
Plain weave in dark blue, 8 warps per cm, S-spun;
6 wefts per cm, S-spun
Decoration:
Two red stripes of 24 weft shots and 19 weft shots
respectively in weft-faced plain weave, 14 wefts per
cm, S-spun, separated by 6 weft shots of plain
weave, S-spun; an additional stripe of 12 yellow
weft shots in weft-faced plain weave, 14 wefts per
cm, S-spun, near finished edge; warp threads
worked into twisted cord along one edge
Dimensions: 26cm (warp) x 40cm (weft)

64

Grave Q 62   X-Group

Tumulus, shaft and end chamber, shaft partly
   covered by brick vault built into wall
Burial: Disturbed
Body: Adult
Objects: All from the chamber:
1. Leather quiver
2. Leather with rosettes
3. Stud
4. Textiles (see entry below) 20178 A–C
5–16, 17, 18–20. Pottery
21. Iron fragment
22. Beads
23. Textile (see entry below) 20399
24. Date pits

4A. Shroud (3 pieces)

Material: Animal
Structure:
Plain weave with increased warps in dark brown, 9
warps per cm, S-spun; 9 wefts per cm, S-spun;
selvages present
Decoration:
At one end (believed to have covered head) tightly
wrapped tassels and a row of countered weft
twining in medium yellow and dark brown; at
other end (believed to have wrapped feet), warps
gathered into medium yellow twisted cord
terminating at both ends in a round tassel; cord
goes through center of this round tassel and is
subsequently terminated with an additional round
tassel suspended from a 7.5cm long cord; at both
selvages cording attached through stitching for
33cm. At end of cording another round tassel
appears
Dimensions: All-over: 180cm (warp) x 114cm (weft)
   including tassels

65

Grave Q 62

4B. Fragments (2 pieces)

Material: Animal
Structure:
Plain weave in dark brown, 8 warps per cm, S-spun;
9 wefts per cm, S-spun; 1 selvage present
Decoration:
Double layered fragment, either a bag or a portion
of a garment (?) with center area of 34cm in dark
brown set off at both ends with red stripes of
1.5cm, 1.8cm, 1.2cm widths (bottom) and 2.5cm,
2cm, 1.5cm (top); separated by brown stripes of
0.5cm, 1cm and 1cm in widths in blue (bottom) and
1.5cm width (top); at both ends appear yellow stripes
of 1.5cm and 1.8cm respectively in width,
terminating in twisted warp thread cord at top and
attached tassels at the bottom
Dimensions: All-over: 56.5cm (warp) x 46cm (weft)

66

Grave Q 62

4Ca. Portion from a Carpet

Material: Animal
Structure:
Plain weave in light brown,* 5 warps per cm, (2-ply),
S-spun; 8 wefts per cm, Z-spun, with slip loops
inserted after 2 weft groupings of 3 each, in shades
of light brown, green and blue
Decoration:
Center field in red,* outlined by continuous "S"
motif in dark green* enframed with arched
architectural elements (to left) and geometric units
at top and bottom, right lower corner shows
traces of branch motifs
Dimensions: All-over: 132cm (warp) x 110cm (weft)

Dye Analysis:
Yellow—weld, Orange—orlean?
Red—purpurin?, carminic acid
Brown₁—tanin, iron; Brown₂—tanin, iron
Green₁—weld, indigo, iron; Green₂—weld, indigo,
iron

67

Grave Q 62

4Cb. Fragments from Carpet (8 pieces)

Material: Animal
Structure:
Plain weave in light brown, 5 warps per cm, (2-ply), S-spun; 8 wefts per cm with slip loops grouped in 4's, Z-spun, in shades of light brown, green and blue; one piece shows a finished edge
Dimensions: All-over: 60cm (warp) x 39cm (weft)

68

Grave Q 62

23. Large Cover Fragments (5 pieces)

Material: Animal
Structure:
Weft-faced plain weave in purple, 10 dark brown* warps per cm (grouped by 2's and individually counted), S-spun with areas of discontinuous wefts, inserted through interlocking and dovetailing; 35 wefts per cm, S-spun; light brown stripes of 48 wefts per cm, S-spun;
Fragment a: selvage present
Fragment c: selvage present
Fragments d–e: remnants of two large circles, dark brown (badly stained) 10/11 warps per cm, S-spun, (grouped by 2's and individually counted), 48 wefts per cm; plied loose hanging threads
Decoration:
Fragments a–c: Two light brown stripes of 10cm each in weft direction, separated by purple stripe of 1/1.5cm; in purple area of 17/18.5cm two narrow stripes of 5 weft shots each (separated by 2 weft shots of purple) in light brown; heading in dark brown present formed through 7 weft shots; dark brown warp threads terminate in twisted cord; light brown stripes show an intertwining design carried out with inlaid purple thread; slit tapestry, interlocking and dovetailing, S-spun
Dimensions:
Fragment a: 52cm (warp) x 63cm (weft)
Fragment b: 48cm (warp) x 48cm (weft)
Fragment c: 43cm (warp) x 28cm (weft)
Fragment d: 75cm (warp) x 114cm (weft)
               (40.5cm diameter of circle)
Fragment e: 60cm (warp) x 46cm (weft)

* Dye Analysis:
Brown—purpurin (alizarin)
Dark Brown—purpurin (alizarin), iron

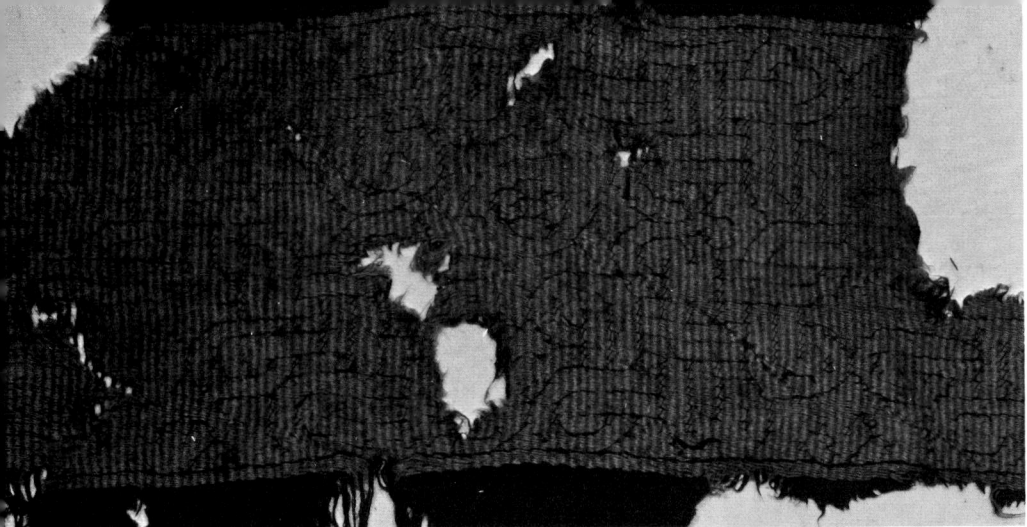

Fragment b

Fragments a–c

Fragments d–e

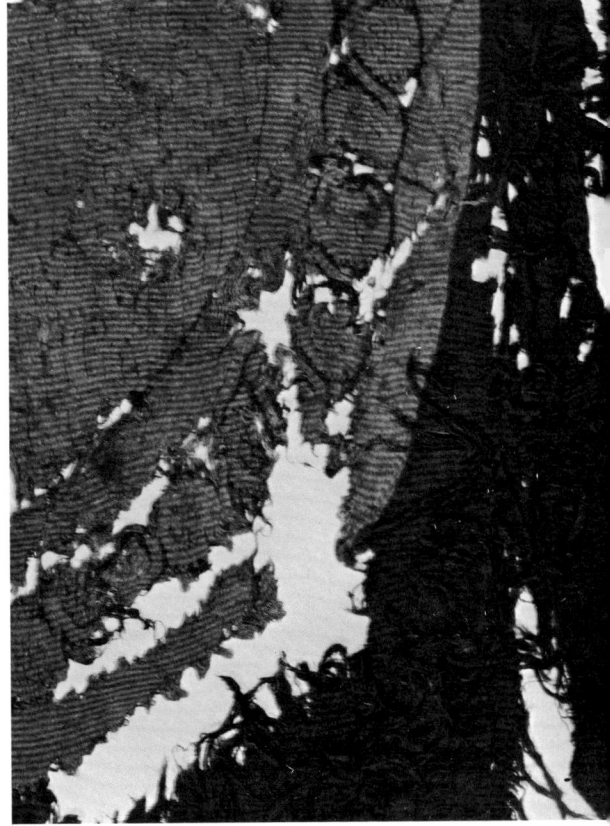

Fragment e

69

Grave Q 68   X-Group

Tumulus, shaft with side-chamber
Burial: Disturbed, head south, semicontracted
Body: Mature, male?
Objects:
1. Pot (*qadus*)
2. Jar
3. Textiles beside body (see entry below)
   20132 A–C
4. Two arrowheads
5. Beads
6. Silver ring
7. Sandals
8. Fragment of bed

3A. Mantle (2 pieces)

Material: Animal
Structure:
Weft-faced plain weave in medium brown,* 9
warps per cm, S-spun; 16 wefts per cm, S-spun;
selvage present on one side
Decoration:
Both fragments show two large notched "L"
shapes in purple, inserted through discontinuous
wefts and dovetailing; 29 wefts per cm, S-spun;
other side is rolled and stitched along edge; warp
threads worked into twisted cord at both ends; two
narrow stripes of 3 and 2 weft shots respectively in
purple separated by 3 weft shots in medium brown
occur at both ends
Dimensions:
Fragment a: 114cm (warp) x 132cm (weft)
Fragment b: 73cm (warp) x 143cm (weft)

* *Dye Analysis:* Brown—gallotanin, iron

70

Grave Q 68

3B. Large Cover Fragments (2 pieces)

Material: Animal and Vegetable (Linen)
Structure:
Plain weave in dark blue,* 10/12 double warp threads (individually counted), S-spun, 10 wefts per cm, Z-spun
Decoration:
Fragment a: square in weft-faced plain weave, in light brown and red inserted through discontinuous wefts, with inner border of 3/3.5cm showing woven three-leafed vine leaves in red and dark green alternating against light brown ground; center design totally worn away; was decorated with inlaid linen thread, in red, 31 wefts per cm, S-spun; 10/12 double warps per cm, S-spun. Area of dark blue plain weave with plied loose hanging threads of 6cm in weft direction; occur after 17/18 weft shots; inserted after 9 warps, overlapping the following 3 warps; *Fragment b:* Plain weave with plied loose hanging threads of 6cm; occur after 17/18 weft shots; inserted after 9 warps, overlapping the following 3 warps

Dimensions: *Fragment a:* All-over: 54cm (warp) x 65cm (weft)
Square: 27cm (warp) x 27cm (weft)
Fragment b: 40cm (warp) x 80cm (weft)

* *Dye Analysis:*
Blue₁—indigo, weld, iron
Blue₂—indigo, weld, iron, tin

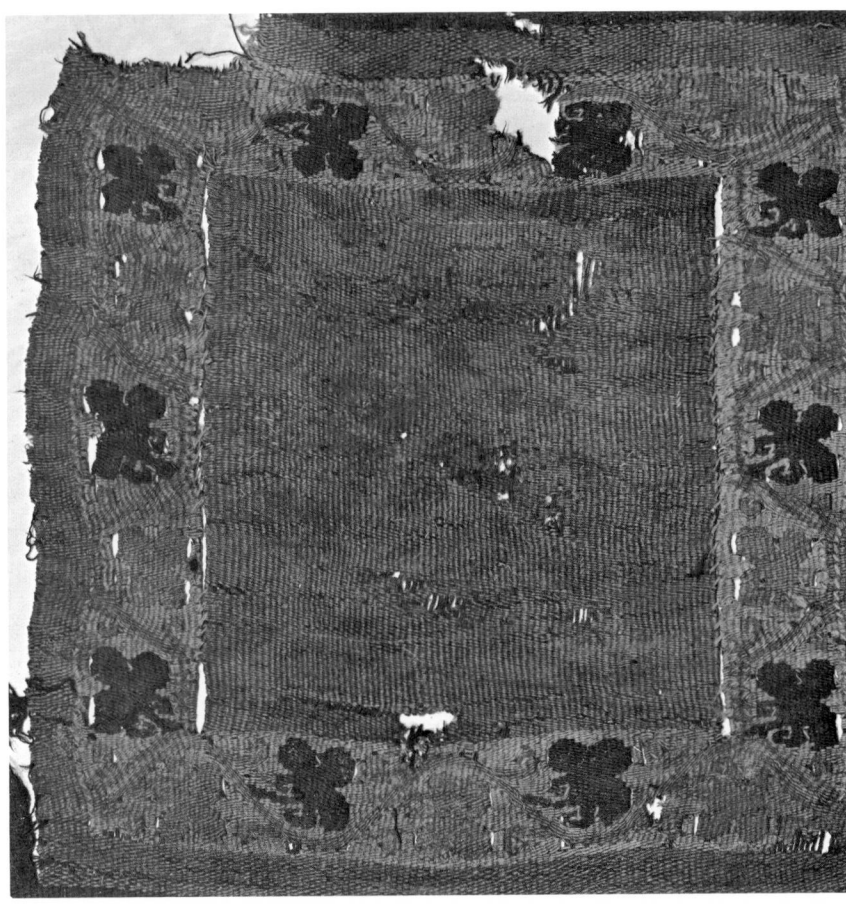

71

Grave Q 68

3C. Small Complete Sheet

Material: Animal
Structure:
Weft-faced plain weave in light brown, 11 warps per cm, S-spun; 40 wefts per cm, S-spun; one complete selvage present, other only in parts, as rest of that selvage edge is torn
Decoration:
At one end 2 weft shots in purple, S-spun; purple however, does not run from selvage to selvage; it stops on left side 14.5cm short; warp threads worked into twisted cord; re-opened and damaged on one side (side with one green glass bead); on left side at six occasions in staggered arrangement countered weft twining occurs; additional countered weft twining occurs on reverse of sheet; three of these are terminated in twisted cords of 10–12cm in length
Dimensions: All-over: 69cm (warp) x 128cm (weft)

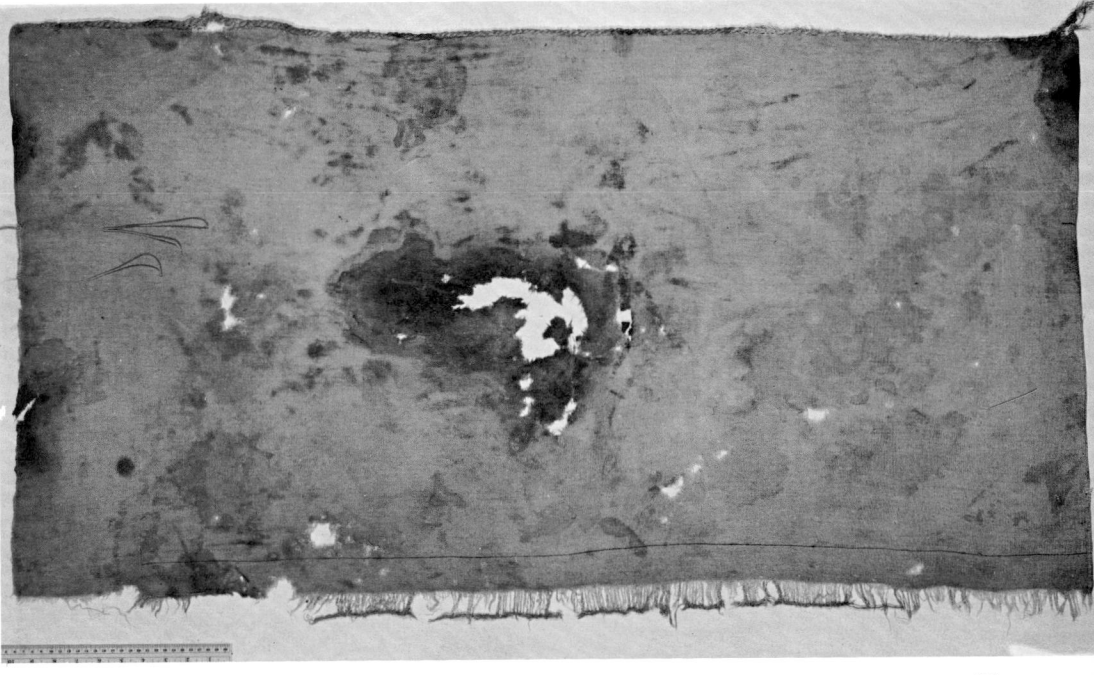

72

Grave Q 74   X-Group

Tumulus, shaft and side-chamber, stone blocking
Burial: Disturbed
Body: Adult, male
Objects in shaft:

1. Textile (see entry below) 20135 A
2. Leather quiver
3. Arrowhead
4. Leather belt
5. Two sandals
6. Strap for quiver
7. Leather fragment
8. 21 arrowheads
9. Textiles (see entry below) 20135 B–C
10, 11. Cups or Bowls
12. Beads

1A. Fragments (9 pieces)

Material: Animal*
Structure:
Weft-faced plain weave in light** brown with stains
of dark brown,** 10 warps per cm, S-spun (double
warps individually counted), 17 wefts per cm,
S-spun; one selvage present
Decoration:
Continuous Sehna knots forming loops of 2.5cm–
4cm in length, inserted at 1.5cm apart in weft
direction; 8 markings, four of which are remnants
of dark blue tape, four others are dark blue weft
inserts along selvage edge
Dimensions: All-over: 132cm (warp) x 122cm (weft)

* *Fiber Analysis:* Wool—Sheep; *Degradation:* Slight

** *Dye Analysis:*
Light Brown (unsoiled)—orlean?
Brown (soiled)—orlean?

73

Grave Q 74

9B. Sheet (?) Fragment

Material: Animal*
Structure:
Plain weave in blue-green, 10 warps per cm,
S-spun; 5/6 wefts per cm, S-spun; one selvage
present
Decoration:
Near selvage two markings in red thread, S-spun
Dimensions: All-over: 46cm (warp) x 25cm (weft)

* *Fiber Analysis:* Wool—Sheep; *Degradation:* Slight

74

Grave Q 74

9C. Shroud or Tunic (?) Fragment

Material: Animal*
Structure:
Plain weave in dark brown, 12/13 warps per cm,
S-spun; 7 wefts per cm, S-spun
Decoration:
Along one edge in weft direction countered weft
twining in yellow and dark brown terminating in
small wrapped tassels
Dimensions: All-over: 33cm (warp) x 48cm (weft)

* *Fiber Analysis:* Wool—Probably Camel;
   Degradation: Severe

75

Grave Q 78   X-Group

Tumulus, shaft and end-chamber, with brick vault
   over shaft built into wall and brick blocking
Burial: Disturbed, included animal
Body: Adult, female?
Objects:
1–5. Pottery including two jugs and two cups
6. Potsherds
7. Date pits
8. Textile (see entry below) 20250
9. Leather cord fragments, tightly wound

8. Sheet or Tunic (?) Fragments (8 pieces)

Material: Animal
Structure:
Plain weave in varying shades of brown,* 7/8 warps
per cm, S-spun; 6/7 wefts per cm, S-spun; selvage
present
Decoration:
Four pieces show portions of medium green*
stripe, of 2.5cm in width of 11 wefts per cm,
S-spun; one piece shows repeated arrangement of
three twisted warp threads as fringe; another piece
shows repeated arrangement of three warp
threads worked into twisted cord
Dimensions: All-over: 76cm (warp) x 93cm (weft)
Remarks:
Remnants were originally knotted. They fell into
eight pieces after knot was opened.

* *Dye Analysis:*
Brown₁—purpurin (alizarin), weld, iron
Brown₂—purpurin (alizarin), iron
Brown₃—purpurin (alizarin), iron
Green—indigo, gallotanin

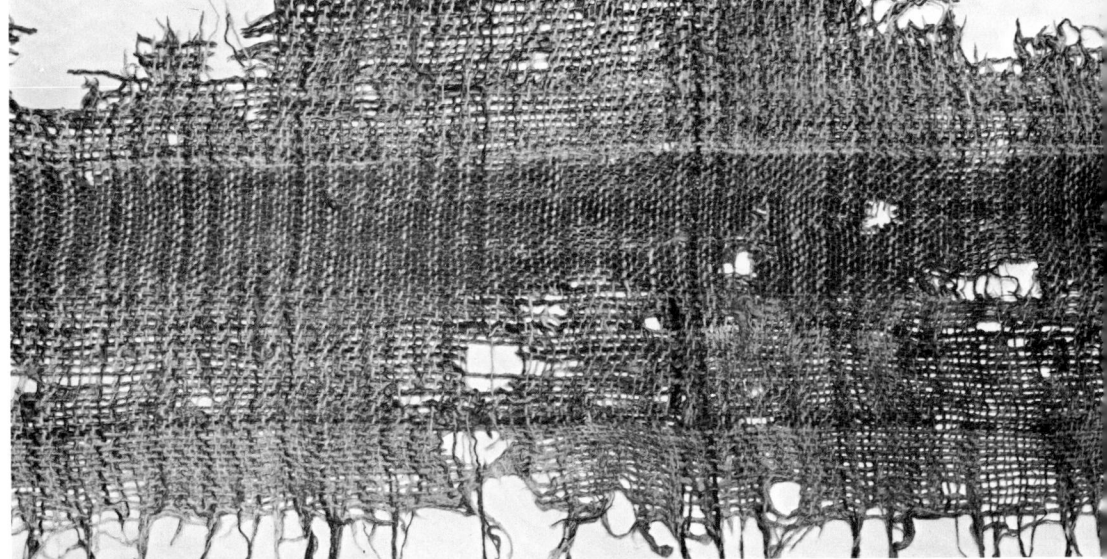

Grave Q 82   X-Group

Tumulus, shaft and side-chamber, stone blocking,
    deposit hole near shaft
Burial: Disturbed
Body: Mature
Objects:
1–6. Pottery
7. Beads
8. Necklace
9. Leather container fragment
10. Twisted straw
11. Textile (see entry below) 20167

11. Fragments (3 pieces)

Material: Animal
Structure:
Plain weave in white, 6/7 warps per cm, S-spun;
7/8 wefts per cm, S-spun
Dimensions: All-over: 7cm (warp) x 12cm (weft)

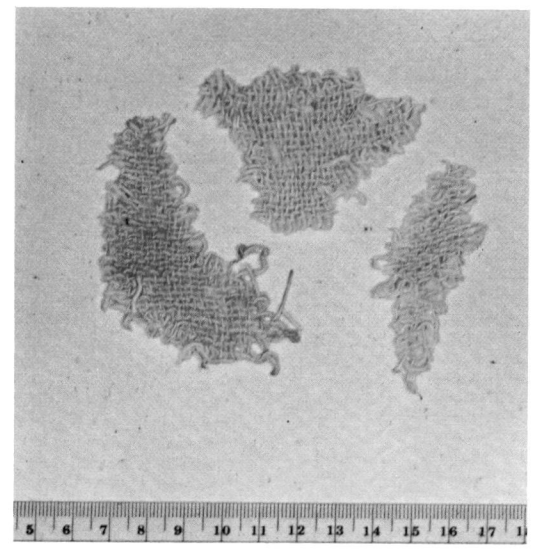

Grave Q 119   X-Group

Tumulus?, shaft and side-chamber, brick blocking
Burial: Disturbed, semicontracted?
Body: Mature female?
Objects:
1, 2. Jars
3. Textiles (see entry below) 20251 A–C
4. Leather sandals
5. Quiver

3A. Tunic or Sheet (?) Fragments (6 pieces)

Material: Animal*
Structure:
Plain weave in dark brown,** 7/8 warps per cm,
S-spun; 8/10 wefts per cm, S-spun; selvages present
Decoration:
Medium yellow border stripe of 16 weft shots
present, separated by dark brown stripe of 10/16
weft shots, followed by two narrow medium yellow
stripes of 2 weft shots each, separated by 2 weft
shots in dark brown; warp threads worked into
twisted cord
Dimensions: All-over: 200cm (warp) x 147cm (weft)

* *Fiber Analysis:* Wool—Sheep; *Degradation:*
  Moderate

** *Dye Analysis:* Brown—purpurin (alizarin)

78

Grave Q 119

3B. Mantle Fragments (8 pieces)

Material: Animal*
Structure:
Plain weave in dark brown, 8 warps per cm, S-spun;
5/8 wefts per cm, S-spun; two selvages present
Decoration:
Two large notched "L" shapes in weft-faced plain
weave on dark brown warps, inserted through
discontinuous wefts and dovetailing in orange,
10 wefts per cm, S-spun; one narrow stripe in plain
weave of 10 weft shots in yellow in weft direction
Dimensions: All-over: 69cm (warp) x 149cm (weft)

* *Fiber Analysis:* Wool—Probably Camel;
  Degradation: Severe

79

Grave Q 119

3C. Tunic or Sheet (?) Fragment

Material: Vegetable (Linen)
Structure:
Plain weave in medium brown, 6 warps per cm,
S-spun; 8 wefts per cm, S-spun; one selvage present
Decoration:
Stripe of 1.2cm in purple, S-spun, of 15 weft shots
appears along edge; grouped warps worked into
twisted cord along same edge and above 2cm of
purple stripe; along selvage 5 rows of purple weft
shots, separated by 2 rows of medium brown appear
in weft direction, 4cm into fabric
Dimensions: All-over: 85cm (warp) x 67cm (weft)

80

Grave Q 132   Probably X-Group

Tumulus probably, shaft with brick vault constructed
  in sides, dromos
Burial: Absent
Objects:
1. Textiles (see entry below) 20307 A–B
2. Potsherds

1A. Sheet or Tunic (?) Fragments (4 pieces)

Material: Animal
Structure:
Weft-faced plain weave in medium brown, 8 warps
per cm, S-spun; 35 wefts per cm, S-spun
Fragment a: One selvage present
Decoration:
Patterned area in purple visible, 20 wefts per cm,
S-spun
Fragment a: Shows warp threads worked into
twisted cord
Dimensions:
Fragment a: 9cm (warp) x 20.5cm (weft)
Fragment b: 5.5cm (warp) x 5cm (weft)
Fragment c: 6cm (warp) x 7cm (weft)

81

Grave Q 132

1B. Fragment with edging for Sheet or Tunic

Material: Animal
Structure:
Weft-faced plain weave in dark brown, 11 warps per
cm, S-spun; 20 wefts per cm, S-spun
Decoration:
Countered weft twining in yellow and brown,
S-spun; terminating with warp threads worked into
twisted cord
Dimensions: 3cm (warp) x 7cm (weft)

82

Grave Q 134   X-Group

Tumulus, wide stepped shaft with side-chamber,
  brick blocking filling shaft, crumbled rectangular
  bed posts in chamber
Burial:
Disturbed, extended on back, head south, covered
with shroud
Body: Mature, female?
Objects:
1, 2. Jars at feet of burial; 10. Contents
3. Iron arrowheads
4, 5. Iron fragments
6. Jug
7, 8. Cups
9. Juglet
11. Ivory bracelet
12. Beads and shell fragment
13. Copper ring
14. Copper spoon
15. Textiles (see entry below) 20344 A–D
16. Leather fragments
17. Animal horn
18. Pendant

15A. Fragments (3 pieces)

Material: Animal
Structure:
Plain weave in dark green,* 6 warps per cm, S-spun;
16 double wefts per cm (individually counted),
S-spun; selvage present
Decoration:
Two stripes of red, S-spun of 2cm and 2.5cm
respectively in width; 20 double wefts per cm
(individually counted)
Dimensions: All-over: 22cm (warp) x 11cm (weft)

* *Dye Analysis:* Green—weld, indigo, purpurin
  (alizarin), iron

15B. Textile—Not available for study; Beyond
    restoration

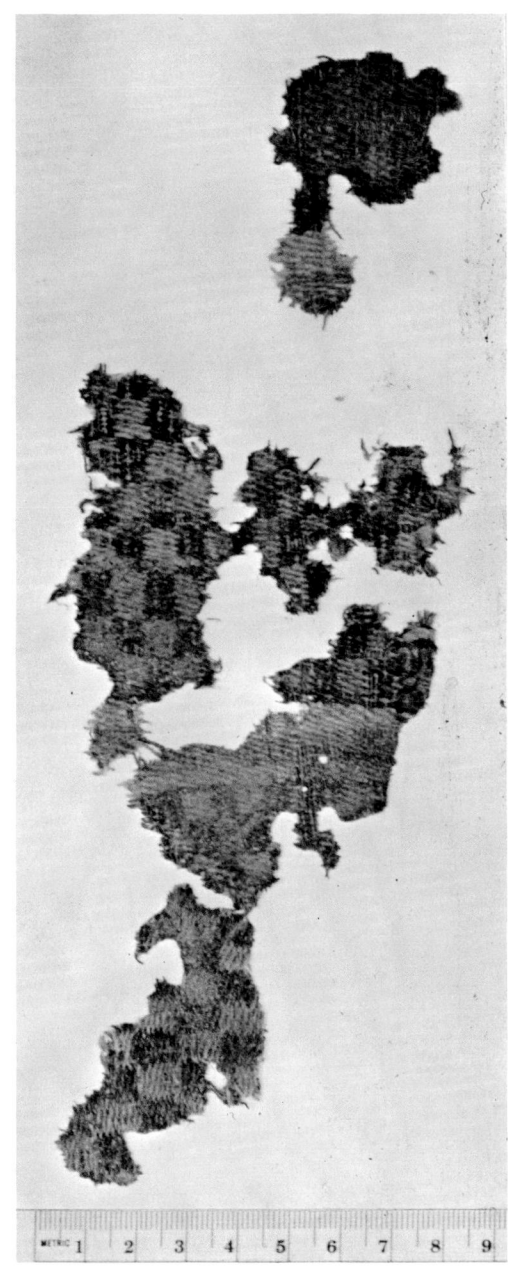

83

Grave Q 134

15C. Tunic Fragment (3 pieces)

Material: Animal
Structure:
Weft-faced plain weave formed by complementary wefts and inner warps in red, blue, green and yellow; 8/10 warps per cm in red and yellow, S-spun; 28 wefts per cm, S-spun; tiny selvage portion present
Decoration:
Small checkerboard pattern in yellow and green, as well as red and blue separated by three narrow stripes of yellow with a center stripe of red, of .5cm respectively (all in weft direction)
Dimensions: All-over: 23cm (warp) x 8cm (weft)
Remarks:
This fragment is identical in structure and patternization to entry 33

84

Grave Q 134

15D. Fragments (7 pieces)

Material: Animal
Structure:
Plain weave in dark blue, 9 warps per cm, S-spun; 9 wefts per cm, S-spun
Dimensions: All-over, 24cm (warp) x 25cm (weft)

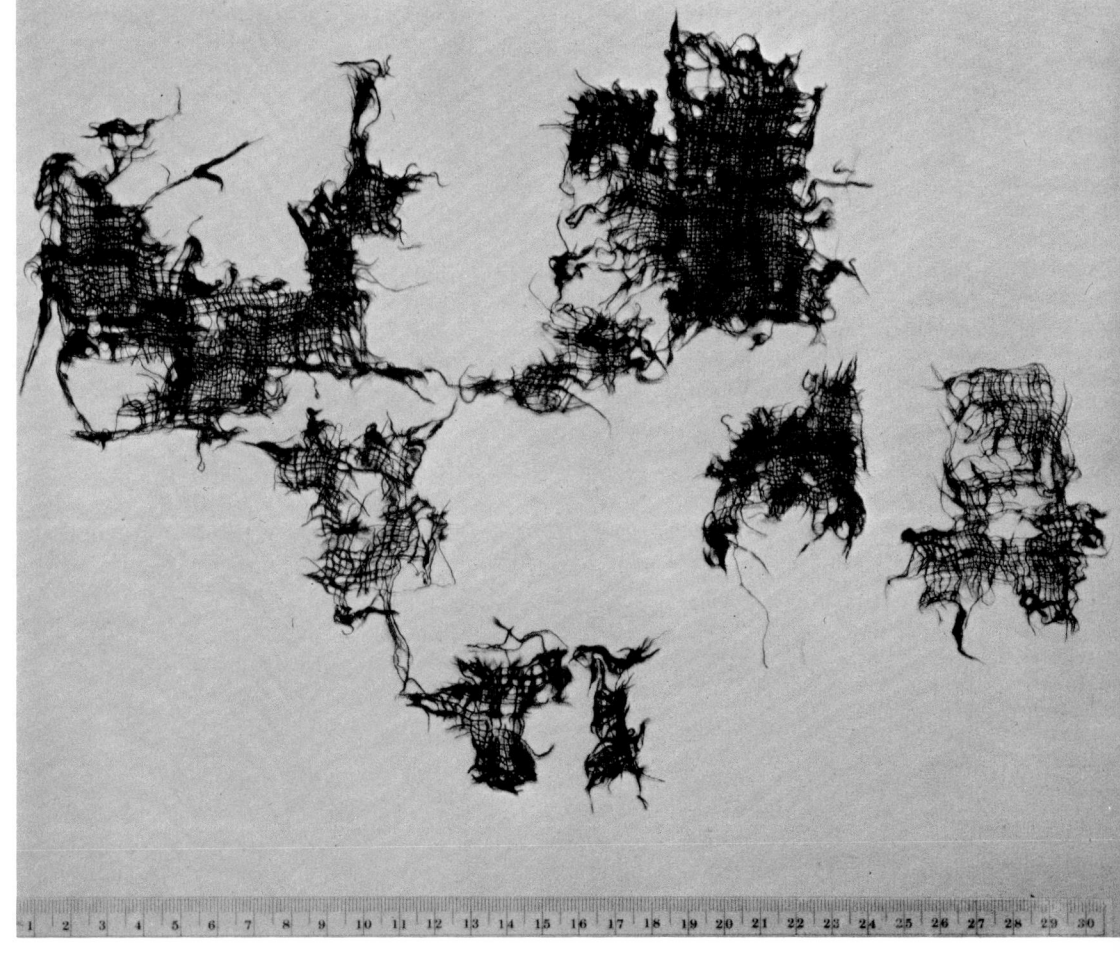

85

Grave Q 136   X-Group

Tumulus, shaft with single step and side-chamber,
  brick blocking
Burial: Disturbed
Body: Adult, female?
Objects, in burial chamber:
1.   Textiles (see entry below) 20326 A–F
2.   Fragment of leather
3.   Fragment of leather bag or garment
4.   Potsherds, including jug
5.   Beads
6.   Horn object

1A. Fragments of a Large Cover or Hanging

Material: Animal
Structure:
Weft-faced plain weave in purple, 8 warps per cm,
S-spun; 32 wefts per cm, S-spun; selvages present
Decoration:
Pattern of geometric and circular motifs with leaves
woven in weft-faced plain weave inserted through
discontinuous wefts in medium yellow or orange,*
32 wefts per cm, Z-spun; joining of various areas
carried out by either leaving slits or dovetailing;
decoration throughout in inlaid purple thread,
S-spun; sewing used in joining purple portions to
patterned area
Dimensions: (Detail): 32cm (warp) x 25cm (weft)
Remarks:
It is unusual that the medium yellow or orange weft
thread was spun in the Z-direction

* *Dye Analysis:* Orange—weld, purpurin (alizarin)

86

Grave Q 136

1B–C. Sheet Fragments (2 pieces)

Material: Animal
Structure:
Fragment a: Weft-faced plain weave in light brown,
10/13 warps per cm, S-spun; 35 wefts per cm, S-spun
Fragment b: Weft-faced plain weave in light brown,
9/10 warps per cm, S-spun; 38 wefts per cm, S-spun;
two selvages present stitched together with brown
thread, S-spun
Decoration:
Fragment a: At one end 2 weft shots in purple,
S-spun
Dimensions:
Fragment a: 66cm (warp) x 67cm (weft)
Fragment b: 25cm (warp) x 13cm (weft)

87

Grave Q 136

1D. Fragment

Material: Animal
Structure:
Plain weave in light brown, 7 warps per cm, S-spun;
11 wefts per cm, S-spun
Dimensions: 20cm (warp) x 16cm (weft)

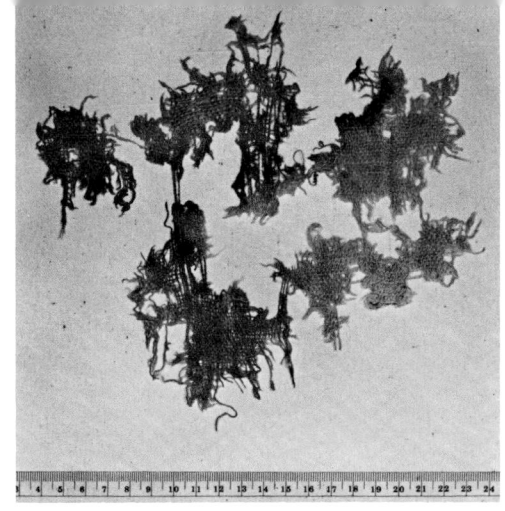

88

Grave Q 136

1E. Fragment

Material: Animal
Structure:
Plain weave in dark blue, 6 warps (?) per cm, S-spun;
8 wefts (?) per cm, S-spun
Dimensions: 15cm (warp) (?) x 16cm (weft) (?)

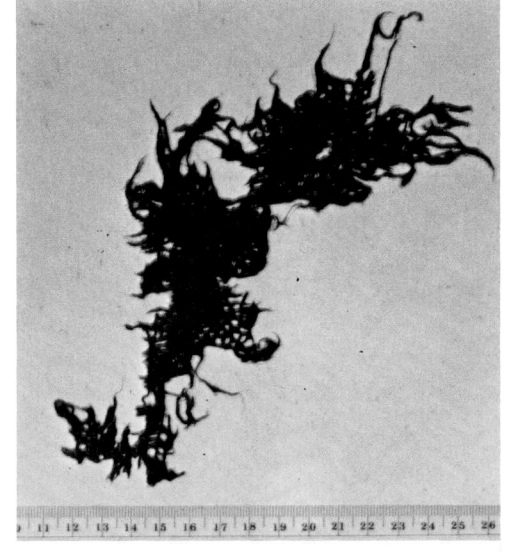

89

Grave Q 136

1F. Tape (2 pieces)

Material: Animal
Structure:
Warp-faced plain weave; 14 dark brown warps per
cm, S-spun; ca. 4 dark blue and brown (combined)
wefts per cm, S-spun
Decoration:
Checkerboard pattern in dark and light brown
Dimensions: All-over: 26cm x 2.5cm

90

Grave Q 137   X-Group

Shaft with side-chamber, brick blocking
Burial: Disturbed
Body: Adult, male?
Objects:
1. Ivory animal head
2. Textile (see entry below) 20285
3. Jar, 9. Contents
4. Jar
5. Animal bone
6. Beads
7. Stud
8. Arrowhead
10. Seeds

2. Edge of Sheet

Material: Animal
Structure:
Weft twining in yellow, brown and red
Dimensions: 4cm (warp) x 1.2cm (weft)

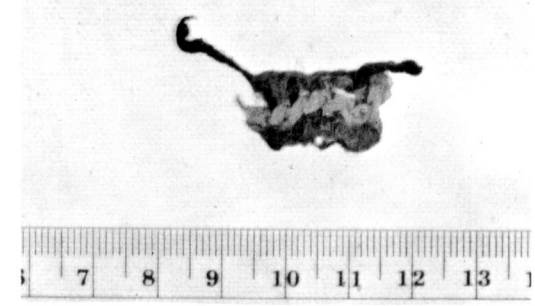

91

Grave Q 141   X-Group

Tumulus, shaft with vault built into the walls, no
   dromos
Burial: Head south, semicontracted on the left side
Body: Adult, female?
Objects:
1. Potsherds
2. Beads, strung, on top of shroud
3. Textiles (see entry below) 20305 A–D
4. Jar
5. Red and blue beads from neck of body
6. Two rings
7. Gut string

3A. Textile—Not available for study

3B. Sheet Fragments (9 pieces)

Material: Animal
Structure:
Plain weave in light brown, 11 warps per cm, S-spun;
17/19 wefts per cm, S-spun; selvages present
Decoration:
Two purple stripes in weft-faced plain weave,
S-spun, of 38 weft shots each, separated by light
brown area of 36.5cm; markings of two short, 1.5cm
long parallel running lines in three corners; in
purple, S-spun; upper and lower edges rolled and
crudely stitched
Dimensions: All-over: 159cm (warp) x 266cm (weft)
Remarks:
Two additional fragments (j and k) exist, both with
one stripe and a selvage of 34cm (warp) x 9cm (weft)
and 33cm (warp) x 10cm (weft). They must be from
another accompanying piece

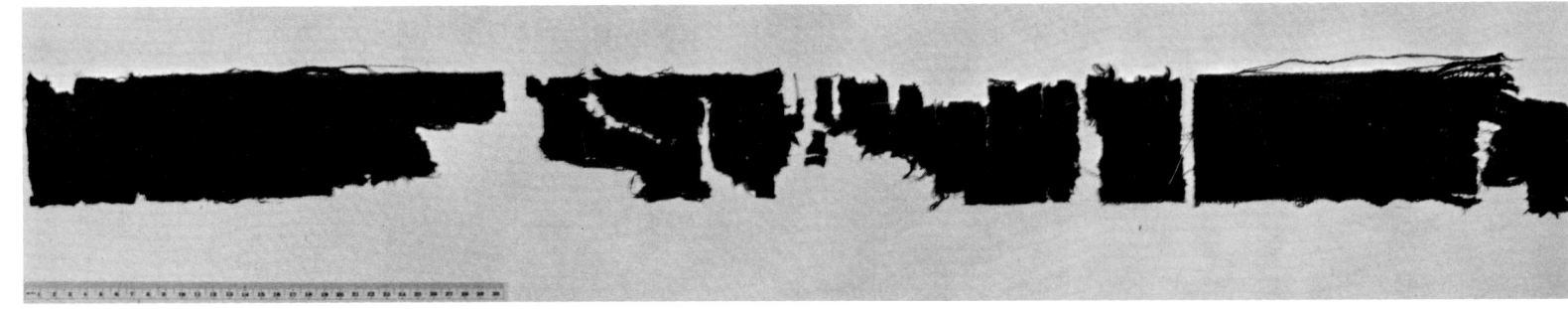

92

Grave Q 141

3C. Fragments (7 pieces)

Material: Animal in parts*
Structure:
Weft-faced plain weave in dark red,** 20 light brown linen warps per cm (double alternating with quadruple; individually counted), S-spun; 30/32 wefts per cm, S-spun; one selvage present
Dimensions: All-over: 9cm (warp) x 98cm (weft)

* *Fiber Analysis:* Warp—Linen; *Degradation:* Severe

** *Dye Analysis:* Red—purpurin (alizarin), iron

93

Grave Q 141

3D. Fragment

Material: Animal
Structure:
Braided string in red,* S-spun
Dimensions: 34cm in length
Remarks:
This string was probably used as an edging on a textile or fabric

* *Dye Analysis:* Red—purpurin (alizarin)

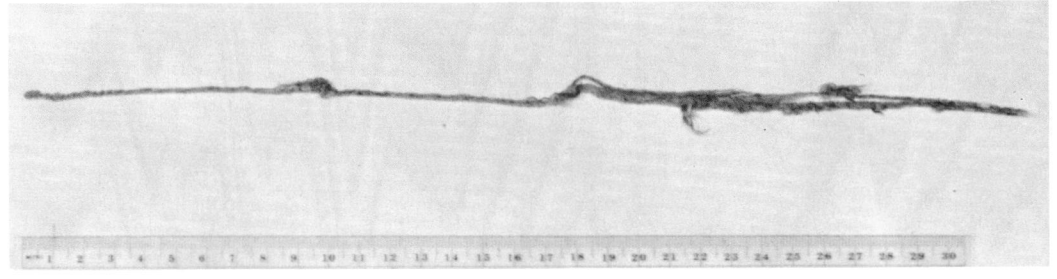

94

Grave Q 149   X-Group

Shaft, side-chamber with brick blocking
Burial:
Head west facing south, semicontracted on the left side, with hands before face
Body: Adult, female?
Objects:
a. In shaft:
1. Leather bag or garment
2. Quiver
3. Archer's loose near the top of the quiver
b. From the burial chamber:
4. Jar
5. Sandals on feet
6. Two rings, third finger of left hand
7. Beads
8. Bowstring?
9. Textiles (see entry below) 20382 A–E

9. Mantle Fragment

Material: Animal
Structure:
Plain weave in light brown, 11/12 warps per cm, S-spun; 10 wefts per cm, S-spun; one selvage present; badly stained
Decoration:
In one corner remnants of a notched "L" shape visible in purple inserted in weft-faced plain weave through discontinuous wefts and dovetailing; at one end warp threads worked into twisted cord (16cm present)
Dimensions: 220cm (warp) x 110cm (weft)

95

Grave Q 149

9B. Sheet (?) Fragments (9 pieces)

Material: Animal
Structure:
Plain weave in dark brown, 8/9 warps per cm,
S-spun; 16/17 wefts per cm, S-spun
Decoration:
5 weft shots in slightly darker brown, S-spun
Dimensions: All-over: 46cm (warp) x 56cm (weft)

96

Grave Q 149

9C. Sheet (?) Fragment

Material: Animal (?)
Structure:
Weft-faced plain weave in medium brown; 7/8
warps per cm, S-spun; 14/15 wefts per cm, S-spun;
(badly stained); one selvage present
Decoration:
Along selvage some overcast stitches in twisted
red wool thread, S-spun; occur in two places
Dimensions: 29.5cm (warp) x 23cm (weft)

97

Grave Q 149

9D. Cord Fragments

Material: Animal (?)
Structure:
Fragment a: 16 fiber strands twisted; in dark brown;
S-spun
Fragment b: several fiber strands twisted in red,
S-spun
Dimensions:
Fragment a: 19cm x 5cm
Fragment b: 3.4cm x .3cm

98

Grave Q 149

9E. Fragment

Material: Animal
Structure:
Plain weave in medium brown, 9 warps per cm,
S-spun; 14/15 wefts per cm, S-spun
Decoration:
Braided edging
Dimensions: 13.5cm (warp) x 3cm (weft)

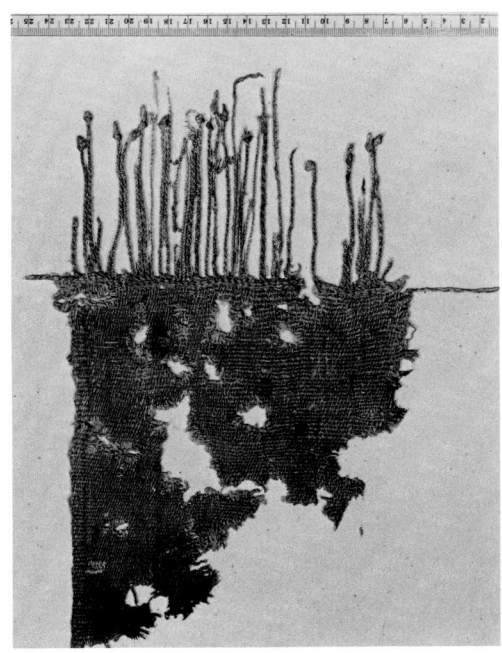

99

Grave Q 152   X-Group

"Emergency burial," mudbrick surrounding body,
   hole left for contracted feet; *rigor mortis?*
Burial: Undisturbed, almost on face, knees semicontracted, shroud
Body: Adult, male
Objects:
1. Textile (see entry below) 20518
2. Sandal
3. Silver anklet
4. Pot—ribbed jar, near head
5. Bow
6. Arrow
7. Beads

1. Fragment

Material: Animal
Structure:
Plain weave in white (off-white), 15 warps per cm,
S-spun; 5 wefts per cm, S-spun; one selvage present

Decoration:
Warp threads worked into twisted fringe of 9.5cm;
two rows of weft twining
Dimensions: 29cm (warp) x 32cm (weft)

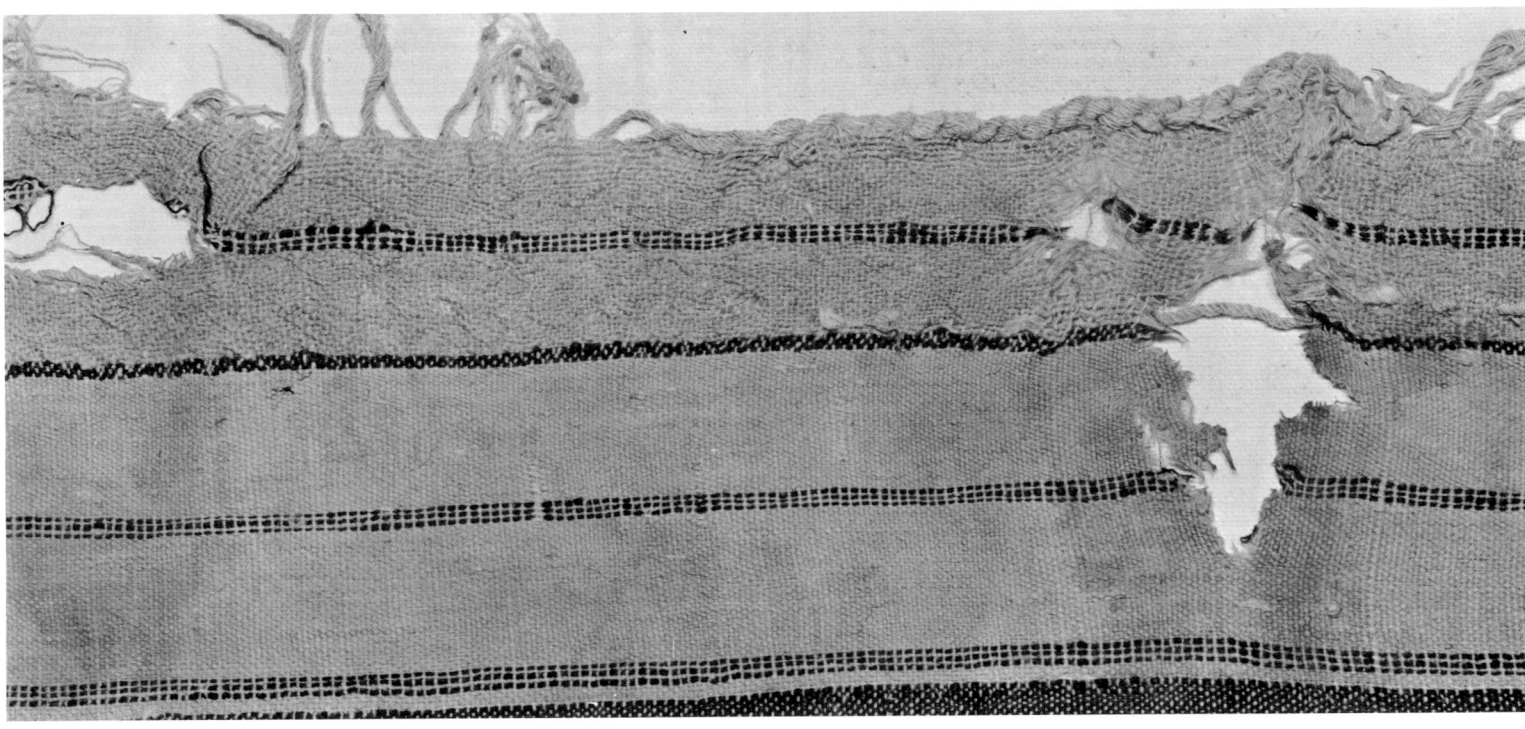

100

Grave Q 164   X-Group

Shaft with side-chamber, no blocking
Burial: Head east, semicontracted on the right side,
    shrouded
Body: Adult, female (definite)
Objects:
a. From shaft:
1. Wooden kohl stick
2. Wooden whorls
b. From burial chamber:
3, 7. Juglets
4, 8. Cup
5. Jar
9. Leather bag
10. Bronze bowl
11. Iron bracelet
12. Frog pendant
13. Iron kohl-stick
14. Carved ivory kohl tube
15. Cloth bag with kohl

16. Silver bracelet
17. Bead anklet
18. Leather sandals
19. Beads from bracelet and necklaces
20. Textiles (see entry below) 20456 A–D
21. Bronze fragment
22. Seed

1A and C. Tunic Fragments, Ties and Twisted Cord (5 pieces)

Material: Animal
Structure:
Plain weave in medium yellow, light brown, dark
blue and orange; warps light brown throughout;
10/12 warps per cm, S-spun; 14 medium yellow
wefts per cm, S-spun; 20 light brown wefts per cm,
S-spun; 23 dark blue wefts per cm, S-spun; 23
orange wefts per cm, S-spun
Fragment a: one selvage present
Fragment b: two selvages present

Fragment c: two selvages stitched together
Decoration:
Grouped stripes of medium yellow, light brown,
dark blue, light brown, orange, light brown, dark
blue, light brown, orange and light brown are
separated by three weft shots of dark blue alter-
nating with light brown; the stripes vary in width
from 1.5cm to 3cm; at one end grouped warp
threads of 6 each worked into twisted cord
Dimensions:
Fragment a: 49cm (warp) x 56cm (weft)
Fragment b: 24cm (warp) x 35cm (weft)
Fragment c: 24cm (warp) x 23cm (weft)
Fragment d: 13cm (warp) x 12.5cm (weft)
Fragment e: 13cm (warp) x 6cm (weft)

101

Grave Q 164

20B. Tunic or Sheet Fragments (2 pieces)

Material: Animal*
Structure:
Fragment a: weft-faced plain weave in light brown, 6/9 warps per cm, S-spun and dark blue, 48 wefts per cm, S-spun; left selvage present
Fragment b: weft-faced plain weave in light brown, 7/9 warps per cm, S-spun; 20/21 wefts per cm; S-spun; left selvage present
Decoration:
Fragment a: Weft-faced plain weave insert of 4 shots, S-spun
Dimensions:
Fragment a: 57cm (warp) x 58cm (weft)
Fragment b: 32cm (warp) x 17cm (weft)

* *Fiber Analysis:*
Brown—Wool, Sheep; *Degradation:* Slight
Blue—Wool, Sheep; *Degradation:* Slight

102

Grave Q 164

20D. Fragment

Material: Animal*
Structure:
Plain weave in medium brown,** 12 warps per cm, S-spun; 8 wefts per cm, S-spun; selvage present
Dimensions: 39cm (warp) x 47cm (weft)

* *Fiber Analysis:* Wool—Sheep; *Degradation:* Slight

** *Dye Analysis:* Brown—gallotanin, iron

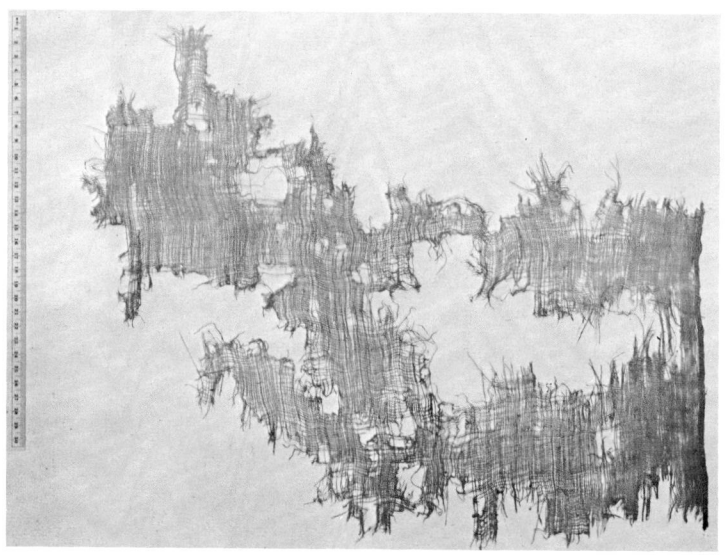

103

Grave Q 191   Late X-Group

Shaft with narrow side-chamber, mixed stone and
  brick blocking
Burials:
A. Head west, extended on back, arms removed
B. Disturbed
Bodies:
A. Mature, female
B. Mature, male?
Objects:
a. From shaft:
1. Stone with Meroitic text reused for blocking
2. Cup

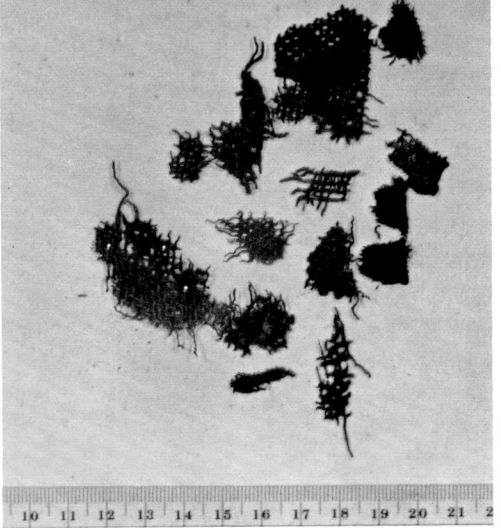

3. Potsherds
b. From intrusive burial B:
4. Textile (see entry below) 20508
c. From burial A:
5. Textile—Not available for study
6. Cup

4. Fragments (15 pieces)

Material: Animal
Structure:
Plain weave in medium brown, 7/8 warps per cm,
S-spun; 7/8 wefts per cm, S-spun
Dimensions: All-over: 12cm (warp) x 9cm (weft)

104

Grave Q 192   X-Group

Shaft and side-chamber, possibly small tumulus
Burial: Disturbed, head south, semicontracted on
right side
Body: Mature, female?
Objects:
a. From shaft:
1. Potsherds
b. From burial chamber:
2. Sandals
3. Jar
4. Textiles (see entry below) 20548 A–B
5. Beads and pendant

4A. Fragment

Material: Animal
Structure:
Weft-faced plain weave in medium brown, 12 warps
per cm, S-spun; 36 wefts per cm, S-spun
Decoration:
Stitching along all four edges
Dimensions: All-over: 17cm (warp) x 14cm (weft)

105

Grave 192

4B. Mantle (?) Fragments (9 pieces)

Material: Animal
Structure:
Plain weave in medium brown, 9 warps per cm,
S-spun; 14 wefts per cm, S-spun
Decoration:
Portions of notched "L" shape in weft-faced plain
weave in dark blue, 26 wefts per cm, S-spun; on
9 medium brown warps per cm, S-spun, inserted
through discontinuous wefts
Dimensions: All-over: 17cm (warp) x 16.5cm (weft)

Grave Q 230 X-Group

East-west shaft with end-chamber
Burials: Disturbed
Bodies:
a. In chamber:
A. Adult, female?
B. Mature, male?
C. Mature, male?
b. In shaft:
D. Mature, male?
E. Mature, male?
Objects:
a. From shaft:
1, 2, 4. Jars
3. Cup

b. From chamber:
5. Jug
6, 7. Cup
8. Ring, from body A
9. Earrings
10. Seed
c. From body D:
11. Traces of textiles (see entry below) 20554

11. Fragments (34 pieces)

Material: Vegetable (Cotton)
Structure:
Plain weave in medium to dark brown (stained),
9 warps per cm, S-spun; 13 wefts per cm, S-spun
Decoration:
Knotted or wrapped border terminating in fringe
Dimensions: 25cm (warp) x 32cm (weft)

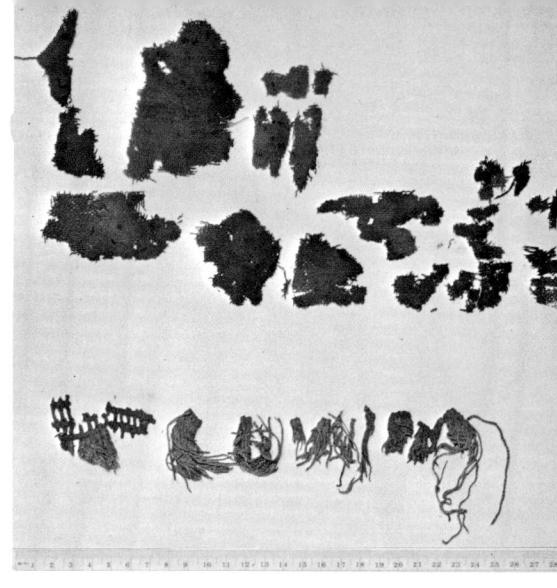

Grave Q 231 X-Group

Nearly rectangular shaft with end-chamber, brick
blocking
Burial: Head south? semicontracted?
Body: Child
Objects:
1. Textiles mixed with blocking (see entry below)
    20521 A–B
2. Neck of jar

1A. Garment or Tunic (?) Fragments (10 pieces)

Material: Animal
Structure:
Weft-faced plain weave in medium brown, 13 warps
per cm, S-spun; 56 wefts per cm, S-spun; selvages
present
Decoration:
Two widths of fabric (one with two selvages and
finished cord formed through twisted warp threads,
the other only fragmentary). Complete width
decorated at one end with two complete roundels of

6 cm diameter in weft-faced plain weave in purple,
inserted through discontinuous wefts and interlocking; ca. 50 wefts per cm, S-spun, with inlaid interior
decoration in light brown thread, S-spun; an additional third of a third roundel appears on the joined
incomplete width; needlework decoration in
medium yellow, blue and dark brown in same area
in parts covering the joined selvages of the two
fabric widths in back stitch, S-spun thread; two
widths joined through crude stitching
Dimensions: All-over: 182cm (warp) x 91cm (weft)

108

Grave 231

1B. Mantle

Material: Animal
Structure:
Very open plain weave (irregular) in light brown,*
8/9 warps per cm, S-spun; 4/5 wefts per cm, S-spun;
two selvages present
Decoration:
"H" markings at opposite ends of sheet in weft-
faced plain weave inserted with discontinuous wefts
and with occasional dovetailing, in purple,* 13 wefts
per cm, S-spun; markings on both sides 45cm apart;
on one side they occur in red, S-spun, on the other
side in purple, S-spun; in warp direction piece is
self-fringed at both ends 4 to 7 warps together
Dimensions: 175cm (warp) x 105cm (weft)

Dye Analysis:
Brown—tanin, iron
Purple—purpurin (alizarin), iron, gallotanin

109

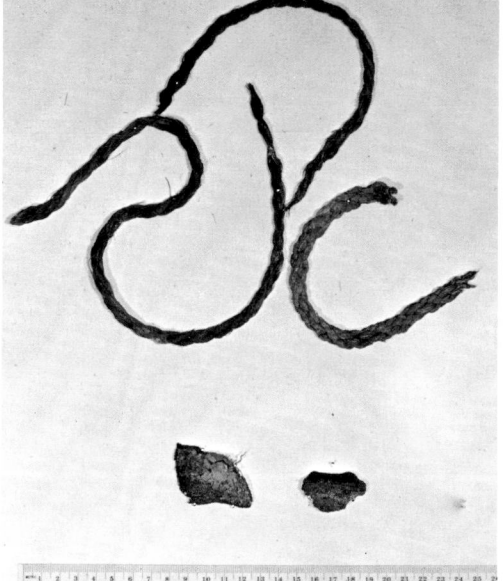

Grave Q 273   Late? X-Group?

Shaft with brick blocking taken from superstructure
  of Q 169
Burial: Head west, semicontracted on left side
Body: Juvenile, female
Objects:
1. Bead bracelet on right wrist
2. Textile (see entry below) 20588 A
3. Rope fragments (see entry below) 20588 B

2A. Fragments

Material: Animal

Construction:
Weft-faced plain weave encrusted and encased with
sand, showing in fragment b a portion of selvage
in red and green
Dimensions:
Fragment a: 5cm x 3cm
Fragment b: 3.5cm x 2.5cm

3B. Fragments

Material: Coarse grass or reed
Structure:
Twisted and braided cording
Dimensions: All-over: 23cm x 15cm

110

Grave Q 301   X-Group?*

Shaft with side chamber
Burials:
a. In chamber:
A. Head west, extended on back, left hand on
    pelvis, right on stomach
b. In shaft:
B. Extended, disturbed
C. Disturbed
D. Disturbed
Bodies:
A. Adult, female?
B. Adult, male
C. Mature—senile, female?
Objects:
a. In shaft:
1. Potsherds
2. Fragment of wood
b. In chamber:
3. Jar at east end of burial
4. Painted cup
5. Cord basket at head
6. Date pits and grape seeds in basket
7. Textile (see entry below) 20614

7. Mantle Fragments (3 pieces)

Material: Animal
Structure:
Plain weave in medium-dark brown, 11 warps per
cm, S-spun; 22 wefts per cm, S-spun; occasionally
uneven weave with irregular double wefts (counted
individually)
Decoration:
One fragment shows portion of rectangular notched
shape in purple, weft-faced plain weave, inserted
through discontinuous wefts and interlocking; 38
wefts per cm, S-spun; one area badly stitched
Dimensions: 60cm (warp) x 44cm (weft)

* The tomb contained a Meroitic painted cup,
which is suspected of having been reused

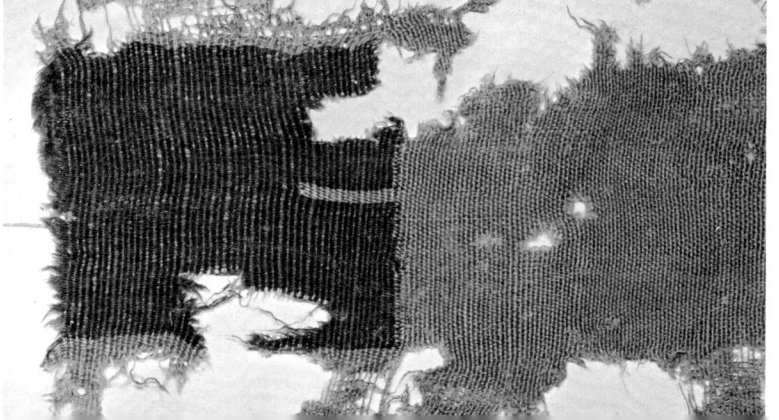

111

Grave Q 321 X-Group

Small shaft with side-chamber
Burial: Head south, semicontracted on the right side
Body: Mature, female?
Objects:
1. Cup
2. Jar—(qadus)
3. Textiles around pelvis (see entry below)
   20818 A–C

3A. Sheet or Tunic (?) Fragments (3 pieces)

Material: Animal
Structure:
Plain weave in shades of dark brown* (uneven coloration throughout), 9/12 warps per cm, S-spun; 6/7 wefts per cm, S-spun; badly stained
Decoration:
Finished on both sides by working warp threads into countered weft twining at both ends in brown and yellow; area with crude repair stitching present
Dimensions: All-over: 84cm (warp) x 126cm (weft)

Dye Analysis: Brown—gallotanin, iron

112

Grave Q 321

3B. Sheet Fragment

Material: Animal
Structure:
Open and irregular plain weave in medium grey, 5/7 warps per cm, S-spun; 7/10 wefts per cm, S-spun
Dimensions: 126cm (warp) x 52cm (weft)

113

Grave Q 321

3C. Garment or Sheet (?) Fragments (4 pieces)

Material: Animal*
Structure:
Plain weave in dark brown (very uneven); difficult
to determine warp and weft direction due to extensive patching and layering; estimated count: 6/11
warps per cm, S-spun; 12/13 wefts per cm, S-spun
Decoration:
None except crude layering and stitching throughout
Dimensions:
Fragment a: 86cm (warp) x 64cm (weft)
Fragment b: 62cm (warp) x 49cm (weft)
Fragment c: 44cm (warp) x 20cm (weft)
Fragment d: 33cm (warp) x 23cm (weft)

* *Fiber Analysis:* Wool—Camel; *Degradation:* None

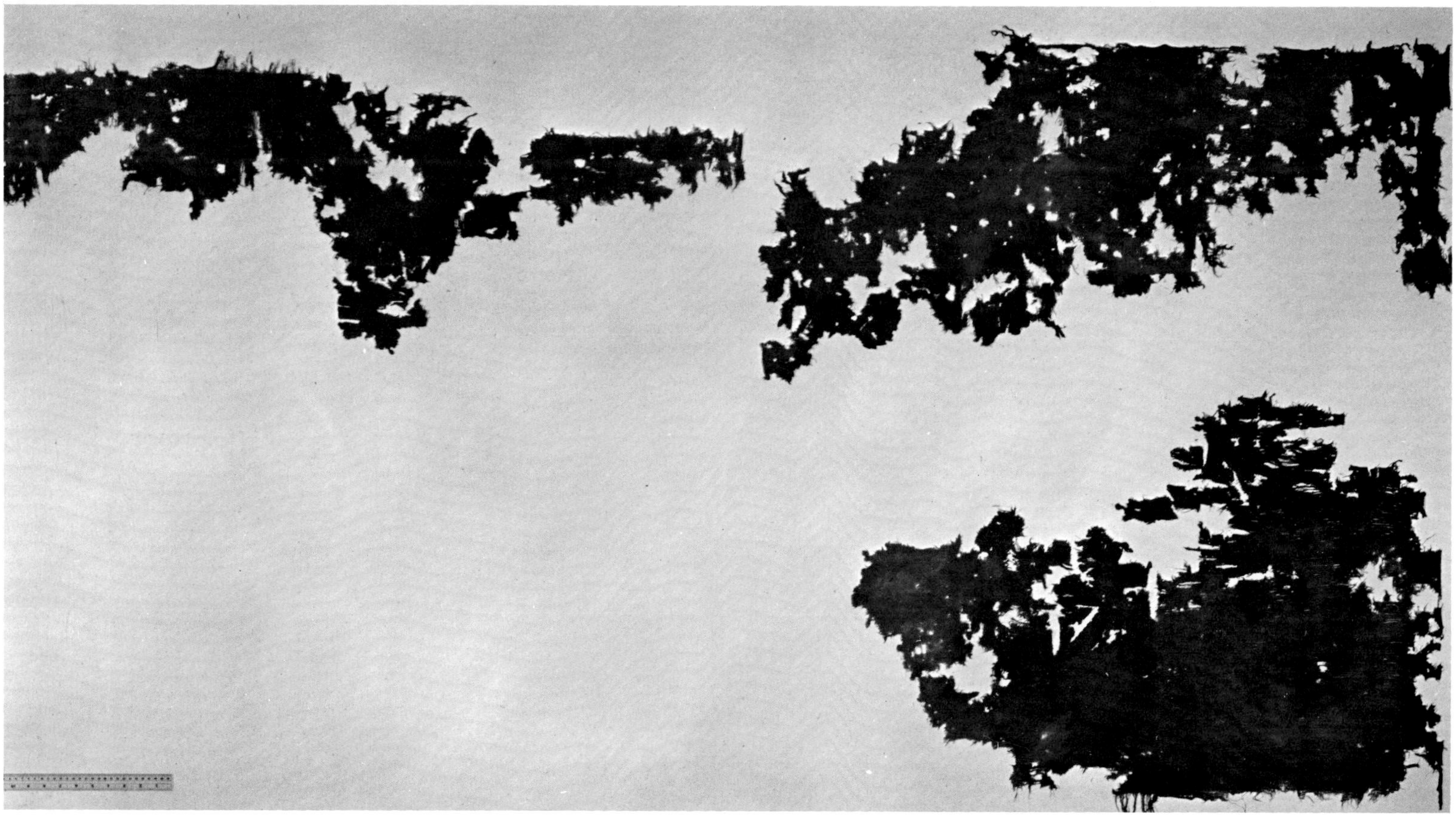

114

Grave Q 325   X-Group?

Shaft and side-chamber
Burial: Disturbed
Body: Mature, female?
Objects:
a. From shaft:
1. Potsherds
2. Leaves
3. Textiles (see entry below) 20817
6. Beads
b. From chamber:
4. Arrowhead
5. Remains of wood

3. Tunic Fragments (4 pieces)

Material: Animal
Structure:
Weft-faced plain weave in medium brown, 8 warps
per cm, S-spun; 36 wefts per cm, S-spun; selvages
present including two for neck opening
Decoration:
Narrow stripe in weft direction of 2/3 shots in
purple, S-spun; warp threads worked into twisted
cord at both ends
Dimensions: All-over: 122cm (warp) x 234cm (weft)

115

Grave Q 332   X-Group

Shaft and end-chamber
Burial: Head south, semicontracted on left side
Body: Juvenile
Objects:
a. From shaft:
1. Sherd (qadus)
b. From chamber:
2. Large carnelian bead
3. Jar
4. Beads
5. Textiles (see entry below) 20812 A–D
6. Ring

5A. Carpet (7 pieces)

Material: Animal
Structure:
Groupings of 3 wefts in light brown* and light red,*
Z-spun; 9 wefts per cm (individually counted), held
in place by two Z-spun S-plied warps in light brown,
7 warps per cm; finishing edges at all four sides of
carpet; warp ends terminate in plied fringes
Decoration:
Design of center field is formed by introducing
slip loops inserted after 2 weft groupings of 3 weft
shots each, in light green,* interspersed with abstract
floral shapes in red; center field of carpet is set
off by two double borders of which outer border
shows running key motif; all design elements are
formed through slip loops with short pile in blue,*
red,* green,* yellow, light and dark brown,* orange,
off-white and green;* in some places loops are
uncut
Dimensions: All-over: 196cm (warp) x 112cm (weft)

Dye Analysis:
Red—purpurin (alizarin), gallotanin
Pink—purpurin (alizarin), iron
Brown—purpurin (alizarin), gallotanin
Blue—indigo, (weld)
Green—weld, iron, gallotanin

116

Grave Q 332

5B. Tunic (?) Fragment

Material: Animal
Structure:
Weft-faced plain weave; 7/8 medium brown* warps
per cm, S-spun; 30 wefts per cm in dark blue,*
S-spun
Decoration:
Narrow stripe of red* of 6 weft shots, S-spun; crude
stitching
Dimensions: 21cm (warp) x 24cm (weft)

Dye Analysis:
Beige—tanin, iron
Red—gallotanin
Blue-Green—gallotanin

113

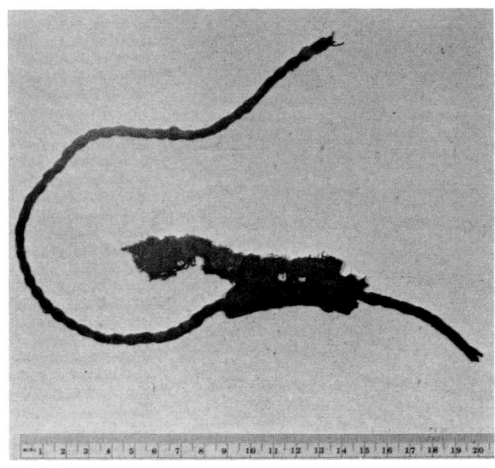

117

Grave Q 332

5C. Fragment

Material: Animal
Structure:
Weft-faced plain weave in dark brown, 9 warps per cm, S-spun; 24 wefts per cm, S-spun
Decoration:
Twisted cord
Dimensions: 5cm (warp) x 40cm (weft)

118

Grave Q 332

5D. Fragments (10 pieces)

Material: Animal
Structure:
Weft-faced plain weave in light brown, dark green, red and blue, 12 warps per cm, S-spun; 40 wefts per cm, S-spun; selvage remnants present
Dimensions: All-over: 16.5cm (warp) x 15.3cm (weft)

119

Grave Q 334   X-Group*

Shaft and side-chamber, stone, brick and mud
  blocking
Burial:
A. Head west, extended on back, disturbed
B.   Disturbed
Body:
A. Adult
B. Mature
Objects:
a. From shaft:
1. Potsherds
b. From plunderer's passage:
2, 3. Fine Meroitic cups
4. Textile (see entry below) 20852
5. Sherds of pot, part found in shaft

* Cups 2 and 3 appear to be reused plunderer's tools

4. Tunic (?) Fragments (4 pieces)

Material: Animal*
Structure:
Plain weave in dark brown, 8/9 warps per cm, S-spun; 7 wefts per cm, S-spun
Fragment a: one selvage present and finished edge
of warps worked into twisted cord
Decoration:
Fragments of a and b: narrow red stripe of 12/13 weft shots each; additional 2/4 weft shots in red and countered weft twining in red and yellow, green and yellow and green and red
Fragment b: twisted warp threads in groups of 3 at one end
Fragment c: decorated with both wider and narrower red stripe, tiny tassels along a double selvage edge and one finishing edge of grouped warps worked into twisted cord
Fragment d: finished edge of grouped warps worked into twisted cord
Dimensions:
Fragment a: 40cm (warp) x 56cm (weft)
Fragment b: 22cm (warp) x 23cm (weft)
Fragment c: 32cm (warp) x 42 cm (weft)
Fragment d: 8cm (warp) x 22 cm (weft)
Remarks:
Fragment c is in parts double. The two layers are not stitched together but fragment seems to have been shaped during weaving process

* *Fiber Analysis:* Wool—probably Camel
Degradation: Severe

120

Grave Q 338   X-Group

Tumulus?, shaft and side-chamber, stone blocking
Burial: Head south, semicontracted on right side
Body: Infant
Objects, from chamber:
1. Small lamp
2. Bowl
3. Jar
4. Textiles (see entry below) 20815 A–B
5. Bead necklace
6. String of beads at foot used to fasten textile
7. Bead bracelets
8. Pendants

4A. Sheet Fragments (2 pieces stitched together)

Material: Animal
Structure:
Plain weave in light brown (irregular in coloring
throughout), 7/8 warps per cm, S-spun; 5/9 wefts
per cm, S-spun; selvages present on both halves
Decoration:
Warp stripe of 12/14cm in weft direction in
irregularly brown colored threads in both sections
of piece appears reversed in final arrangement
of sheet as it was cut and then reattached
through coarse stitching in yellow thread; one half
shows stripe of 10 weft shots in green, 1cm wide,
S-spun; two green markings at both selvages on one
half; two stitched repairs
Dimensions: All-over: 167cm (warp) x 124cm (weft)

121

Grave Q 338

4B. Child's Tunic Fragment

Material: Animal*
Structure:
Weft-faced plain weave in varying shades of
medium brown, 6/7 warps per cm, S-spun; 13 wefts
per cm, S-spun; selvages present including those
needed for neck opening
Decoration:
Two weft-faced plain weave stripes of 1.5cm are
present 19cm apart; in addition, 3 rows of countered weft twining in red and green as well as light
red and yellow
Dimensions: 49cm (warp) x 84cm (weft)

Fiber Analysis: Mixture of Coarse Camel and
Sheep (?); *Degradation:* Severe

122

Grave Q 345   X-Group

Shaft with two side-chambers, one on south
   filled in and covered with brick, north one
   covered with stones
Burial: Head west, semicontracted on left side
Body: Adult, male
Objects:
a. From shaft:
1. Fragment of stone offering table
2. Potsherds
6. Lamp
b. From chamber or blocking:
3. Meroitic stela reused as blocking
4. Beads
5. Leather strap
7. Leather cord fragment
8. Textile—Discarded
9. Jar
10. Bowstring
11. Sandals on feet
12. Textile (see entry below) 20966
13. Archer's loose
14. Two arrowheads
c. From south burial chamber:
15. Textile fragment (see entry below) 20962
16. Beads

12. Sheet or Tunic (?) Fragments (3 pieces)

Material: Animal
Structure:
Plain weave in light brown, 7 warps per cm, S-spun;
15 wefts per cm, S-spun
Decoration:
Fragment a: two narrow stripes in medium brown
of 4 weft shots each, separated by light brown
stripe of 5 weft shots
Fragment c: three narrow stripes of medium brown
of 7/8 weft shots each, separated by light brown
stripe of 9 weft shots
Repeated in *Fragment b*
Dimensions: All-over: 48.5cm (warp) x 44cm (weft)

123

Grave Q 345

15. Portions from a Sheet or Tunic used to make Tying Tapes (2 pieces)

Material: Animal
Structure:
Weft-faced plain weave in purple,* 11 warps per cm, S-spun, in dark brown; 41 wefts per cm, S-spun; selvages present at one end (warp direction) on both pieces
Dimensions:
Fragment a: 9.5cm (warp) x 83.5cm (weft)
Fragment b: 9.5cm (warp) x 63cm (weft)

* *Dye Analysis:* Red—purpurin (alizarin), iron

124

Grave Q 350   X-Group

Tumulus, shaft and side-chamber, brick blocking
Burial: Head south, semicontracted, face down, knees bent, so that feet required special niche to be dug, *rigor mortis?*
Body: Adult, male
Objects:
a. From shaft:
1. Sealed jar
2. Wooden container with beads and seeds
4. Leather sandals
b. From burial chamber:
5. Beads
6. Textiles (see entry below) 20919 A–E
7. Pendant
8. Bead-bracelet on right arm
9. Juglet
10. Two rings
11. Bead necklaces
12. Textile—Discarded
13. Beads

6A and C. Belt or Sash (3 pieces)

Material: Animal
Structure:
Fragments a and b: Weft-faced plain weave in shades of dark brown,* 6/8 warps per cm, S-spun; 17/18 wefts per cm, S-spun; selvages present
Decoration:
Twisted weft threads at one end with tassels and three beads, two with light blue glaze, one with white glaze; weaving uneven and striated in shades of dark brown; countered weft twining in yellow
Dimensions:
Fragment a: 12cm (warp) x 41cm (weft)
Fragment b: 13.5cm (warp) x 33cm (weft)
Fragment c: 2cm (warp) x 20cm (weft)

* *Dye Analysis:* Brown—tannin, iron

125

Grave Q 350

6B. Tunic (?) Fragments (2 pieces)

Material: Animal*
Structure:
Fragment a: Weft-faced plain weave in medium brown; 6/8 warps per cm, S-spun; 25/26 wefts per cm, S-spun; left and right selvages present
Fragment b: Portion of sleeve (?); weft-faced plain weave, 10 warps per cm, S-spun; 20 wefts per cm, S-spun; left and right selvages present

Decoration:
Fragment a: Along parts of left selvage in red** over first 5 warps small pattern formed through slits; 1cm of weft-faced plain weave insertion along that same selvage, part of damaged area and at lower center portion of fabric embroidered motif; both in red
Fragment b: Twisted cord incorporating warp threads; extended on one side while some terminate in fringe; red and yellow countered weft twining along heading which is incorporated at one end of twisted cord; three weft stripes of varying widths of 4, 5 and 32 shots in red forming decorative design; widest stripe's pattern is formed by wrapping every 6th warp
Dimensions: 37cm (warp) x 26cm (weft)

* *Fiber Analysis:*
Wool—Camel; *Degradation:* None
Wool—Camel (CIBA no. 5)

** *Dye Analysis:*
Red—purpurin (alizarin)
Brown—gallotanin

126

Grave Q 350

6D. Fragment

Material: Vegetable (Cotton)
Structure:
Plain weave in dark brown, 10/11 warps per cm, S-spun; 11 wefts per cm, S-spun
Decoration:
Plaited or twisted threads worked into geometric design
Dimensions: 4cm (warp) x 12.5cm (weft)

127

Grave 350

6E. Tunic (?) Fragments (3 pieces)

Material: Animal
Structure:
Weft-faced plain weave in off-white 5/6 warps
per cm, S-spun; 11 wefts per cm, S-spun
Fragment c: with repaired section and section of
selvage

Decoration:
Stripes in purple, 22 wefts per cm, S-spun (sometimes double wefts, counted individually), set off by
stripes in medium brown, 32 wefts per cm, S-spun;
separated by narrow stripes of red (Fragments a, b
and c) and green (Fragment b), 3 weft shots each
time
Dimensions:
Fragment a: 28cm (warp) x 53cm (weft)
Fragment b: 26cm (warp) x 18cm (weft)
Fragment c: 22cm (warp) x 22cm (weft)

128

Grave Q 356   X-Group

Tumulus?, shaft and side-chamber with stone
    blocking? with brick weight above
Burial: Disturbed
Body: Child
Objects:
a.   From shaft:
1.   Lock of brown hair
2.   Leaves
b.   From chamber:
3.   Jug
4.   Painted bowl or cup with date pits (5)
6.   Textiles (see entry below) 20947 A–C
7.   Beads

6A. Fragment

Material: Animal
Structure:
Plain weave in medium brown,* 7 warps per cm,
S-spun; 9 wefts per cm, S-spun
Dimensions: 22cm (warp) x 23cm (weft)

* *Dye Analysis:* Brown—orlean?, iron

129

Grave Q 356

6B. Fragments (3 pieces)

Material: Animal
Structure:
Weft-faced plain weave in two shades of dark
brown (the darker of the two browns may have
been originally purple); 12 warps per cm, S-spun; 42
wefts per cm, S-spun
Decoration:
The fragments are slightly shaped and give
appearance of having originally been part of a
medallion; small-scaled intertwining "S" design
inlaid in lighter brown thread against darker color
Dimensions: All-over: 11.5cm (warp) x 11cm (weft)

119

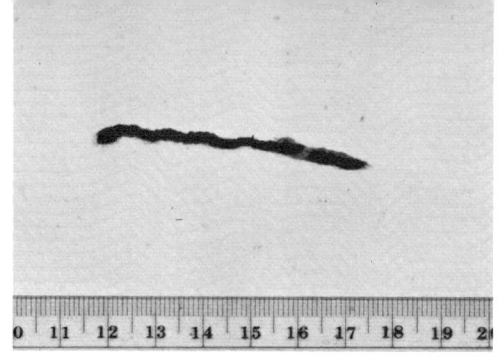

130

Grave Q 356

6C. Fragment

Material: Animal
Structure:
Twisted cord of dark and light brown fiber
Dimensions: 6cm x 0.3cm

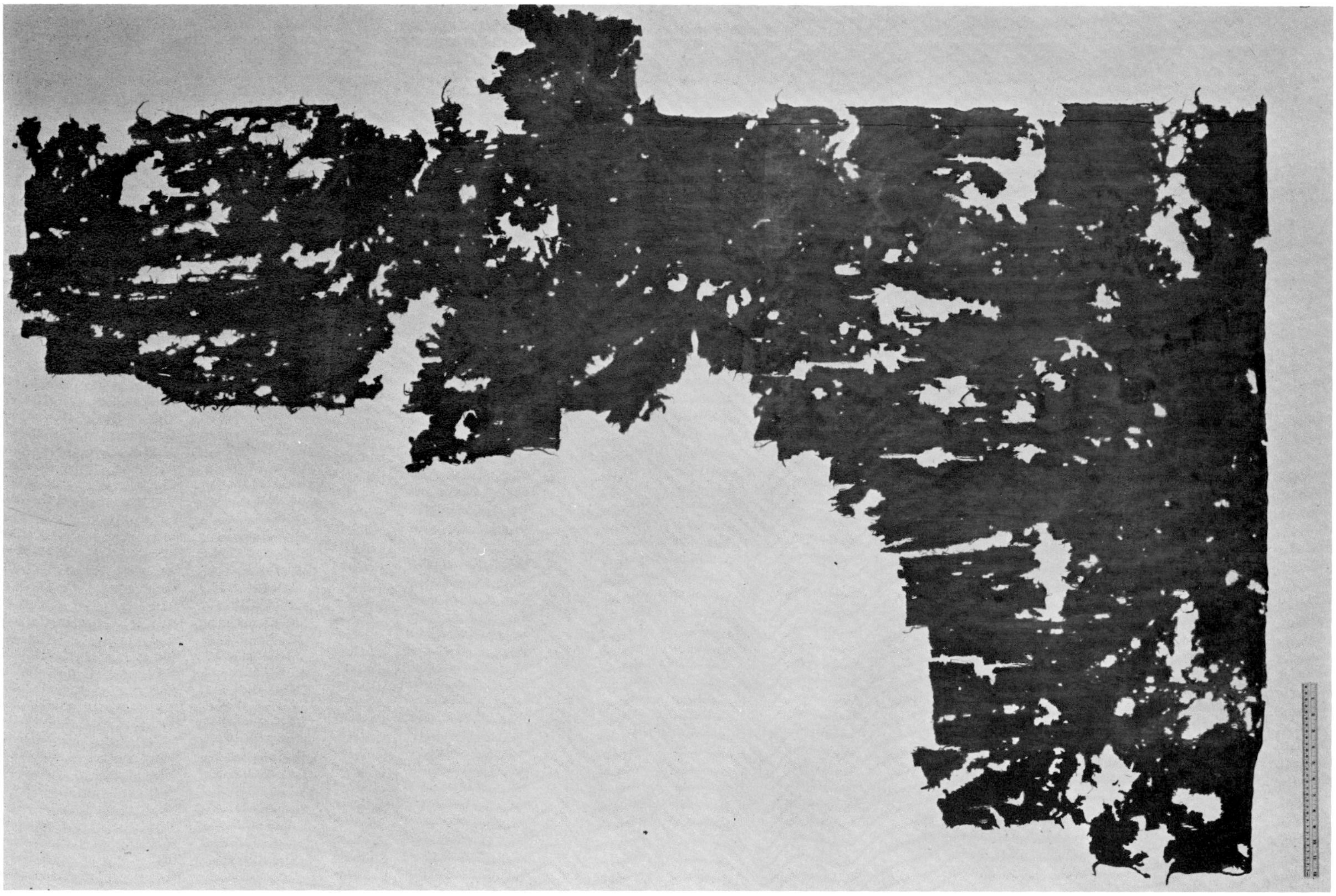

131

Grave Q 378   Meroitic Tomb, X-Group Burial

Rectangular brick superstructure, shaft and side-
chamber blocked with stone, brick and mud
Burials:
A. Broken up in shaft
B. Head east, semicontracted on left side, wrapped
   in several layers of cloth
Bodies:
A. Adult, male?
B. Adult, male
Objects:
a. From shaft, associated with burial A:
1, 2. Incomplete stela, reused
3. Broken *ba* statue below first stela
4. Sherds of painted Meroitic cup
5. Sherds
b. From chamber:
6. Textile (see entry below) 21234
7. Textile (see entry below) 21281
8. Remains of bow
9. Remains of basket
10. Jar
11. Iron spearhead
12. Four arrows

13. Arrow-feathers
14. Bracelet on right wrist
15. Bead necklace
16. Anklet of string and feathers
17. Pair of sandals

6. Tunic Fragment

Material: Animal*
Structure:
Weft-faced plain weave in light brown, 11 warps
per cm, S-spun; 28 wefts per cm, S-spun; selvages
present
Decoration:
At top and bottom of fragment narrow stripes of
purple occur, 3 weft shots each; run entire width of
fragment with exception of sleeve area; stripe occurs
once 2cm and once 2.5cm in from finished edge;
weft twining terminating in cords appear twice;
warp threads worked into twisted cord on one side
in weft direction; rolled edge with crude stitching
on other side
Dimensions: All-over: 238cm (warp) x 205.5cm
(weft)
* *Fiber Analysis:* Wool—Sheep; *Degradation:*
Moderate

132

Grave Q 378

7. Tunic Sleeve Fragment

Material: Animal
Structure:
Weft-faced plain weave in medium brown, 14 warps
per cm, S-spun; 33 wefts per cm, S-spun; selvages
present
Decoration:
Centered in lower portion of fragment two stripes
of 3/3.4cm in widths respectively inserted through
dovetailing in weft-faced plain weave with discontinuous wefts, 35 wefts per cm, S-spun; warp
threads worked into twisted cord along edge
Dimensions: 31cm (warp) x 29cm (weft)

133

Grave Q 387   X-Group

Tumulus?, shaft with side-chamber, mudbrick
   blocking
Burial: Disturbed, head east, semicontracted
Body: A. Male
Objects:
a.   From chamber:
1.   Textiles (see entry below) 20968 A–B
2.   Ring, iron?, on second toe of left foot
b.   From shaft:
3.   Sherds, cup
4.   Basket

1A. Sheet or Tunic (?) Fragments (2 pieces)

Material: Animal
Structure:
Plain weave in dark brown,* 7 warps per cm, S-spun;
10 dark brown wefts per cm; selvages present; sewn
and repaired areas
Dimensions: 58cm (warp) x 53cm (weft)

* *Dye Analysis:* Brown—tanin, iron

134

Grave Q 387

1B. Fragment

Material: Animal
Structure:
Plain weave in medium brown, 10 warps per cm,
S-spun; 8 wefts per cm, S-spun
Dimensions: 48cm (warp) x 12cm (weft)

135

Grave Q 388   X-Group

Tumulus?, shaft and side-chamber
Burial: Disturbed, head south, contracted on right side
Body: Juvenile
Objects:
1. Date pits
2. Textiles (see entry below) 20969
3. Beads
4. Cup
5. Jug

2. Sheet Fragments (3 pieces)

Material: Animal
Structure:
Plain weave in medium brown, 8 warps per cm, S-spun; 7/9 wefts per cm, S-spun
Decoration:
Fragment b and c: with traces of green* stripe, 9 weft shots each, S-spun
Fragment b: warp threads worked into twisted cord
Dimensions: All-over: 45.5cm (warp) x 36cm (weft)

* *Dye Analysis:* Green—weld, iron

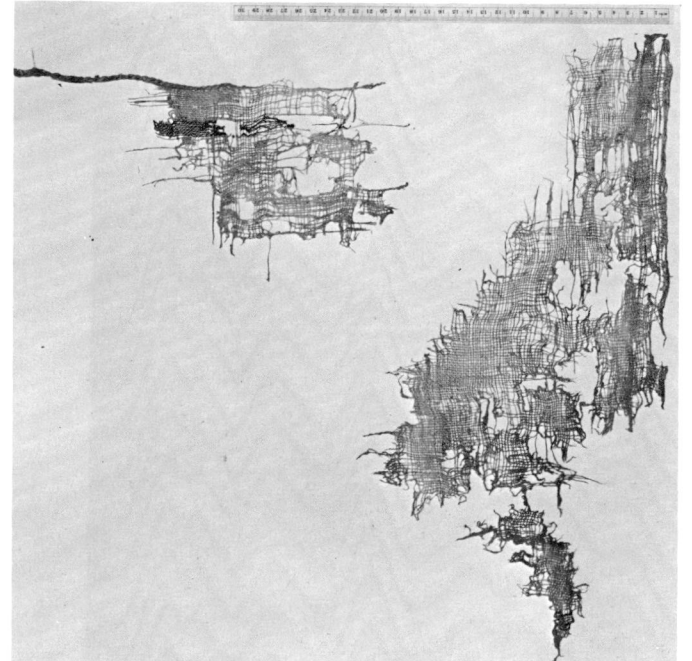

136

Grave Q 390   X-Group

Tumulus, shaft with brick vault built into walls
Burial: Disturbed
Body: Mature, male?
Objects:
a. From shaft:
1. Potsherds
b. From chamber:
2. Textile (see entry below) 21232
3. Sherds
4. Cup

2. Mantle Fragment

Material: Animal
Structure:
Weft-faced plain weave in dark brown, 7/9 warps per cm, S-spun; 14 wefts per cm, S-spun; one selvage present
Decoration:
Portions of two large notched "L" shapes in red in weft-faced plain weave, 22 wefts per cm, S-spun on dark brown warps, with two small areas in light brown (filling in two notched openings), inserted through discontinuous wefts and interlocking, 18 wefts per cm, S-spun on dark brown warps; warp threads worked into twisted cord
Dimensions: 146cm (warp) x 200cm (weft)

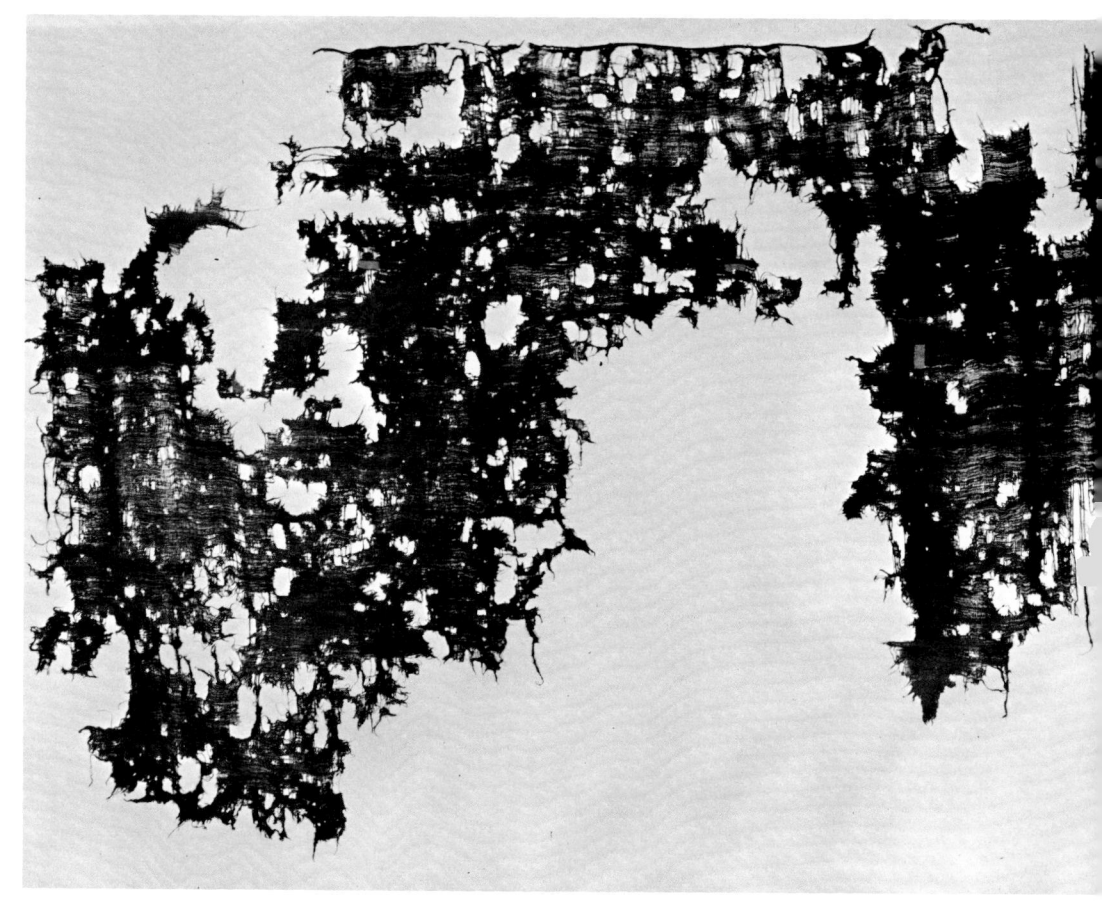

137

Grave Q 393   X-Group

Tumulus, shaft with side-chamber
Burial: Disturbed, head south, semicontracted on
left side
Body: Adult, female?
Objects:
a. From shaft:
1. Sherd
b. From chamber:
2. Textile (see entry below) 21237
3. Jug handle

2. Mantle Fragments (3 pieces)

Material: Animal
Structure:
Plain weave in medium brown, 10 warps per cm,
S-spun; 13/14 wefts per cm, S-spun; one selvage
present
Decoration:
Portion of a large notched "L" shape in weft-faced
plain weave, inserted through discontinuous wefts
and interlocking, in dark blue, 28 wefts per cm,
S-spun on medium brown warps
Dimensions: All-over: 42cm (warp) x 34cm (weft)

138

Grave Q 394   X-Group

Tumulus?, shaft and side-chamber with brick
blocking
Burial: Disturbed, head south, right side, semicontracted
Body: Adult, male?
Objects:
a. In shaft:
1. Potsherds
2. Textile—Discarded
3. Leather fragments
4. Loaves (and in burial chamber)
b. From burial chamber:
5. Textile 21233—Not available for study;
Totally disintegrated
6. Sandal strips
7. Jar *(qadus)*

139

Grave Q 422   Late? X-Group

Tumulus?, shaft and side-chamber (E–W), brick
blocking
Burial: Disturbed, head west, semicontracted on
right side, 1 and 2 on back
Body: Mature, male
Objects:
a.   In shaft:
1.   Two sherds
2.   Leather fragments
b.   In chamber:
3.   Textiles (see entry below) 21230 A–B

3A. Mantle Fragments

Material: Animal
Structure:
Plain weave in light brown,* 9 warps per cm,
S-spun; 8/9 wefts per cm, S-spun; selvages present
Decoration:
Four notched rectangles, two at both ends, weft-
faced plain weave in red, inserted through discon-
tinuous wefts and dovetailing, 20 wefts per cm,
S-spun; two of these inserts are nearly complete; the
other two are only fragmentary; warp threads
worked into twisted cord at one end
Dimensions: All-over: 220cm (warp) x 134cm (weft)

* *Dye Analysis:* Brown—tanin, iron

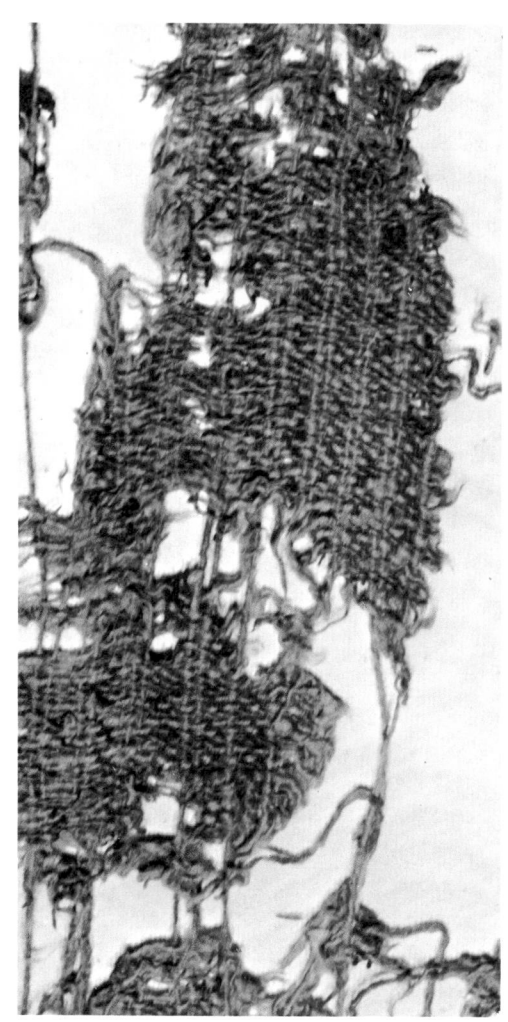

140

3B. Sheet (?) Fragments (3 pieces)

Material: Animal*
Structure:
Plain weave in light brown, 7/8 warps per cm,
S-spun; 11/13 wefts per cm, S-spun; selvage present
Decoration:
Uneven weave produces striated effect in warp
direction of alternating two lighter and two darker
colors; near one selvage narrow paired stripes in
green appear, of 6 weft shots each, separated by
four light brown weft shots
Dimensions: All-over: 76cm (warp) x 73cm (weft)

* *Fiber Analysis:* Wool—Camel; *Degradation:* Slight

141

Grave Q 479   X-Group

Tumulus?, shaft with side-chamber
Burial: Head south, semicontracted on right side
Body: Child
Objects:
1. Jar *(qadus)*
2. Textile (see entry below) 21487

2. Sheet or Tunic (?) Fragments (3 pieces)

Material: Animal
Structure:
Plain weave in a variety of shades of brown,*
8/11 warps per cm, S-spun; 6/7 wefts per cm,
S-spun; uneven weaving; (where sewing occurs
fragment is double)
Dimensions: All-over: 88cm (warp) x 55cm (weft)

* *Dye Analysis:*
Brown$_1$—purpurin (alızarin);
Brown$_2$—tanin, iron

142

Grave Q 501   X-Group

Tumulus, shaft and side-chamber
Burial: Disturbed
Body: Juvenile, female?
Objects:
a. In shaft:
1. Jar
2. Cup
3. Sandal
b. In chamber:
4. Beads
5. Silver ring
6. Pair of sandals
7. Textile (see entry below) 21646
8. Potsherds
9. Sandal sole

7. Fragments (9 pieces)

Material: Animal*
Structure:
Plain weave in dark blue and red, of double warps,
14 per cm, S-spun; single wefts, 8 per cm, S-spun;
selvage
Decoration:
Six weft shots in red, S-spun; other areas show
traces of an unidentifiable design in yellow, red,
blue and green
Dimensions: All-over: 35cm (warp) x 29cm (weft)

* *Fiber Analysis:* Dark Blue—Wool, probably Sheep
   Red—Wool, Sheep; *Degradation:* None

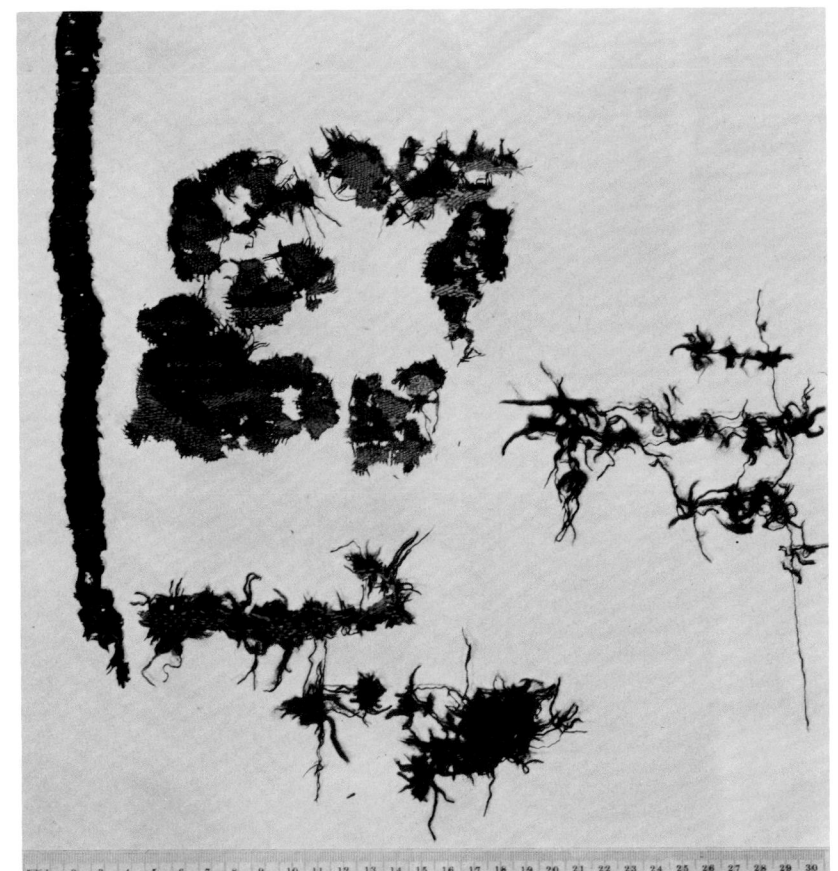

143

Grave Q 503   X-Group

Tumulus, shaft and side-chamber, brick blocking
Burial: Disturbed in shaft
Body: Infant (reused tomb?)
Objects from shaft:
1. Cup
2. Jar *(qadus)*
3. Textile (see entry below) 21665
4. Beads

3. Infant Tunic (?) Fragments (3 pieces)

Material: Animal*
Structure:
Plain weave in dark brown,** 9/10 warps per cm,
S-spun; 7/8 wefts per cm, S-spun
Fragment a: one selvage present
Fragment b: one selvage present
Fragment c: one selvage present
Decoration:
Fragment a: two stripes of yellow and red near fin-
ishing edge; *red stripe:* 17 wefts in plain weave,
S-spun; *yellow stripe:* 7 weft shots in plain weave;
warp threads worked into twisted cord
Fragment b: two stripes, one yellow, one red near
edge; *red stripe:* 24 weft shots in plain weave;
S-spun; *yellow stripe:* 6/7 weft shots in plain weave,
S-spun; warp threads worked into twisted cord
Fragment c: laid in geometric pattern in red wool,
S-spun
Dimensions:
Fragment a: 34cm (warp) x 26cm (weft)
Fragment b: 25cm (warp) x 22cm (weft)
Fragment c: 23.5cm (warp) x 22cm (weft)

* *Fiber Analysis:* Wool—Camel; *Degradation:*
   Moderate
** *Dye Analysis:* Brown—gallotanin, iron

144

Grave Q 582   X-Group

Tumulus, shaft and side-chamber (E–W) stone and
  brick blocking
Burial: Disturbed
Body: Infant
Objects:
1.   Leaves
2.   Date pits
3.   Textiles (see entry below) 21793 A–C

3A. Textile—Not available for study

3B. Textile—Not available for study

3C. Edging for Sheet or Tunic (2 pieces)

Material: Animal
Structure:
Counted weft twining in dark brown, red and
yellow; all fibers S-spun; small tassels at end
Dimensions: All-over: 19cm x 5cm

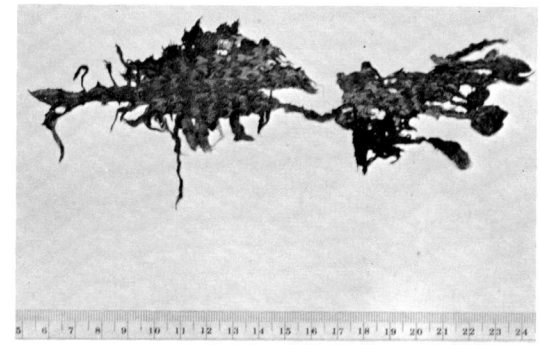

145

Grave Q 594   Meroitic Tomb, X-Group Burial

Shaft and side-chamber, brick blocking
Burials:
A. (Meroitic) Extended on back, hands at pubis
B. Disturbed, in shaft
Bodies:
A. Adult-mature, male?
B. Adult
Objects:
a. With burial A:
1.   Shells of Dom palm seed
2.   Jug
3.   Ring
4.   Textile (see entry below) 22027
5.   Small glass vessel
6.   Sherds
7.   Beads
b. With burial B:
8.   Textile—Discarded
9.   Quiver fragments
10. Twisted leather cords
11. Sherds*
12–14. Arrowheads
* Possibly plunderer's tools; one was part of a pot
  also found in the burial chamber

4. Tunic or Sheet (?) Fragment

Material: Animal and Vegetable (Cotton)
Structure:
Plain weave in medium brown, 16/18 warps per
cm, S-spun; 8 wefts per cm, S-spun; one selvage
present
Decoration:
Two stripes of 1.7cm each in dark blue, weft-faced
plain weave, 33 wefts per cm, S-spun on medium
brown warps, separated by two 4 medium brown
weft shots with 4 center light blue cotton weft shots;
near twisted warp thread end, 2 narrow stripes of
3 dark blue weft shots each, separated by 3 medium
brown weft shots; warp threads grouped by 6/7,
twisted and terminated
Dimensions: 51.5cm (warp) x 28cm (weft)

146

Grave Q 600   X-Group

Tumulus?, shaft with side-chamber, mudbrick
   blocking
Burial: Disturbed, head south, semicontracted?
Body: Senile, male
Objects from burial chamber:
1. Textile (see entry below) 20029
2. Wood fragments

1. Ball

Material: Animal
Structure:
Ball or pom-pom in medium brown pile; probably
originally part of horse-trappings
Dimensions: Diameter: 3cm

147

Grave R 6   X-Group

Shaft with side-chamber
Burial: Head south, semicontracted on right side
Body: Mature, male
Objects:
1. Textile, loincloth with bands holding it to waist
   of body   20813
2. Two-handled jar
3. Cup
4. Toilet kit
5. Braided leather

1. Sheet or Tunic (?) Fragments (7 pieces)

Material: Animal
Structure:
Four fragments of weft-faced plain weave in dark
brown,* 8/9 warps per cm, S-spun; 10/11 wefts per
cm, S-spun; three fragments with weft-faced plain
weave inserted through discontinuous wefts and
interlocking in light brown* and light pink;* *light
brown area:* 7/8 dark brown warps per cm, S-spun;
22/28 wefts per cm, S-spun; *light pink area:* 7/8 dark
brown warps per cm, S-spun; 28/34 wefts per cm,
S-spun

Decoration:
Judging from the insertions the sheet must have
been decorated with a stripe or stripes and
geometric shapes
Dimensions: All-over: 60cm (warp) x 85cm (weft)

* *Dye Analysis:* Beige—gallotanin
Red—gallotanin, iron
Brown—purpurin (alizarin)

148

Grave R 15   X-Group Burial

Vaulted chamber built in shaft, stone and brick
  blocking
Burial: Head west?, wrapped, disturbed
Body: Mature, female?
Objects:
1. Textile (see entry below) 20853
2. Jar
3. Jar
4. Cup in jar neck
5, 6. Cups
7. Beads

1. Tunic or Sheet (?) Fragment

Material: Animal
Structure:
Plain weave in dark brown, 10/11 warps per cm,
S-spun; dark brown warps throughout; 12 wefts
per cm, S-spun; one selvage present
Decoration:
Stripe in light brown at one end, in weft-faced plain
weave, 26 wefts per cm, S-spun, of 8cm in width;
warp threads worked into twisted cord along one
edge
Dimensions: 60cm (warp) x 63cm (weft)

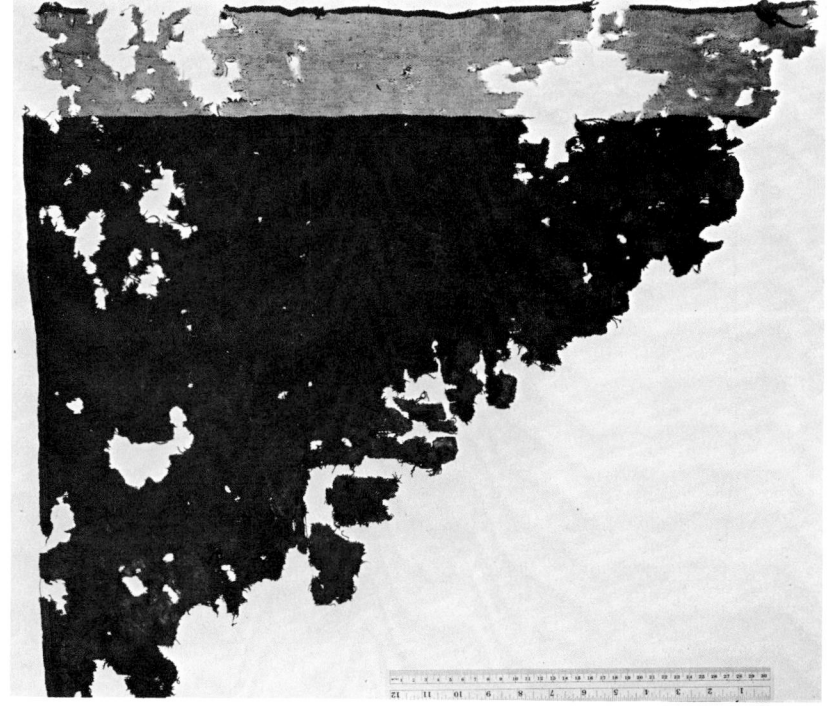

149

Grave R 16   X-Group

Tumulus, shaft and side-chamber, stone blocking
Burial: Head west, extended on back, head facing
  south 3/4
Body: Mature, female
Objects:
1. Iron ring on third finger of left hand
2. Two iron rings on index finger of left hand
3. Bone beads
4. Textile (see entry below) 20814

4. Tunic or Sheet (?) Fragments (7 pieces)

Material: Animal
Structure:
Weft-faced plain weave in dark brown, green, red*
and medium brown on dark brown warps, 5/8
warps per cm, S-spun; 28 red wefts per cm, S-spun;
26 green wefts per cm, S-spun; 18/22 medium
brown wefts per cm, S-spun; 16/18 dark brown
wefts per cm, S-spun
Decoration:
Stripes of medium brown (11.2cm), green (12.5cm),
dark brown (12cm), red (10cm ?), green (12cm),
red (10.5cm), dark brown (10.5cm); separated by
narrow stripes of 15 weft shots in dark brown, 7 weft
shots in medium brown, 4 weft shots in dark brown,
4/6 weft shots in medium brown; at top warp
threads worked into twisted cord
Dimensions: All-over: 83.5cm (warp) x 70cm (weft)

* *Dye Analysis:* Red—iron

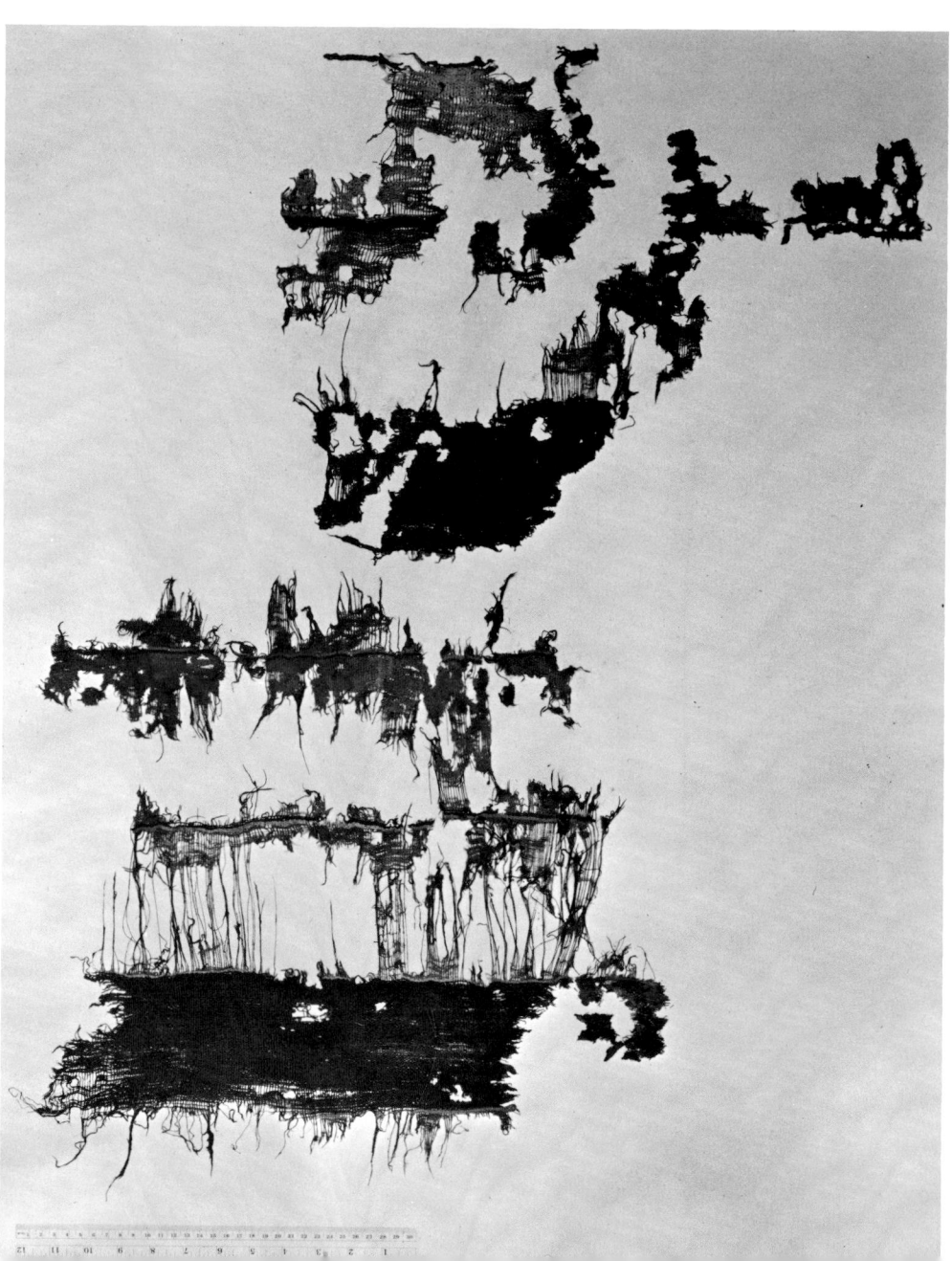

150

Grave R 22   X-Group

Tumulus?, shaft and side-chamber
Burial: Head west, semicontracted on right side
Body: Mature, male
Objects:
1, 2. Jars
3, 4. Cups, inverted over the necks of the jars
5. Leather garment or armor
6. Decorated quiver
7. Adze head
8. Beads
9. Saw
10. Sandals
11. Textile (see entry below), 20965

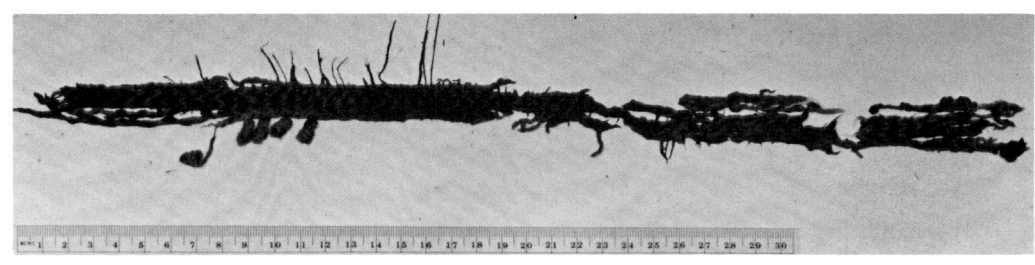

11. Edging for Sheet or Tunic (?)

Material: Animal
Structure:
Countered weft twining in yellow and red; with
light green tassels in warp direction at one end; all
fibers S-spun
Dimensions: All-over: 40cm x 4cm

151

Grave R 60   X-Group

Shaft and side-chamber, stone blocking
Burial: Head west? extended?, wrapped in winding
    sheet, disturbed
Body: Mature female
Objects:
1. Cup
2. Jar
3. Beads
4. Textiles (see entry below) 21236 A–B

4A. Sheet Fragment

Material: Animal*
Structure:
Plain weave in dark brown with weft-faced stripe
in red; warps dark brown throughout, 6/8 warps
per cm, S-spun
Decoration:
Stripe of red of 5.5cm; 19 red wefts per cm, S-spun
Dimensions: 36cm (warp) x 67cm (weft)

* *Fiber Analysis:*
Brown-Wool—Camel; *Degradation:* Moderate
Red-Wool—Sheep; *Degradation:* Slight

152

Grave R 60

4B. Tunic or Sheet (?) Fragments (5 pieces)

Material: Animal*
Structure:
Weft-faced plain weave in medium and dark brown,
6/7 warps per cm in dark brown, S-spun; 23/25
wefts per cm in medium brown to white, S-spun
Decoration:
Warp threads worked into twisted cord along the
edge of four fragments
Dimensions:
Fragment a: 5.5cm (warp) x 39cm (weft)
Fragment b: 1cm (warp) x 34cm (weft)
Fragment c: 3cm (warp) x 31cm (weft)
Fragment d: 6cm (warp) x 31cm (weft)
Fragment e: 2cm (warp) x 22cm (weft)

* *Fiber Analysis:* Medium Brown—Wool, Sheep;
   Degradation: None
Dark Brown—Wool, probably Camel
   Degradation: Moderate

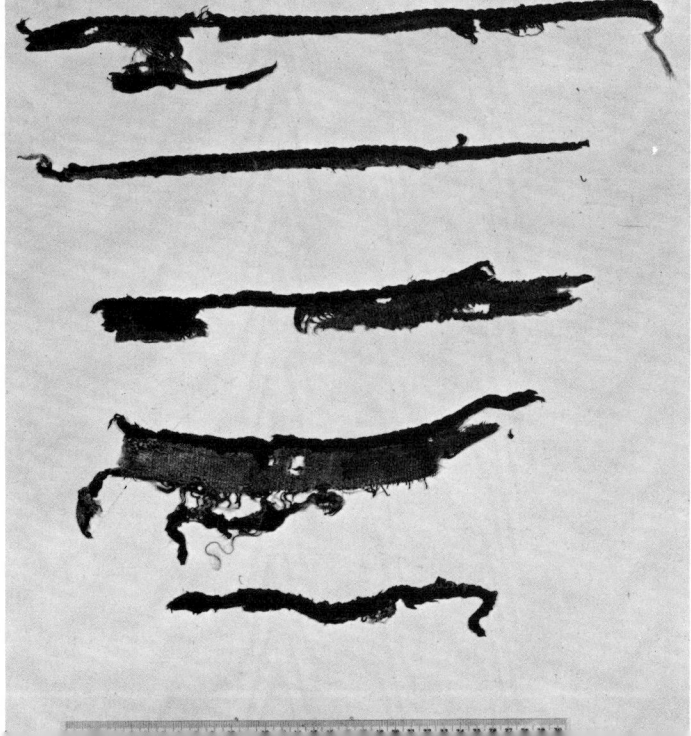

153

Grave R 111   X-Group

Shaft with side-chamber, stone blocking
Burial: Head north, extended on back, hands at
  pubis
Body: Adult, female
Objects:
1. Large jar
2. Bowl inverted over neck of jar
3. Textile wrapping from pelvis (see entry below)
    23514

3. Tunic or Sheet Fragment (2 pieces)

Material: Animal
Structure:
Weft-faced plain weave, 6/7 warps per cm, S-spun
Fragment a: one selvage present
Decoration:
Badly worn weft stripes in dark blue alternating
with a light brown* stripe of 20 wefts per cm in a
total of 53 weft shots, and three red* stripes of
18 wefts per cm in a total of 38, 32 and 24 weft
shots respectively

Fragment a: warps worked into twisted cord along
one edge
Fragment b: warps worked into twisted cord
Dimensions:
Fragment a: 40cm (warp) x 75cm (weft)
Fragment b: 70cm (warp) x 56.5cm (weft)

* *Dye Analysis:*
Red-Brown—purpurin (alizarin), iron
Brown—gallotanin, iron
Dark Beige—gallotanin, iron
Beige—gallotanin, iron

154

Grave R 113   Probably X-Group

Shaft
Burial: Disturbed
Body: Infant
Object:
1.   Textiles (see entry below) 23707 A–B

1A. Tunic or Sheet Fragment

Material: Animal
Structure:
Weft-faced plain weave in stripes of light and
medium brown and purple; warps medium brown*
throughout; 7 warps per cm, S-spun; 30 light brown
wefts per cm, S-spun; 12/14 medium brown wefts
per cm, S-spun; 30 purple wefts per cm, S-spun
Decoration:
Stripes of varying widths: light brown: 7cm;
medium brown: 1.5cm; purple: 7cm;
medium brown: 8cm; purple: 8cm; medium
brown: 1.5cm; purple: 8cm; medium brown: 20cm
Dimensions: 63cm (warp) x 68cm (weft)

* *Dye Analysis:* Brown—tanin, iron

155

Grave R 113

1B. Complete Carpet or Cover (5 pieces)

Material: Animal

Structure:
Plain weave in medium brown of double warps alternating with single warps, (2-ply), Z-spun, 11 warps per cm (individually counted); double wefts alternating with single wefts, (2-ply), Z-spun, 11 wefts per cm (individually counted); selvages present

Decoration:
At both ends two parallel positioned dark blue stripes inserted in weft direction through double wefts, 27 wefts per cm, S-spun, of 3/3.5cm each, separated by medium brown stripe of 1.5cm which does not run entire width of cover but ends 5/6cm at both sides before reaching selvages; warp threads worked at both ends into countered weft twining and subsequently braided fringe; main field of cover decorated with heavier weft threads inserted after each 18th weft shot (individually counted); rows of slip loops inserted in weft direction after each 2nd row of plied weft threads, held in place through warp floats that skip over heavy weft threads; center field further decorated with two parallel running weft stripes of cut slip loops at both ends in dark blue of 5cm each, separated by light brown weft stripe of 4/5 cm; this light brown stripe does not go all the way to selvage but stops 5/6cm before reaching the selvage on both sides; a gammadion or flyflot design formed by cut slip loops appears in all four corners 5/6cm in from selvage

Dimensions: All-over: 244cm (warp) including fringe at both ends x 168cm (weft)

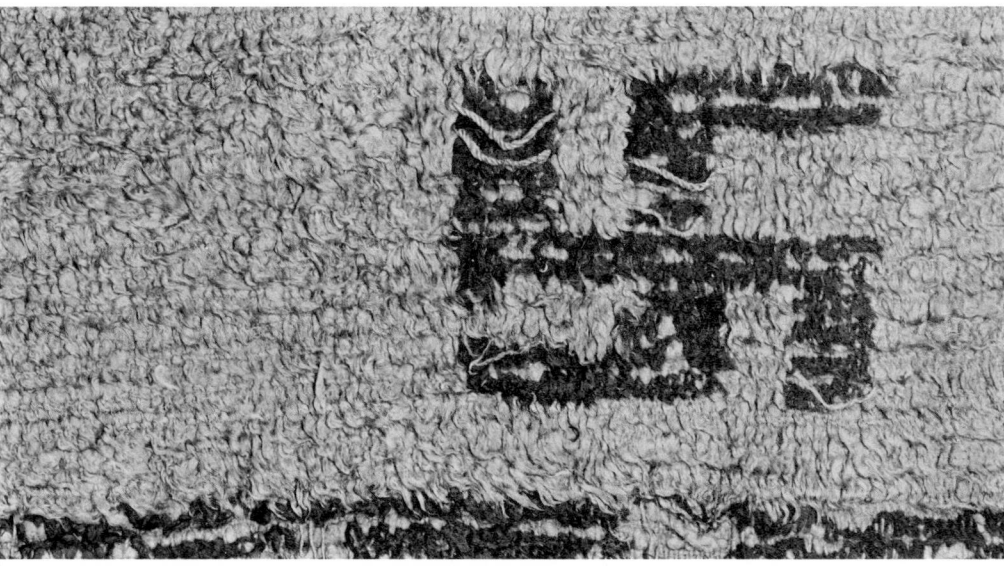

156

Grave R 118   X-Group

Shaft and side-chamber
Burial: Head east, semicontracted on right side, arm
    straight out
Body: Child, ca. 6 years, boy
Objects:
1.   Small globular jar at head
2.   Footed bowl with ring base, painted
3.   Textiles (see entry below) 24877 A–B

3A. Child's Mantle Fragments (2 pieces)

Material: Animal
Structure:
Plain weave in light brown,* 10/11 warps per cm,
S-spun; 7 wefts per cm, S-spun
Fragment a: one selvage present
Decoration:
Fragment a: rectangle of 18cm x 12cm inserted in
purple in weft-faced plain weave, 26/28 wefts per
cm, S-spun; inserted through discontinuous wefts;
interlocked and irregularly dovetailed; warps
grouped unevenly; form short fringe at one end
Dimensions:
Fragment a: 92cm (warp) x 72cm (weft)
Fragment b: 31cm (warp) x 31cm (weft)

* *Dye Analysis:* Light Brown—tanin
Dark Brown—tanin

157

Grave R 118

3B. Border Fragment

Material: Animal
Structure:
Plain weave in dark brown, 10/11 warps per cm,
S-spun; 10/11 wefts per cm, S-spun
Decoration:
Fringe worked in yellow and red threads, S-spun;
some stitching and tiny wrapped tassels
Dimensions: 5cm (warp) x 2.5cm (weft)

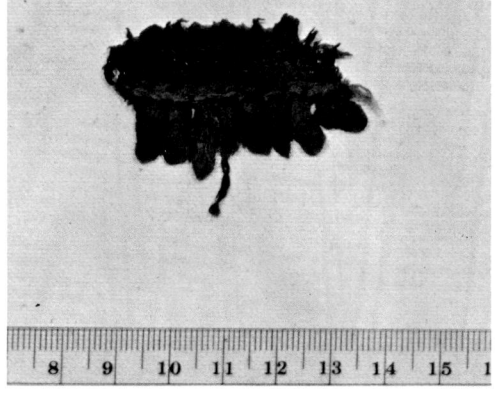

158

Grave V 122 X-Group Tomb—Burials (?)

Shaft and side-chamber, brick blocking
Burials:
A. Disturbed in chamber
B. Head west, extended on back
Bodies:
A. Adult, female?
B. Adult, female?
Objects:
1. Textiles (see entry below) 23846 A–C
2. Jar
3. Bowl
4. Leather quiver

1A. Carpet Fragments (2 pieces)

Material: Animal
Structure:
Plain weave in shades of red* formed by 2-ply warps, 6 per cm, S-spun and grouped wefts of 3/4, 12 wefts per cm, Z-spun (individually counted); after each weft grouping slip loops inserted in weft direction in blue,* green,* yellow and red forming pile
Fragment a: Selvage present
Decoration:
Traces of a large-scaled geometric pattern are visible
Dimensions:
Fragment a: 33cm (warp) x 30cm (weft)
Fragment b: 22cm (warp) x 25cm (weft)

* Dye Analysis: Red—purpurin (alizarin)
Pink—purpurin (alizarin)
Blue-Green—indigo

159

Grave 122

1B. Tunic or Sheet (?) Fragment

Material: Animal
Structure:
Plain weave in dark brown, 12 warps per cm, S-spun; 16/17 wefts per cm, S-spun
Decoration:
Two stripes in weft-faced plain weave in red, 24 wefts per cm, S-spun; stripes 4cm apart
Dimensions: 34cm (warp) x 17cm (weft)

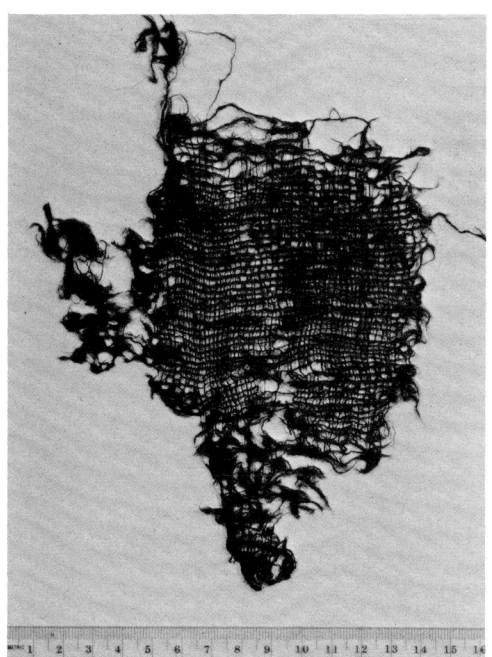

160

Grave V 122

1C. Fragment

Material: Animal
Structure:
Plain weave in dark blue,* 5 warps per cm, S-spun; 7 wefts per cm, S-spun
Dimensions: 16cm (warp) x 14cm (weft)

* Dye Analysis: Blue—indigo, purpurin (alizarin)

161

Grave W 71   X-Group

Shaft and side-chamber, stone blocking
Burials:
A. Wrapped
B. Wrapped
Bodies:
A. Child, ca. 12 years, probably female
B. Infant, ca. 7½ years
Objects:
1. Textile from A—Discarded

2. Textile from B (see entry below) 24878

2. Sheet or Tunic (?) Fragments (7 pieces)

Material: Animal*
Structure:
Open plain weave in dark blue, 8/9 warps per cm,
S-spun; 12/22 wefts per cm, S-spun
Decoration:
Fragments b, c and e: Show three red stripes and

one light brown stripe of 3, 3.5 and 3.5–4cm
respectively in weft-faced plain weave; 19/25 red
wefts per cm, S-spun, and 18/28 light brown wefts
per cm, S-spun
Dimensions: All-over: 125cm (warp) x 176cm (weft)

* *Fiber Analysis:*
Dark Blue—Wool, Camel (Coarse); *Degradation:*
Moderate-Severe
Wool, Sheep (CIBA, no. 2)

162

**Grave Q 40   Intrusive late X-Group or Christian
             Burial**

Tumulus?, shaft with side-chamber, stone blocking;
second chamber begun but left incomplete; holes
for the prepared bed burial in completed chamber
Burial: Disturbed, extended on back, head south,
    arms missing
Body: Adult, male
Objects:
a. In shaft or fill:
1. Jar
5. Two dates in a cord
b. In chamber:
2. Cord of twisted leather and strips
3. Jar at right shoulder
4. Textile fragments near pelvis (see entry below)
    20012
6. Bed, below body

4. Fragments (14 pieces)

Material: Vegetable (Cotton)*
Structure:
Plain weave in dark brown, with double wefts
throughout; 9 warps per cm, S-spun; 16 wefts per
cm, S-spun (individually counted)
Decoration:
Plaited or knotted (?) borders; some warp threads
form a fringe
Dimensions: All-over: 48cm (warp) x 50cm (weft)

* *Fiber Analysis:* Cotton; *Degradation:* Severe

163

Grave Q 174   Late X-Group—Christian

Shaft, narrow side-chamber with mud-brick sealing
Burials:
A. In wooden coffin, extended on back, hands on
   pelvis, head west
B. Intrusive, stuffed into burial chamber, extended
Bodies:
A. Juvenile, male?
B. Infant
Objects:
a. From chamber:
1. Coffin remains
2. Textile (see entry below) 20525
3. Pendant-bead
b. From shaft:
4. Cup

2. Fragments (7 pieces)

Material: Vegetable (Cotton)
Structure:
Plain weave in dark brown, 11/12 double warps per
cm (individually counted), S-spun; 11/12 wefts per
cm, S-spun
Dimensions: All-over: 9cm (warp) x 12cm (weft)

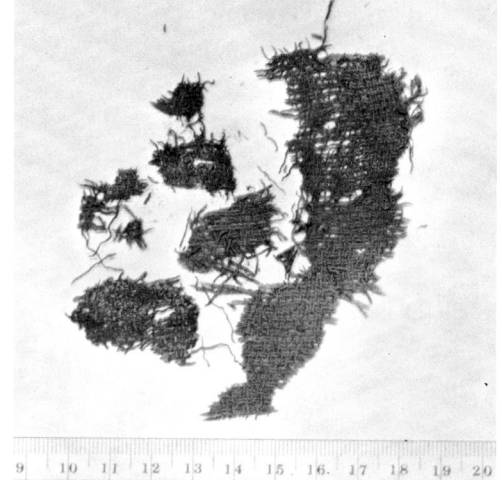

164

Grave Q 186   Late X-Group—Christian

Shaft with narrow side-chamber, brick blocking
Burial: Disturbed
Body: Juvenile, female?
Objects:
1. Beads
2. Jar
3. Textiles (see entry below) 20566 A–B
4. Date pits
5. Potsherd

1A. Fragments

Material: Animal
Structure:
Loose red and brown weft threads in what was
formerly a weft-faced plain weave (too disintegrated
to get accurate count)
Dimensions: 30cm (warp) x 40cm (weft)

1B. Textile—Not available for study

Totally disintegrated

165

Grave Q 286 A   Uncertain, probably partly Christian

Trench with brick cist
Burials:
A. In cist, head west, extended on back, hands at side
B. In trench, head south, extended on back, hands
   on pubis, head resting on two bricks
Bodies:
A. Juvenile, female?
B. Mature, male?
Objects:
1. Textiles (see entry below) 20847 A–B

1A. Fragments (3 pieces)

Material: Animal
Structure:
Plain weave with 3 grouped warps, 6 warps per cm,
S-spun (individually counted); spaced widely; 27
wefts per cm, S-spun
Decoration:
Red and yellow and green and yellow checkerboard
   design

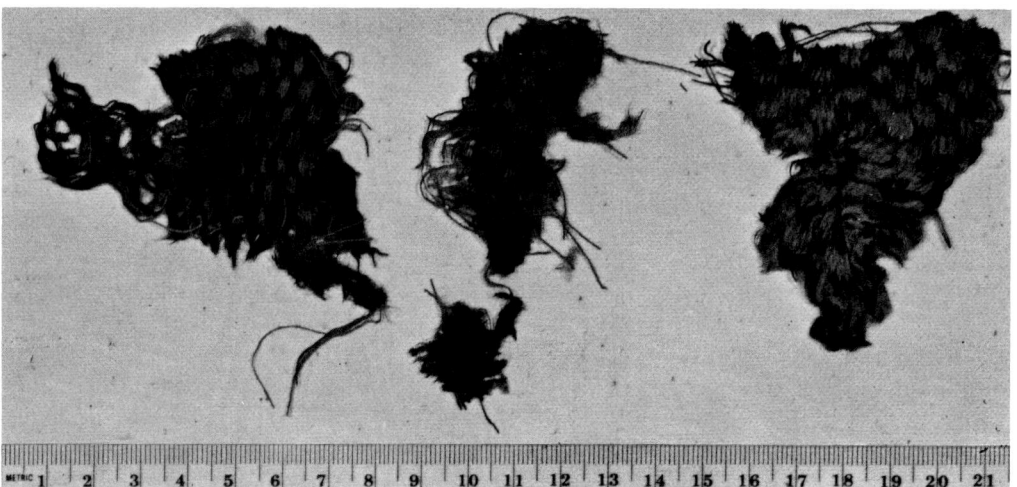

Dimensions: All-over: 13cm x 14cm

166

Grave Q 286 A

1B. Fragments (3 pieces)

Material: Animal
Structure:
Plain weave in dark brown, 11 warps (?) per cm,
S-spun; 18 wefts (?) per cm, S-spun
Dimensions: All-over: 6.5cm (warp) (?) x 7cm
(weft) (?)

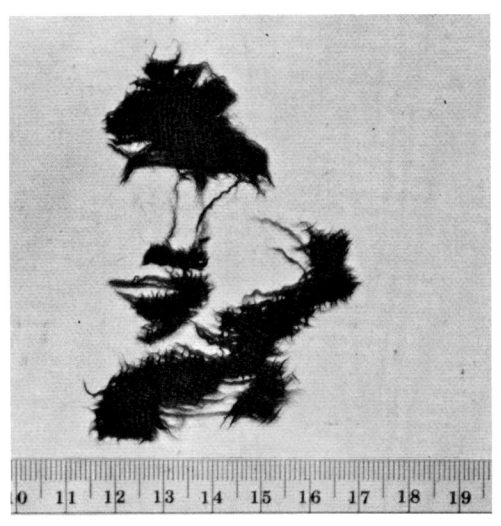

167

Grave Q 348   X-Group-Christian

Tumulus? shaft and side-chamber, blocked with
stone flags and brick
Burial: Head south, extended on back, hands at
sides
Body: Mature-senile male, upper right skull
smashed, moustache and beard
Objects:
1.   Stele reused as blocking
2.   Textiles (see entry below) 20918 A–B

2A. Fragments (6 pieces)—

Material: Animal
Structure:
Plain weave, 8/9 warps per cm, S-spun; 14 double
wefts per cm (individually counted), S-spun
Decoration:
Along top in weft direction one single green thread,
S-spun; warp threads worked into braid with a
few braided fringe elements
Dimensions: All-over: 7cm (warp) x 15cm (weft)

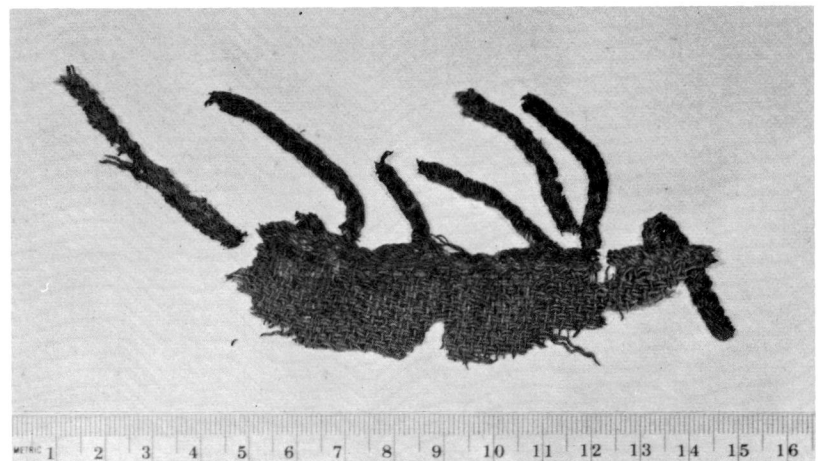

168

Grave Q 348

2B. Fragments (12 pieces)

Material: Vegetable (Cotton)
Structure:
Plain weave in medium brown, 12 warps per cm,
S-spun; 8 wefts per cm, S-spun
Decoration:
Twining ending in knotted or wrapped border with
long fringe
Dimensions: All-over: 33cm (warp) x 44cm (weft)

169

Grave Q 425 Very late X-Group (?)

Tumulus?, shaft with floor-chamber (E–W)
Burial: Disturbed, head west, extended on back
Body: Mature
Objects:
a. From chamber:
1. Leaves and straw near head
2. Cup near head
3. Sherds
4. String near head and waist
5. Textile (see entry below) 21308
b. From shaft:
6. Sherds
7. Textile—Discarded

5. Tunic or Sheet Fragments (?) (2 pieces)

Material: Vegetable (Cotton)*
Structure:
Plain weave in medium brown, 9/10 warps per cm,
S-spun; 20/24 wefts per cm, grouped by two's,
S-spun
Decoration:
Fragment a: narrow red stripe of 6 weft shots in
animal fiber, S-spun; braided 10cm long cords
terminating in five knots at end attached through
sewing
Fragment b: twisted warp threads worked into
cording along one edge; one sewn edge
Dimensions:
Fragment a: 76cm (warp) x 75cm (weft)
Fragment b: 42cm (warp) x 86cm (weft)

* Fiber Analysis: Cotton; Degradation: Slight

170

Grave Q 436   Early Christian or End of X-Group

Shallow rectangular shaft
Burial: Head east, extended on back, hands at sides,
 toes tied together, textile on upper body, leather
 on legs
Body: Adult, male, bearded, with much body hair
Objects:
1.   Textile on upper body
a.   Outer hide
b.   Second layer, textiles (see entry below) 21464 A
c.   Third layer, textiles (see entry below) 21464 C–F
2.   Textile on legs (see entry below) 21464 B

1A. Mantle or Sheet (?) Fragments (3 pieces)

Material: Animal
Structure:
Plain weave in medium brown of several badly worn
and stained fabrics; 8/10 warps per cm, S-spun;
23/24 wefts per cm, S-spun
Fragment a: One selvage present
Decoration:
Some of the patched areas show weft-faced plain
weave insertions in purple and dark blue; 7/8 warps
per cm, S-spun; 27 purple and dark blue wefts per
cm, S-spun

Fragment a: Warps worked into twisted cord along
one edge
Fragment b: Several sewn and layered portions
Fragment c: Several sewn and layered portions
Dimensions:
Fragment a: 74cm (warp) x 87cm (weft)
Fragment b: 65cm (warp) x 78cm (weft)
Fragment c: 24cm (warp) x 17cm (weft)

171

Grave Q 436

2B. Tunic or Sheet (?) Fragment

Material: Animal
Structure:
Plain weave in light brown, 6/9 warps per cm,
S-spun; 9/11 wefts per cm, S-spun; selvage present

Decoration:
At one end two stripes of dark blue in weft-faced
plain weave; both stripes of 1.5cm; 12/13 wefts per
cm, S-spun, separated by 3 weft shots of light brown;
warp threads worked into twisted cord; incomplete
red stripe of 4cm, 11 wefts per cm, S-spun
Dimensions: 35cm (warp) x 59cm (weft)

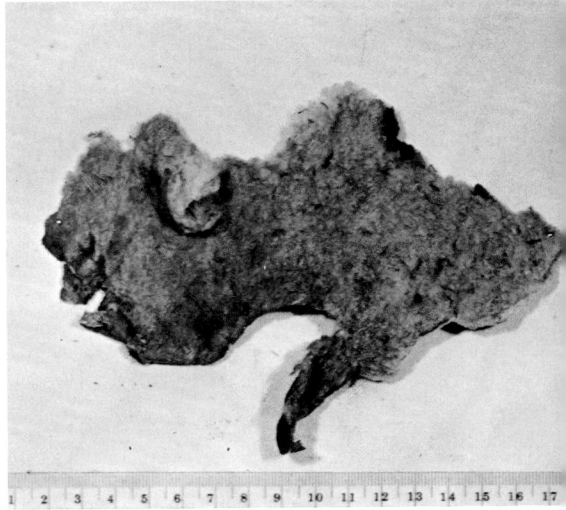

172

Grave Q 436

1C–E. Mantle Fragments (3 pieces)

Material: Animal
Structure:
Plain weave in light brown, 11 warps per cm,
S-spun; 8 wefts per cm, S-spun
Decoration:
Fragment c: portion of notched "L" shape in dark

brown, inserted through weft-faced plain weave,
of discontinuous wefts occasionally dovetailed and
interlocked
Fragment e: warp threads worked into twisted cord
along one edge; stripes
Dimensions:
Fragment c: 63cm (warp) x 98cm (weft)
Fragment d: 24cm (warp) x 23cm (weft)
Fragment e: 15cm (warp) x 9cm (weft)

173

4F. Piece of Sheepskin*

Dimensions: All-over: 16cm x 9cm

* *Fiber Analysis:* Sheepskin; *Degradation:* None

139

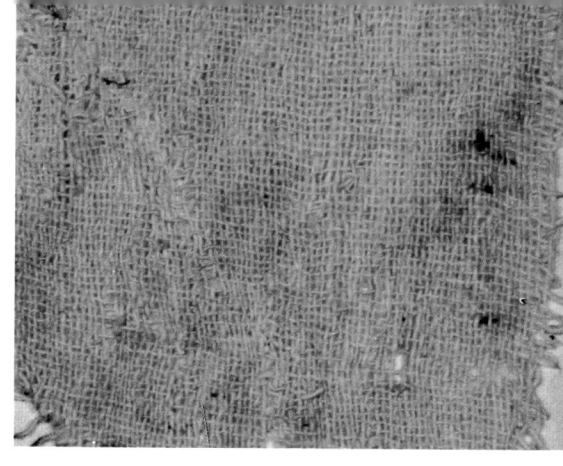

174

Grave Q 476   End of X-Group or Early Christian

Shaft with side-chamber
Burial: Head east? disturbed
Body: Adult
Objects:
a.   From shaft:
1.   Sherds
2.   Textiles—Discarded
3.   Branch, straw and thorns
b.   From chamber:
2.   Textiles (see entry below) 21463 A–C

2A.   Tunic or Sheet (?) Fragments (2 pieces)

Material: Animal

Structure:
Plain weave in dark brown
Fragment a: 7 warps per cm, S-spun; 8/9 wefts per cm, S-spun
Fragment b: 11 warps per cm, S-spun; 8 wefts per cm, S-spun; one selvage present
Decoration:
Fragment a: 3 stripes in weft direction with worn off medium brown wefts in plain weave, S-spun; warp threads worked into twisted cord
Fragment b: 3 stripes in weft direction in medium brown of 21 weft shots, and twice 6 weft shots each in plain weave, S-spun; grouped warps worked into twisted cord
Dimensions: 13cm (warp) x 20cm (weft)

175

Grave Q 476

2B-C.   Sheet (?) Fragments (4 pieces)

Material: Vegetable (Cotton)
Structure:
Plain weave in white with brown* stains throughout; 7 warps per cm, S-spun; 7/8 wefts per cm, S-spun
Dimensions: All-over: 89cm (warp) x 116cm (weft)

* *Dye Analysis:* Brown—gallotanin

Grave Q 35B   Christian Burial

Intrusive in X-Group tumulus, shaft with side-
    chamber, blocking of stone flags
Burial: Head south, extended on back, face east,
    hands on pubis, wrapped in textile
Body: Mature
Objects:
1. Textiles (see entry below) 20039
2. Pottery lamp

1. Sheet or Tunic (?) Fragment

Material: Animal
Structure:
Weft-faced plain weave in dark brown, 5 warps per
cm, S-spun; 18 wefts per cm, S-spun
Decoration:
Three red stripes of 1.5cm in width (measured in
warp direction), of 15/17 wefts per cm, S-spun;
they are separated by 3cm wide stripes (measured

in warp direction), in dark brown; one additional
stripe in light brown of 1.5cm (measured in warp
direction), of 22 wefts per cm, S-spun
Dimensions: 32cm (warp) x 84cm (weft)

Grave Q 91   Christian

Rectangular mudbrick superstructure over shaft,
    with floor chamber, flagstone blocking
Burial: Extended on back, hands at pubis, head west
Body: Mature
Objects:
1. Jar
2. Textile (see entry below) 19943

2. Fragments

Material: Animal
Structure:
Very open plain weave in two medium browns,* 5
warps per cm, S-spun; 4/5 wefts per cm, S-spun;
portion of selvage present
Decoration:
Stripes of orange* and yellow* of 5/6 weft shots
each
Dimensions: 80cm (warp) x 93cm (weft)

* *Dye Analysis:* Brown—gallotanin
    Orange—purpurin (alizarin)
    Yellow—tanin, iron

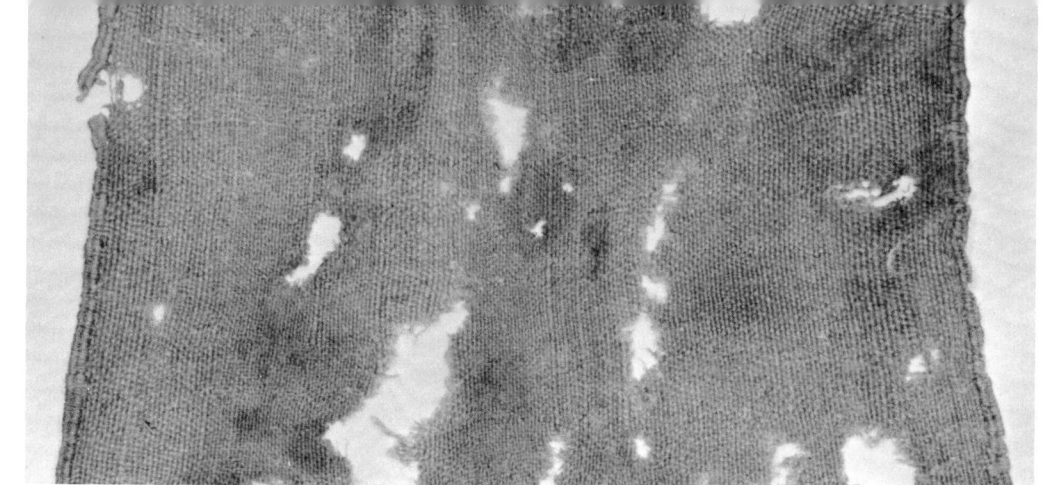

178

Grave Q 92   Christian

Rectangular mudbrick superstructure over shaft
  with narrow floor-side chamber; stone blocking,
  leaning floor to wall
Burial:
Extended on back, face up, hands folded at pubis,
  wrapped in cloth
Body: Mature
Objects:
1. Textile (see entry below) 20265

1. Loincloth (?) (4 pieces)

Material: Animal
Structure:
Weft-faced plain weave with increasing or decreas-
ing warp count in medium brown, 12/13 warps per
cm, S-spun; 24 wefts per cm, S-spun
Fragment a: occasionally two warps reduced to one;
selvage and heading present
Fragment b: selvage present
Fragment c: heading and selvage present
Fragment d: two selvages present
Dimensions:
Fragment a: 33cm (warp) x 57cm (weft)
Fragment b: 53cm (warp) x 26cm (weft)
Fragment c: 26cm (warp) x 28cm (weft)
Fragment d: 35cm (warp) x 18.5cm (weft)
Remarks:
Fragments a, b and c were knotted together; based
on the drastic warp thread reduction, the piece
must have been an elongated triangle

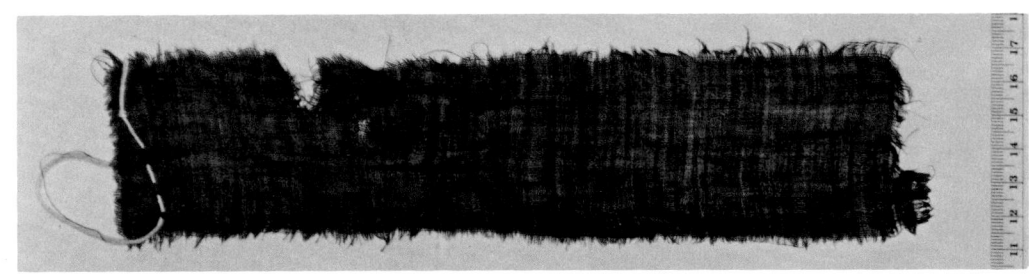

179

Grave Q 98   Christian

Rectangular mudbrick superstructure covering shaft
with floor-niche with flagstone blocking
Burial:
Head west, extended on back, face up, hands at
pubis, wrapped
Body: Mature, female
Object:
1. Textile (see entry below) 20258

1. Fragment

Material: Vegetable (Cotton)*
Structure:
Plain weave in black,** 25 warps (?) per cm, S-spun;
25/26 wefts (?) per cm, S-spun

Decoration:
Yellow cotton thread of four filaments twisted
together, S-spun; stitched along one side
Dimensions: 6cm (warp) (?) x 26cm (weft) (?)

* *Fiber Analysis:* Black—Cotton
　　Yellow—Cotton; *Degradation:* None
** *Dye Analysis:* Black—modern chromium

Remarks:
The existence of this so very different looking textile
can only be explained as being of much later date
and intrusive; the fineness of both warp and weft
cotton threads as well as the modern chromium in
the black dye point to a fabric of modern age which
was probably torn off an intruder's clothing

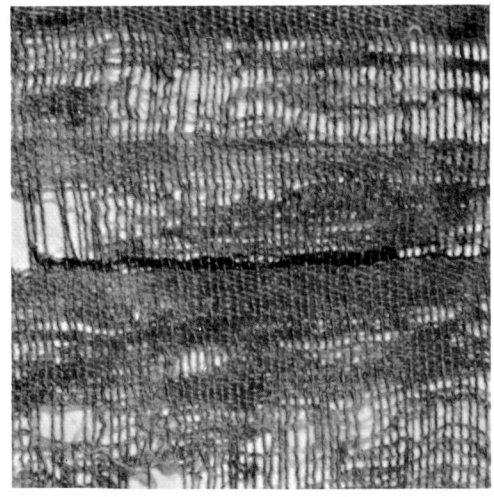

180

Grave Q 159   Christian and Later

Narrow shaft with side-chamber
Burials:
Appear to have been moved from elsewhere;
stacked, but do not fit one another as though
done before they stiffened; upper extended,
right side, hands above pubis; middle on back,
head opposite, same position; bottom same as
middle
Bodies:
C. (upper) Senile, female?
B. (middle) Adult, male
A. (lower) Adult, male
Objects:
1. Textile (see entry below) 20437
2. Potsherds (added with fill)

1. Sheet Fragments (3 pieces)

Material: Animal*
Structure:
Plain weave (uneven and irregular), in medium
brown, 6/7 warps per cm, S-spun; 10/13 wefts per
cm, S-spun
Decoration:
Traces of 3–5 weft shots in purple, S-spun; two
smaller pieces were knotted to one another
Dimensions: All-over: 60cm (warp) x 110cm (weft)

* *Fiber Analysis:*
Wool—Sheep (with Sand); *Degradation:* Slight

181

Grave Q 167   Christian?

Shaft with narrow side-chamber partly covered with
   mudbrick
Burials:
Disturbed, skulls of four, one in burial chamber,
   extended on back, head detached
Objects:
1. Textile (see entry below) 20572

1. Fragments (ca. 35 pieces)

Material: Vegetable (Cotton)
Structure:
Plain weave in medium brown, 12 warps per cm,
S-spun; 15 wefts per cm, S-spun
Dimensions: All-over: 22cm (warp) x 19cm (weft)

182

Grave Q 206 a   Christian

Stone rectangular bench superstructure, shaft and
   floor-chamber partly blocked with flagstones
Burial:
Head west, extended on back, hands on hips; body
   shrouded and bound around and lengthwise
Body: Child
Object:
1.   Textile (see entry below) 20300 A–B

1A. Fragment

Material: Vegetable (Linen)
Structure:
Plain weave (uneven) in light brown* (stained), 13
warps (?) per cm, S-spun; 16 wefts (?) per cm,
S-spun
Dimensions: 9cm (warp) (?) x 11cm (weft) (?)

* Dye Analysis: Grey—tanin?

1B. Portion of Tape

Material: Animal (?)
Structure: Woven
Dimensions: 7.5cm x 1cm

183

Grave Q 398   Christian Burial

Shaft and side-chamber, stone and mud blocking
Burials:
A. Disturbed and destroyed
B. Extended, head west, ¾ on back, hands at sides,
    swathed and bound
Bodies: Both senile, females?
Objects:
1. Sherds in both shaft and burial chamber
2. Leaves
3. Textiles (see entry below) 21235 A–B

3A. Tunic or Sheet (?) Fragment

Material: Animal
Structure:
Weft-faced plain weave in dark brown,* 11 warps
per cm, S-spun; 30 wefts per cm, S-spun
Decoration:
Three green stripes (top one totally worn away),
of 3/3.3cm, 34 wefts per cm, S-spun, alternating
with dark brown stripes of 3/3.8cm, 44 wefts per
cm, S-spun; at one end warp threads worked into
twisted cord
Dimensions: 65.5cm (warp) x 52cm (weft)

* *Dye Analysis:* Brown—gallotanin, iron

184

Grave Q 398

3B. Sheet Fragments, Tapes (4 pieces)

Material: Animal
Structure:
Fragment a (left): Plain weave in light to medium
brown, 8 warps (?) per cm, S-spun; 11 wefts (?) per
cm, S-spun
Fragment b (right): Plain weave in light to medium
brown, 8 warps (?) per cm, S-spun; 11 wefts (?) per
cm, S-spun;
Fragments c and d (center): Plain weave in light
brown, 8 warps per cm, S-spun; 12 wefts per cm,
S-spun
Decoration:
Fragment b (right): Traces of inlaid decoration
in purple visible in two spots; weft twining in
medium brown
Dimensions:
Fragment a: 55.5cm (warp) (?) x 5cm (weft) (?)
Fragment b: 47cm (warp) (?) x 4cm (weft) (?)
Fragment c: 15cm (warp) x 7cm (weft)
Fragment d: 35cm (warp) x 13cm (weft)

185

Grave Q 456   Christian

Burial:
Shaft with layer of stones above body, no shelf
Head west, extended on back, hands on pelvis,
   wrapped and tied with tapes
Body: Mature, male
Objects:
1. Textile (see entry below) 21666

1.   Tunic (?) Fragments (2 pieces)

Material: Animal
Structure:
Plain weave in dark brown, 8 warps per cm,
S-spun; 7/10 wefts per cm, S-spun
Fragment a: selvages present
Fragment b: one selvage present
Decoration:
Fragment a: five rows of countered weft twining or
loom needlework (?), 4/5 cm apart in green, red and
yellow, S-spun; (decoration does not run from
selvage to selvage)
Fragment b: five rows of countered weft twining or
loom needlework (?), 3.5/4cm apart in green, red
and yellow, S-spun; (decoration does not run from
selvage to selvage)
Fragment c: warp threads worked into cording
Dimensions:
Fragment a: 54cm (warp) x 62cm (weft)
Fragment b: 53cm (warp) x 58cm (weft)
Fragment c: 18cm (warp) x 40cm (weft)

186

Grave R 77   Christian?

Shaft with side-chamber
Burial:
Head west, extended on back, right hand across
  pelvis, left at pubis, wrapped in cloth
Body: Adult, male
Objects:
1. Textiles (see entry below) 23513 A–B
2. Leather cords, one at neck, one at pelvis, one
    attached to textile

1A. Tunic or Sheet (?) Fragment

Material: Animal
Structure:
Plain weave in different shades of medium to dark
brown,* 6/7 warps per cm, S-spun; 7 wefts per cm,
S-spun; one selvage present
Decoration:
Narrow stripe in weft direction in dark brown of
2 weft shots
Dimensions: 35cm (warp) x 34.5cm (weft)

* *Dye Analysis:*
Brown$_1$—tanin?, iron
Brown$_2$—tanin?, iron
Brown$_3$—gallotanin, iron

187

Grave R 77

1B. Tunic or Sheet (?) Fragment

Material: Animal
Structure:
Plain weave in dark brown, 6 warps per cm, S-spun;
8/9 wefts per cm, S-spun
Decoration:
Wide stripe in weft direction in medium brown, 21
wefts per cm, S-spun; two narrow stripes of red in
weft direction of 21 weft shots each, separated by
3 dark brown weft shots; warp threads worked into
twisted cord along one edge
Dimensions: 26cm (warp) x 44.5cm (weft)
Remarks:
This fragment was found near the hip area and was
wrapped inside entry 186

188

Grave Q 327   Surface burial

Surface placement
Burial: Head west, placement uncertain
Body: Infant
Object:
1. Textile 20816—Not available for study
    Totally disintegrated

DISCARDED TEXTILES

Meroitic
Q 172
Q 176
Q 181
Q 185
Q 250
Q 302 A
Q 313
Q 328
Q 335
Q 340
Q 347
Q 351
Q 353
Q 392
Q 415 B, C
Q 417 A
Q 427 B
Q 430
Q 464 B
Q 474
Q 475 A, B
Q 493
Q 508
Q 509
Q 510
Q 519
Q 525
Q 526
Q 532
Q 661
Q 670
Q 675
B 2
B 8 B
B 9
B 11 A
B 13
B 14
B 29
B 65
B 66 A, B
B 67
B 87 A, B
B 90 A, E, F
B 109 C
B 144
B 179
B 333 A

Meroitic?
Q 236
Q 245
Q 272
Q 275
Q 290
Q 298
Q 300
Q 302 A
Q 303 A, B
Q 339
Q 507
Q 512
Q 542
Q 547

Q 552
Q 554
Q 557
Q 558
Q 562
Q 564
Q 569
Q 579 A, B
Q 584
Q 586
Q 590
Q 591
Q 601
Q 607
Q 609
Q 624
Q 642
Q 646
Q 654
B 201
B 234

**Late Meroitic
or X-Group**
Q 158

X-Group
Q 16
Q 20
Q 29
Q 31
Q 33
Q 41
Q 42
Q 45
Q 46
Q 47
Q 48
Q 58
Q 60
Q 65
Q 66
Q 67 A, B
Q 71
Q 73
Q 75
Q 76
Q 101 B
Q 133
Q 135
Q 150
Q 161
Q 164
Q 279
Q 282
Q 309
Q 316
Q 320
Q 348
Q 360
Q 381
Q 385
Q 387
Q 391
Q 405
Q 410

Q 434
Q 454
Q 485 B
Q 504
Q 567
Q 600
Q 643
B 135
B 205
R 7
R 8
R 14
R 23
R 24
R 26
R 36
R 49
R 50
R 62
R 67
R 74
R 78
R 82
V 9
V 14
V 41
V 42
V 96
V 128
M 1
W 39
W 60 B
W 83
W 88

X-Group?
Q 69
Q 72
Q 287
Q 357
Q 377
Q 447
R 80
W 66

X-Group-Christian
V 90
W 79

Christian
Q 90
Q 109
Q 121
Q 125
Q 127 B
Q 131
Q 200
Q 201
Q 203 A, B
Q 208
Q 212
Q 214
Q 411 B
B 100
V 1
V 4 A, B
V 11

V 88
V 89
V 104

Christian?
Q 143 B
Q 157
Q 307
Q 524
V 2
W 34

Unknown
Q 140
Q 371
Q 376
Q 419
Q 492
Q 518
Q 534
Q 655
Q 669
Q 681
B 294